2004
EDITION

California

CONSTRUCTION LAW

Compiled and Written By
Sam K. Abdulaziz

Edited By
Kenneth S. Grossbart

Sam K. Abdulaziz

Abdulaziz & Grossbart

Emphasizing All Phases of Construction Law

6454 Coldwater Canyon Avenue

North Hollywood, CA 91606-1187

Phone (818) 760-2000

Fax (818) 760-3908

BNi PUBLICATIONS, INC.

LOS ANGELES
10801 National Blvd., Ste.100
Los Angeles, CA 90064

ANAHEIM
1612 S. Clementine St.
Anaheim, CA 92802

NEW ENGLAND
PO BOX 14527
East Providence, RI 02914

WASHINGTON,D.C.
502 Maple Ave. West
Vienna, VA 22180

1-800-873-6397

ISBN 1-55701-4655

ABOUT THE AUTHOR

SAM K. ABDULAZIZ is an acknowledged expert in the field of construction law in general and, in particular, Mechanics' Lien and Contractor's Licensing. Because of his in-depth knowledge of the law in this area, Sam represents numerous construction trade associations and contractors. His advice and opinion is sought by industry, regulatory agencies, legislators and the media. His latest achievement was being appointed to the Advisory Committee for Office of Administrative Hearings, which is where all contractor discipline and other licensing cases are handled. Unfortunately, as a result of budget problems in the state of California, most advisory committees are no longer meeting.

In addition to having authored numerous articles which have appeared in industry publications as well as publications provided by the State of California, Sam has written three books on the subject used by the construction industry. Some of his legal publications are now being used by attorneys and other law professionals.

Sam has been and still is counsel for numerous construction trade associations and exchanges. The last year, Sam has been very heavily involved in the attack on Mechanic's Liens that was sponsored by Assembly Member Dutra (this is discussed elsewhere in this book) as well as advising construction trade associations regarding pending legislation.

In 1989 Sam Abdulaziz was named Chairman of the Advisory Committee to the California State Assembly Select Committee on Unlicensed Contractors. Because of the success of that committee its scope was enlarged to cover all construction issues, not just unlicensed contractors. Sam remained as chair of the committee until it was disbanded as a result of Proposition 140. Much of the proposed construction legislation was handled in that committee.

Sam Abdulaziz was honored with one of the highest awards from American Building Contractors Association, the Gold Card Award. This award is given to people for contributions made to the construction industry, mankind and the ABCA. Sam was also honored twice by the California Association of Plumbing, Heating, Cooling Contractors for his efforts and contribution to the industry.

Sam, a frequent lecturer on the subject of construction law, has spoken at local and national conventions on numerous occasions. Some of the lectures have now been approved for credit towards Continuing Education for Attorneys.

Sam Abdulaziz has litigated and arbitrated numerous construction cases from the very small case to the large multi-party cases. He has also served as an Arbitrator on similar cases. He has argued cases successfully before appellate courts including the California Supreme Court.

Sam has also represented construction licensees before various boards and regulatory agencies as well as successfully appealing decisions of the regulatory agencies.

Sam Abdulaziz was honored by his peers when he was named LAWYER OF THE YEAR by the Los Angeles County Bar Association's Constitutional Rights Foundation for the year 1978-79.

Any questions regarding this book should be directed to the Author.

Sam K. Abdulaziz
ABDULAZIZ & GROSSBART
6454 Coldwater Canyon Avenue
North Hollywood, CA 91606-1187
Phone (818) 760-2000
Fax (818) 760-3908
WEB SITE: www.abdulaziz-grossbart.com
E MAIL: aglaw@earthlink.net

TABLE OF CONTENTS

What's New In 2004 7

I. Introduction 55

II. Summary of the Contractors' License Law 57

III. Licensing and Regulation of Contractors 86

IV. Enforcement 109

V. Home Improvement and Swimming Pool Contracting 116

VI. Contracting with Public Entities in California 147

VII. Construction Contracts 156

VIII. Indemnification 182

IX. Bonding in the Construction Industry 193

X. Insurance 202

XI. Disputes 217

XII. Mechanics' Liens, Stop Notices and Bonds 222

XIII. Prompt Payment Laws 252

XIV. Contractors' Board's Discipline and Disciplinary Statutes 257

XV. Appendix 281

- A. Private Works Mechanics' Lien, Stop Notice and Bond Checklist 283
- B. Private Works Stop Notice, Mechanics' Lien and Bond Flow Charts 290
- C. Prompt Pay Law Flow Chart - Public Works 292
- D. Prompt Pay Law Flow Chart - Private Works 293
- E. Index of Selected Cases 294
- F. Sample Citation 353
- G. Disciplinary Guidelines 363

Index 399

WHAT'S NEW IN 2004

The year 2003 was a bad year for California and most California businesses. The budget problems and insurance issues were in the forefront. Legislation was not far behind. Highlights are as follows:

LIABILITY INSURANCE

Again, our prophecy in 2003 has turned out to be accurate. Just like workers compensation insurance, liability insurance is becoming very hard to get if it is obtainable at all, and very expensive. It was hoped that the Legislature would have looked at the liability insurance problem in 2003. However, the Legislature used the budget problem as an excuse not to do anything in this area. We suspect that the Legislature just did not want to make more people mad (insurance companies and trial lawyers) this year.

We again advise any contractors that need to obtain insurance, that they should start the process of interviewing carriers well in advance of the time needed. Not only is it more expensive, it is much more restrictive containing more exclusions.

WORKERS' COMPENSATION

As we indicated in our 2003 book, there was a substantial workers compensation increase. The increases, in many cases, were more than double the premium. Insurers have withdrawn from the California market and the regulators are totally out of control. The Legislature passed a substantial package of law dealing with the issue (see new legislation) but it is nothing more than a start. Let's see if our government has the guts to do the right thing.

Note: The following analysis of this new mammoth and complicated legislation merely states highlights and opinion dealing with these issues. You should seek the aid and advice of you attorney or workers' compensation provider.

WORKERS' COMPENSATION AND "PAY-OR-PLAY" HEALTH INSURANCE

Background

The legislature enrolled and the Governor signed three bills, SB 2, SB 228, and AB 227, all dealing with the troubled workers' compensation ("workers' comp") system in California. These three laws all became effective January 1, 2004. Democratic legislators who passed these bills hail them as "a big first step" towards reforming the California's workers' comp system. However, the changes put forth by this package are really only baby steps towards any real reform of a system badly in need of some repair.

The California workers' comp system was adopted during the second decade of this century, making it the oldest social insurance program in the state. In California, workers' comp was intended to be a pure no-fault system, meaning that injured employees do not have to prove that their injury was someone else's fault. Rather, the injured employee only needs to show that they have an injury in order to receive workers' comp benefits for an on-the-job injury. Ideally, the workers' comp system is a compromise between employees and employers. Employees are entitled to prompt receipt of the workers' comp benefits for their on-the-job injuries. In return, employees agree not to bring any sort of litigation against the employer, even if the employer negligently caused the employee's injury.

However, while this no-fault structure effectively eliminated the then prevalent litigation over employer's negligence in causing the employee's injury, a whole crop of other litigation has arisen over workers' comp. For example, there is much litigation over issues such as whether the injury was in fact sustained on the job, or how much in benefits an injured worker is entitled to receive. In addition, workers' comp rates for businesses in the past several years has skyrocketed 200-300-400%. Premiums are at an all-time high, as total premiums in California cost $6.6 billion in 1998, and will exceed $20 billion next year according to the latest figures from the Workers' Compensation Insurance Rating Bureau.

As a result of these escalating rates, workers' comp was the biggest single issue in the California Legislature in 2003. Of the various bills dealing with workers' comp in 2003, three have been chaptered. These three are SB 2 (Burton), SB 228 (Alarcon), and AB 227 (Vargas). We will briefly discuss the new laws, then explain why they are not enough to save the workers' comp system in California.

The New Laws

SB 2

SB 2 has been termed "Pay-or-Play" health insurance. While SB 2 is not technically linked to workers' comp, it is still connected to the workers' comp bills since our government has stated that the reduction in workers' comp premiums that will allegedly come about because of the workers' comp bills will offset the massive burden that is facing businesses as a result of the SB 2 health care mandate. Essentially, SB 2 requires employers to either pay into a state healthcare fund that provides coverage or to provide health coverage directly. For employers of 20-99 employees, only the employees will receive this benefit. However, for employers of 200 employees or more, both the employee and the employee's dependents will receive the benefits. An employee is defined as a person who works at least 100 hours per month for an individual employer (23 hours per week), and the employee must have worked for that employer for a minimum of three months. For large employers, those with 200 or more employees, this law will be implemented on January 1, 2006. For employers with 50-199 employees, this law will take effect on January 1, 2007. While this law will also affect employers with 20-49 employees on January 1, 2007, this group is exempt from the requirement until a tax credit is passed to reduce their net costs by 20%. SB 2 mandates the coverage of some nontraditional recipients, including domestic partners and children of any age, including adults who are deemed dependents. SB 2 also requires that both employees and employers contribute a fee to the Employment Development Department. This fee consists of at least 80% from employers and a fee no more than 20% from employees. Low-wage workers (those employees earning less than 200% of the Federal Poverty Level) cannot be required to pay a fee more than 5% of their wages.

However, benefit packages defined in collective bargaining agreements and health coverage provided by the University of California to students of the University of California who are employed by the University of California are exempted from the provisions of this law.

Workers' Compensation -- From the Legislative Workers' Compensation Conference Committee Summary

The following are highlights of some of the provisions of SB 228:

Requires medical providers pay a $100 fee when they file a lien with the Workers' Compensation Appeals Board (WCAB). These fees will be used to off set user funding requirements imposed on employers.

Mandates adoption of interim utilization (use) guidelines and attaches a presumption of correctness to the utilization guidelines.

Mandates a study of utilization guidelines by the Administrative Director of the Division of Workers' Compensation, and mandates adoption of those guidelines. Attaches a presumption of correctness to the utilization guidelines.

Repeals the treater's presumption of correctness for medical treatment for all dates of injury, except in cases where the employee has "pre-designated" his or her personal physician.

Limits chiropractic treatment and physical therapy treatments to 24 visits for the life of the claim. Implements this limitation on injuries occurring on or after January 1, 2004. Provides that insurers may authorize supplemental treatments in writing.

Requires all employers to adopt utilization review systems, consistent with a specific utilization schedule. In cases involving spinal surgery, denials will go to an expedited second opinion process. In all other cases, the existing process will continue to apply.

Establishes procedure for employers to obtain second opinion on recommendations for spinal surgery.

Allows self-referral to outpatient surgery center where the provider discloses the financial relationship to the employer and the employer pre-authorizes the treatment at the center.

Requires the Division of Workers' Compensation to adopt the medical billing and provider fraud referral protocol within the California Department of Insurance.

Clarifies that all dispensers of workers' comp prescription drugs must dispense generic, unless a brand name has been specifically prescribed.

Repeals existing pharmaceutical schedule language, and creates a new pharmaceutical fee schedule.

Reduces time to pay medical bills from 60 days to 45 working days from date of complete billing. Increases penalty for late payment from 10% to 15%. Provides for repayment by the defendant of the lien filing fee if any contested amount is determined payable by the WCAB.

Exempts large government employers.

Requires Administrative Director to adopt regulations on electronic payment by January 1, 2005. All employers must accept electronic billing by July 1, 2006. If bills are sent electronically, and are within the fee schedule, payment must be made within 15 days of receipt.

Repeals Official Medical Fee Schedule language.

Provides for a 5% reduction to Official Medical Fee Schedule rates for physician services, to be implemented in the aggregate, but for that, no reduction shall be made to physician services currently below the Medicare fee schedule rate.

Creates a new outpatient facility fee schedule based on Medicare with a 120% conversion factor.

Requires insurer review of insured's injury and illness prevention plan within four months of commencement of initial policy term.

Some Highlights of Provisions of AB 227:

Provides for 100% employer funding for the Division of Workers' Compensation.

Repeals existing vocational rehabilitation statute as part of repeal of vocational rehabilitation mandate.

Implements a new supplemental job displacement benefit for injuries occurring on or after January 1, 2004.

Provides that employees who do not return to work for their employer within 60 days of the end of temporary disability period will receive an additional lump-sum benefit of $4,000 for permanent partial disability of less than 15%; $6,000 for permanent partial disability between 15% and 25%; $8,000 for permanent partial disability between 26% and 49%; and $10,000 for permanent partial disability between 50% and 99%. The benefit must be used for retraining, skill enhancement, job placement assistance, purchase of employment-related tools, in any combination.

Provides that the employer will not be liable for the supplemental job displacement benefit if, within 30 days of the end of TD, it offers, and the employee rejects, or fails to accept, an offer of modified or alternative work.

Excludes the California Insurance Guarantee Association (CIGA) from attorneys fee awards based upon actions of insolvent insurer.

Authorizes the California Infrastructure and Economic Development Bank (the Bank) to issue up to $1.5 billion worth of bonds at any one time in order to generate funds to be borrowed by the CIGA.

Increases maximum fine for workers' comp fraud from $50,000 to $150,000.

Requires the Insurance Commissioner to take into account the projected savings from the changes enacted this session in determining the advisory pure premium rates.

Expands the definition of "insolvency" to also mean the inability of an insurer to meet its financial obligations when they are due.

Expands the definition of "common trade or business," in the context of group workers' comp insurance, to include specified manufacturing facilities.

Exempts CIGA from certain penalties and attorney fees awards.

Requires the Insurance Commissioner, on or before July 1, 2004, to establish and maintain on the California Department of Insurance's web site, an online rate comparison guide showing workers' comp insurance rates for the 50 insurance companies writing the highest volume of business in this line during the two preceding years.

Requires the Workers' Compensation Insurance Rating Bureau to determine the cost savings achieved in the 2003 workers' comp reform legislation. Requires each insurer to certify that its rates reflect those cost savings. Provide that these certifications shall be made available to the public on the California Department of Insurance's web site. Specifies that the positions funded by the State Compensation Insurance Fund are exempt from any hiring freezes and staff cutbacks otherwise required by law.

As an aside, AB 1262 requires the Insurance Commissioner to set out minimum standards for workers' compensation insurance adjusters

Other Opinions

The package of SB 228, AB 227, and SB 2, while admittedly on its way towards reforming the workers' comp system, is still not enough of a reform. Senator Charles Poochigian stated it best when he remarked that "[w]hile [he] commends [his] colleagues for seeking to confront some escalating medical costs, yet to be addressed are major cost drivers dealing with indemnity or permanent disability that represent billions in potential savings to the ailing [workers' comp] system." In an effort to fully remedy the workers' comp problem, Senator Poochigian proposed SB 899, which he believed would have addressed the magnitude of the workers' comp crisis by providing $11 billion in cost savings. However, SB 899 ultimately failed, although all members of the Workers' Compensation Reform Conferees Committee recognized that the system needs additional reforms in order to truly fix the system. In fact, Republicans urged Governor Davis to call for a special legislative session to tackle issues that went unaddressed, including litigation and indemnity costs.

The promoters of this new worker's comp package claim that these new laws will represent about $5.3 billion in savings associated with pharmaceuticals, vocational rehabilitation, physical fees, utilization, physical therapy and other medical costs. State Insurance Commissioner John Garamendi has further contended that this overhaul will hold off a 12% insurance rate increase proposed for January 1, as well as roll back current premiums by 7%. Some have stated that the savings would not approach $5.3 billion. As of the date of this writing, this estimate has not yet been fully validated or confirmed by analysis from the Worker's Compensation Insurance Rating Bureau (WCIRB). In fact, the WCIRB has stated:

> Given a) the complexity of the medical process for workers' comp in California, b) the relative lack of specificity of utilization standards such as that proposed, c) the nature of the medical dispute resolution process within the WCAB, and d) that the effect of the AB 749 repeal of the primary treating physician presumption on injuries occurring after January 1, 2003 has not yet been reflected in medical loss experience, the WCIRB is *unable to estimate the cost effects of these provisions related to medical utilization.*

Therefore, it is uncertain as to how much in savings these laws will really provide.

While it is commendable that the legislators in Sacramento have taken this first step towards reforming our troubled workers' comp system, AB 227 and SB 228 do not fully comprehend the problems that the system faces. For example, there is currently a lack of consistency in treatment, where workers with similar injuries get vastly different amounts of care, depending on who is their medical practitioner. Supporters of the workers' comp bills say that the utilization review system will solve this. However, while it may weed out some unnecessary procedures, it does not even make a dent in the problem. The problem here is with the standard of treatment in the California workers' comp system. This standard states that everything necessary must be done to "cure and relieve" a worker's injury. With this definition of "cure and relieve," it is extremely difficult to acquire consistency in treatment. What is "necessary" to "cure and relieve" is in the eyes of the beholder. A clearer statement would provide more consistency and therefore fewer disputes with their attendant cost. Neither SB 228 nor AB 227 address this problem since they do not create a new definition for "cure and relieve." Even Insurance Commissioner Garamendi has stated that without changes to the definition of "cure and relieve," the utilization savings are seriously diminished. This is just one example of the inadequacy of this workers' comp package in reforming the system.

As such, the California's Workers' comp system is desperately in need of new reforms that will completely address all the problems. Originally, workers' comp was to be a true no-fault system. It was intended to facilitate both employees and employers efficiently and effectively. For example, a secretary who injures the pinky on her major hand due to an accident on-the-job, and cannot do the typing required for her job, should be able to merely refer to a chart, look up her injury and figure out how much she is entitled to in workers' comp benefits. The employer would then pay the benefits to the employee. There is no need for any sort of litigation in that instance. Instead, the workers' comp system today has evolved into a morass of litigation and contention over such issues as disability pay, whether the injury in fact occurred "on-the-job," etc. Attorneys have swarmed round the workers' comp system and flourished, leading to higher costs and premiums to be paid for by the employers. This is exactly why the system has incurred such heavy premiums and made California such a bad environment for businesses. Reforming the workers' comp system necessarily needs to take into account the original intent of workers' comp – a system whereby there is a finite set of rules to work off of, where there is a lesser requirement for litigation and attorneys. Only then will California truly solve its workers' comp system and entice businesses back into California.

CONTRACTORS BOARD AND THEIR BUDGET

With respect to budget and personnel, the Contractors State License Board was the victim of the ineptness of the Legislature and the governor. As a result of budget woes, the governor placed a hiring freeze on governmental entities including the Contractors Board and an additional reduction in staff. This came at a time when the Contractors Board already had numerous vacancies that they were not able to fill.

The licensing area had suffered and is suffering significant delays. That section is pledging to keep licensed contractors in business. Therefore, the delays should not hurt licensed contractors. They shifted some of the personnel from other areas including enforcement to licensing.

Secondly, as a result of budget concerns, further layoffs took place. The staff of the License Board has now gone from some 450 employees to under 300 employees. This severely limits the Contractors Board in their day-to-day operations.

Some good may come out of adversity. The Contractors Board staff is now conducting a "triage" in order to prioritize complaints received. Repeat offenders, more egregious claims, including those against the elderly, are given top priority along with health and safety issues. The Contractors Board is now telling people that they may not be able to get to their complaints quickly and they may wish to utilize small claims court procedures.

LEGISLATION THAT DID NOT PASS

Sometimes, and probably most often, things that the Legislature does not do are more beneficial than the things that it does. One of those areas is in the Mechanic's Lien area. Another dealt with service and repair contractors.

Mechanic's Liens

For approximately two years, the California Law Revision Commission (CLRC) studied the issue of mechanic's liens. The CLRC studies technical and complex areas of law and makes recommendations to the Legislature for legislative action. After approximately two years of studying, the Commission made its recommendation to the Legislature to do away with mechanic's liens on owner-occupied single-family residences up to the amount of $15,000.00. Assemblyman Dutra took that bill and modified it substantially to increase the floor to $25,000.00 and made other changes. In that Assembly member Dutra could not make the changes quickly enough, that bill was dropped and it was re-introduced in 2003. It was also amended to cover only the first $15,000.00 of the mechanic's lien claims. Throughout the year 2003, Assembly member Dutra had stated that he would work with the affected people in the industry to try to work out a piece in legislation that everybody could support. Unfortunately, nothing was worked out. As a result of a personal emergency, the bill was not heard and is now a two-year bill.

Significantly, Legislative Counsel, the attorney for the Legislature, has twice opined that this type of Bill would require a constitutional amendment. But why should the Legislature do anything that is logical?

This office has been involved in this issue during the entire period of time since it was referred to the California Law Revision Commission, where we attended each and every meeting, and then in all meetings with legislative personnel. We will continue to argue contractor's rights in the future.

Service and Repair Contractors

SB 30 was introduced by Senator Figueroa to take care of some of the problems involved in service and repair work. However, when the people with lack of experience started to re-write SB 30 and essentially make it worse than it presently is, that legislation was put on hold for 2004. One of the inane ideas that was requested by these inexperienced regulators was asking for a "bill of materials" to be used on service and repair work. I am not sure if they understand what the term "bill of materials" means. Would a service and repair contractor have to list all of the flux, or washers used in changing out a faucet.

CONSTRUCTION IN THE CLASSROOM

Congratulations to the California Coalition for Construction in the Classroom, Executive Director Curt Augustine, and its members.

This could have been a real doom and gloom year that could have extended for a long period of time. However, the California Coalition for Construction in the Classroom (CCCC) has made significant contributions to the construction industry that might alleviate the situation. As many of you know, vocational education in high schools is virtually non-existent. Our legislators believe that everyone should have a college degree. This flies in the face of the fact that the construction industry is the largest industry in the state of California. Framing does not require a college degree.

The CCCC gathered its troops and fought recent Federal Legislative proposals and Bush proposals, which threatened the very existence of vocational education in high schools. The administration was essentially proposing a college prep curriculum only. That would eliminate funding for vocational education in high school. Since vocational education in California schools is almost entirely funded from Federal funds, this would eliminate virtually all vocational education in California. Further, the legislation would have allowed current high school vocational education funds to be spent on administrative costs for the One Stop Centers that provide adult education.

The CCCC itself and its industry allies, most notably California SMACNA, began an aggressive push to affect the legislation. This included letter writing campaigns and meeting with various California legislators. As a result, the Work Force Reinvestment Act that would have allowed the Governor of a state to take high school vocational education funds for administrative costs was amended to remove the provision allowing the transfer of funds away from high school vocational education.

Secondly, the Bush administration was pushing a college prep only high school agenda in the budget. In late June, both the House and Senate Appropriations Committee voted on bills to fund career education. Both bills maintain the funding presently in the budget. This in the face of the Bush administration's proposal to cut the funding by 25%.

With California specific legislation, there is a somewhat different story. Because of the state budget crisis, most of the spending bills will be heard next year. However, all of the budget proposals that would have adversely affected the amount of funding for local high schools, have been defeated. The current budget bill maintains the same funding, distribution and levels as last year.

Congratulations and thanks to the California Coalition for Construction in the Classroom, and Curt Augustine.

NOTICE OF COMPLETION LAW

After about five years of trying, the American Subcontractors Association of California achieved a partial victory by sponsoring and having passed into law what they call "Fair Notice" legislation.

The law requires private project owners to notify the prime contractor and all subcontractors and suppliers who properly serve a 20-day Preliminary Notice, that a Notice of Completion or a Notice of Cessation has been recorded within ten days after a Notice of Completion is recorded. The recording of a Notice of Completion or a Notice of Cessation substantially reduces the time within which one may record a mechanic's lien. Typically, one has to record a mechanic's lien within 90 days after completion of the project. However, for subcontractors and material suppliers, the time within which one must record a mechanic's lien is reduced from 90 days to 30 days, if a Notice of Completion or a Notice of Cessation of Labor is recorded.

If the owner does not send the Notice of the recording of the Notice of Completion or Notice of Cessation, then the time period within which to record a mechanic's lien is extended back to the original 90-day requirement as if a Notice of Completion or Notice of Cessation is not recorded.

The law, however, exempts home improvement contracts from this requirement.

LEGISLATION THAT DID PASS

Highlights of Construction Related Legislation

The following are portions of the law and/or highlights of changes in the law. They should not be taken at face value. If the law appears to relate to an issue that you are concerned about, you should read the entire law and discuss it with your attorney.

AB 14 (Jerome Horton)

Topic: Public contracts: job order contracting.

The Public Contract law provides various procedures, including competitive bidding, for different types of contracts involving state and local public entities, including school districts.

This law authorizes, until December 1, 2007, job order contracting, as defined, by the Los Angeles Unified School District as an alternative bidding procedure. The law requires the district to report to the Legislature regarding implementation of the job order contracting process.

AB 17 (Kehoe)

Topic: State Contracts: acquisition of goods or services

This law prohibits a state agency from entering into a contract for the acquisition of goods or services in the amount of $100,000 or more with a contractor who, in the providing of benefits, discriminates between employees with spouses and employees with domestic partners, or discriminates between the domestic partners and spouses of those employees.

AB 76 (Corbett)

Topic: Employment discrimination

This law adds to the term "unlawful employment practice," an employer who knows or should have known of an incident of harassment by a non-employee but fails to take corrective action.

AB 88 (Corbett & Steinberg)

Topic: Contracts.

The federal Telemarketing Sales Rule prohibits a seller or telemarketer from engaging in deceptive or abusive telemarketing acts or practices, including, but not limited to, 1) causing billing information to be submitted for payment, directly or indirectly, without the express informed consent of the customer or donor, as specified, and 2) keeping, for 24 months, certain authorizations or records.

This law provides that any contract with a consumer located in California that is made in connection with a telephone solicitation for the purchase of certain goods or services is unlawful if the telemarketer fails to comply with the provisions of the Telemarketing Sales Rule except as specified.

AB 196 (Leno)

Topic: Discrimination.

Existing law prohibits various types of discrimination and harassment based on sex, as defined, in housing and employment.

This new law expands the prohibition on sexual discrimination and harassment by including gender, as defined, in the definition of sex.

AB 223 (Diaz)

Topic: Employment

Under existing law, if an employee believes an employer has failed to pay wages required by contract or statute, the employee may either file a civil action against the employer or file a wage claim with the Labor Commissioner seeking administrative relief.

This law provides that an employee is successful in a lawsuit as long as the employee recovers a judgment in his or her favor. This law overturns the holding in Smith vs. Rae-Venter Law Group. It restores the prior holding in Cardenas v. Mission Industries and another case called Triad Data Services, Inc. v. Jackson.

AB 227 (Vargas)

Topic: Workers' Compensation

The following explanation of the new Workers' Compensation law (AB 227 and SB 228) is from the Governor's office.

> Governor Gray Davis signed into law a comprehensive workers' compensation legislative package that he alleges will give employers savings of more than $4 billion and protects benefits enacted last year for injured workers.
>
> "By signing this bill package, California's workers' compensation system will get a major overhaul," Gov. Davis said. "We're saving money for businesses, non-profits and cities. We're rebuilding the engines of our economy. As I've said before, our system is like a 90-year old busted-up jalopy. It's ugly. It barely runs. It needs more than tune up and a paint job, it needs a complete overhaul."
>
> The package contains a significant portion of the reforms Governor Davis and Insurance Commissioner John Garamendi jointly proposed in May of this year. It also meets the Governor's goals of preserving quality medical care for workers while reversing the rise in premium costs for employers.
>
> "By signing this bill package, our workers' compensation system gets reforms even industry analysts recognize will save more than $5 billion next year and over $4 billion each year after." Gov. Davis said. "This reform package offers relief to employers and keeps jobs in California. It will decrease expensive litigation, contain medical costs, curb fraud and support return-to-work programs."
>
> The legislation, which emerged after hearings by a joint legislative conference committee, contains reforms lawmakers call a "first step" in righting a system that subjected employers to soaring premium increases over the last few years as medical costs skyrocketed and California-based insurance companies were forced out of the market.
>
> Contained in the proposed package and signed by the Governor are reforms that include:
>
> - Implementing HMO-like utilization management tools;

- Establishing a three-year pilot for an independent second opinion on recommendations for spinal surgery;
- Prohibiting doctors from referring patients to outpatient surgery clinics where the doctors have financial interests;
- Setting an outpatient surgery facility fee schedule based on the Medicare fee plus 20 percent;
- Setting a pharmaceutical fee schedule based on 100 percent of the Medi-Cal fee and requiring greater use of generic drugs;
- Increasing the penalty from 10 to 15 percent to insurance companies for late payment to health care providers;
- Reducing fraud through increased penalties, information-sharing among state programs, consistent medical billing and fraud referral protocols;
- Requiring insurance commissioner to adopt minimum standards of training, experience and skill for workers' compensation claims administrators and bill reviewers. Insurers are required to certify compliance;
- Expanding alternative workers' compensation dispute resolution processes to other unionized industries besides construction;
- Requiring listing of insurance companies and rates on the Internet.

  The legislation also provides a new supplemental job displacement benefit for training, education and skill enhancement to substitute for vocational rehabilitation, estimated to save $1.2 billion per year, a cap of 24 visits to a chiropractor, and a cap of 24 visits for physical therapy for the life of a claim unless authorized by the insurance carrier;

The above is from the Governor's office. There are other opinions on the effect of this law. See our treatment of "***WORKERS' COMPENSATION AND 'PAY-OR-PLAY' HEALTH INSURANCE***" on preceding pages.

AB 274 (Koretz)

Topic: Employment

Under existing law, it is unlawful for a person to retaliate against an employee for exercising his or her employment rights. This law creates a rebuttable presumption that an adverse employment action taken within 60 days after an employee exercises his or her employment rights is retaliatory, unless there is clear and convincing evidence that the employee made up the claim in order to prevent the employer from taking adverse employment action. This presumption does not apply to the criminal penalty for retaliation and does not apply to a discharge upon the completion of a limited-term employment. This law creates a greater burden on the employer, requiring the employer to prove that the employer's actions were not retaliatory.

AB 276 (Koretz)

Topic: Penalties for Labor Code violations.

Under existing law, if an employer fails to pay wages or unlawfully withholds wages, the penalty for a first violation is $50, and the penalty for subsequent or willful or intentional violations is $100 and the penalty recovered is placed in the General Fund.

This law increases the penalties to $100 for the first violation and $200 for subsequent or willful or intentional violations.

AB 309 (Chu)

Topic: Contracts: foreign language

Existing law requires a person in a trade or business who negotiates certain contracts or agreements primarily in the Spanish language to deliver to the other party prior to execution of the contract, a Spanish language translation of the contract or agreement, with some exceptions.

This law, on July 1, 2004, extends these provisions to the foreign languages of Chinese, Tagalog, Vietnamese, and Korean. See also SB 146 which requires that the translation provided in this law extend to every term and condition in that contract or agreement, with specified exceptions. Thus, AB 309 and SB 146 incorporate the other.

AB 334 (Goldberg)

Topic: Water softening and conditioning appliances

Existing law authorizes a local agency, by ordinance, to limit the availability or prohibit the installation of residential water softening or water conditioning appliances that discharge the community sewer systems if the local agency makes certain findings and includes them in the ordinance. The law has changed to revise the findings that the local agency is required to make and include under this provision. The importance is that residential water softening or water conditioning appliances can only be installed if certain conditions are met.

AB 341 (Aghazaria)

Topic: Contractors: landscape contractors.

This law authorizes a landscape contractor working within his or her license classification to subcontract with a swimming pool contractor for the construction of a swimming pool, spa, or hot tub that is included within a landscape project the landscape contractor is supervising, and are subcontracted to a single licensed swimming pool contractor or are performed by the landscape contractor who is a licensed swimming pool contractor.

AB 447 (Vargas)

Topic: Lien claims: release: attorneys' fees.

This law increases the amount of attorneys' fees that may be recovered from one who records a lien and does not remove it when it has become stale, to $2,000.00.

AB 453 (Yee)

Topic: Public works contracts bidding: compensation of contractors.

This law provides that when a project for the construction, alteration, repair, or improvement of any structure, building, or road, or other improvement of any kind is competitively bid and a protest is made, the contract may be entered into pending final decision on the protest. If the contract is later determined to be invalid due to a defect or defects in the competitive bidding process caused solely by the public entity, this law entitles the contractor who entered into the contract with the public entity to be paid the reasonable cost, not including profit, of the labor, equipment, materials, and services furnished by the contractor prior to the date of the determination, subject to specified conditions.

AB 544 (Montanez)

Topic: Contractor: temporary labor.

This law expands the term "contractor" to include certain work activity provided by a temporary labor service agency that as the employer, provides employees for the performance of the work covered. This provision does not apply if a properly licensed contractor exercises proper supervision and control over the employees.

AB 591 (Strickland)

Topic: Curriculum: graduation requirements: career technical education

This law encourages the advisory group to Superintendent of Public Instruction to identify career technical courses that meet the state-adopted academic content standards and that satisfy high school graduation requirements and admission requirements of the University of California and the California State University. What the Legislature is trying to do is have students study courses that will let them enter the University of California and the California State University.

AB 722 (Matthews)

Topic: Public contracts: electronic bids: reverse auctions.

This law authorizes the Department of General Services to utilize reverse auctions for the acquisition of goods, services, and information technology. The law defines "reverse auction" as a competitive online solicitation process for *fungible* goods, information technology, or services in which vendors compete against each other online in real time in an open and interactive environment. Vendors are required to register before the reverse auction opening date and time and as part of that registration requirement agree to the terms of conditions. The Department of General Services may require vendors to be pre-qualified. The reverse auction process may not be used for bidding on any construction contract that is subject to the State Contract Act, Chapter 1 of the Public Contracts Code. For example, historic restoration projects and certain state projects are subject to the State Contract Act, and thus not allowed under reverse auctions.

AB 774 (Wiggins)

Topic: Vocational Education.

Existing law requires the minimum day in specified vocational education programs to consist of four periods totaling at least 180 minutes in duration. This new law additionally provides that for a pupil who attends a school in which the regularly scheduled period is greater than 60 minutes in length, the minimum day is one or more periods totaling at least 180 minutes in duration.

AB 852 (Lieber)

Topic: Prevailing rate of per diem wages: determinations.

With certain exceptions which are in this law, the Director of Industrial Relations must determine the prevailing wage rates to any state or political subdivision that agrees by contract with a private entity that the employees are to be paid the general prevailing rate of per diem wages, to determine that rate including holidays and overtime work, and to provide those wage rates to the state or political subdivision.

AB 902 (Diaz)

Topic: Public Works – Subcontractor Substitution

In California, first tier subcontractors must be listed in the prime contractor's bid to a public entity. One cannot substitute a listed subcontractor unless the awarding authority (the public entity) allows that substitution. In addition to the other means by which one can substitute a subcontractor, this new law would allow the prime contractor to substitute the subcontractor when the listed subcontractor fails or refuses to execute a written contract for the scope of the work specified in the subcontractor's bid and at the price specified in the subcontractor's bid.

AB 903 (Steinberg)

Topic: Construction defect cases.

This law among other things, revises and recasts various provisions governing home construction defect actions that relate to a builders election to inspect, the applicable statute of limitations, affirmative defenses, and the exclusivity of these provisions. It also revises the definition of "builder."

AB 1262 (Matthews)

Topic: Workers' compensation insurance; claims adjusters.

This law requires the insurance commissioner to adopt regulations dealing with the minimum standards of training, experience and skill that workers' compensation claims adjusters must posses. The law also requires every insurer for workers' compensation to certify to the commissioner that the personnel employed by the insurer to adjust workers' compensation claims or employed for that purpose by a medical billing entity meets those standards.

AB 1382 (Correa)

Topic: Contractors: arbitration, civil penalties, and licensing.

This is a very long and complicated piece of legislation and below are just the highlights.

This law provides for the revocation of a contractor's license within 90 days following notification of the contractor by the board, but authorizes the registrar of the board, for good cause, to delay the revocation for not more than one year. This law also deletes the authority of an arbitrator to order specific performance of a contract but specifies that it would not prevent an arbitrator from awarding a complainant all direct costs and expenses for the completion or repair of the project.

Until January 1, 2004, the failure of a contractor to comply with an arbitration award would result in a suspension within 30-days following notification of the contractor by the Board. And would thereafter result in a revocation. Similar provisions deal with failing to pay a civil penalty or failing to comply with an order of correction or to pay a specified sum to an injured party in lieu of correction. As of January 1, 2003, the law would provide for the revocation of the license within 90-days. The Registrar shall notify the contractor certified mail that the failure to comply with the arbitrators award and that the license shall be automatically suspended 30 calendar days from the date of the notice. Reinstatement may be made at any time following the suspension by complying with the arbitrator's award and the final order of the Registrar. If no reinstatement is made of the license within 90-days of the date of the automatic suspension, the contractor's license and any other contractor's license issued to the licensee shall be automatically revoked. The Registrar may delay the revocation for good cause.

This law requires the board to pay the expenses of one expert witness in an arbitration proceeding upon the request of either party only if the case involves workmanship issues. While existing law authorizes the board to assess a civil penalty not exceeding $2000 upon its licensees for specified violations of the Contractor's State License Law, this new law increases the amount to $5000.

If a qualifying partner, responsible managing officer, or responsible managing employee, leaves the company after an act or omission has occurred that resulted in a citation, the disassociated qualifying partner, responsible managing officer, or responsible managing employee shall not be relieved for responsibility for complying with the citation.

Additionally, while existing law allows a suspended contractor's license to be renewed only as an inactive license and prohibits a contractor from engaging in licensed activity until the license is reinstated, this new law instead authorizes the renewal of an expired license which has been suspended as an active license but would prohibit a contractor with a suspended license from engaging in any activity relating to the license until the license is reinstated.

AB 1386 (Horton)

Topic: Contractors

This law, with some exceptions, authorizes a person who utilizes a contractor with a suspended or revoked license to bring an action in any court of competent jurisdiction in this state for recovery of compensation paid to the suspended or revoked licensee for performance of any act or contract.

This law also requires a contractor to demonstrate that he or she acted promptly and in good faith to reinstate his or her license upon learning it was invalid in order to meet substantial compliance with the licensure requirements.

AB 1418 (Laird)

Topic: Public works: prevailing wage

This law requires the Contractor's State License Board to disclose, on the Internet, information regarding a licensee's willful or deliberate violation of the Labor Code. This law imposes interest and penalties under specified conditions on all due and unpaid wages at the specified rate until those wages are paid.

AB 1536 (Goldberg)

Topic: Discrimination.

Under the existing Fair Employment and Housing Act, when a complaint alleging an unlawful practice is filed with the Department of Fair Employment and Housing, the Department is required to serve the complaint upon the person, employer, labor organization, or employment agency alleged to have committed the unlawful practice, and service is to be completed within 45 days.

This law provides that where a person claiming to be aggrieved by an unlawful practice is represented by private counsel, their private counsel, and not the department, would instead serve the complaint, and in either case, service is to be completed within 60 days.

AB 1538 (Berg)

Topic: Construction contractors.

This new law requires a construction contractor, except for plumbing, electrical sign and well drilling contractors, to display his or her contractor's license number, and business name, and permanent business address in or on each commercially registered motor vehicle used in his or her construction business. The reason that plumbing, electrical sign, and well drilling contractors are exempted from the new law is that they were already required to comply with similar requirements.

AB 1573 (Corbett)

Topic: School construction: design-build

Existing law, until January 1, 2007, authorizes a school district governing board to enter into a design-build contract, as defined, in which factors in addition to price and cost may be considered in awarding a contract for the design and construction of a school facility that exceeds $10,000,000. Existing law also requires the school district governing board to be the employer of the project inspector. The project inspector must be fully independent from any member of the design-build entity and prohibits the inspector from having any affiliation with any member of the design-build entity or any of the project subcontractors.

This new law requires the project inspector to act under the direction of either the Director of the Department of General Services or a competent, qualified agent of the school district.

AB 1745 (Dutra)

Topic: Public Contracts: bonds

The State Contract Act requires that every contract provide for the filing of separate performance and payment bonds, as provided, and that the performance and payment bonds each equal at least half of the contract price, subject to certain exceptions.

This law gives the Department of Transportation discretion to specify that, for projects with a contract price greater than $250,000,000, the payment bond shall be the lesser of half the contract price or $500,000,000.

This law declares that it is to take effect immediately as an urgency statute.

SB 2 (Burton)

Topic: Pay-or-Play Health Insurance

Among other things this law enacts the Health Insurance Act of 2003 to provide health coverage to specified individuals (and in some cases their dependents) who do not receive job-based coverage and who work for large and medium employers, as defined. Imposes a fee on employers, as specified, and makes available a credit against that fee for employers who provide coverage.

See our more detailed explanation in preceding pages.

SB 110 (Margett)

Topic: Public contracts: contract specifications.

This law authorizes a bid specification of a certain product if the awarding authority makes a finding that a particular material or service is designated by a brand or trade name in order to: (1) Obtain a genuinely necessary and unique item that is only available from one source, (2) Obtain an item under circumstances in which competition is completely unavailing, or (3) Respond to a local or state declared emergency.

SB 113 (Ackerman)

Topic: Mechanic's liens.

This deals with a technical pleading matter that really should be left to an attorney. Essentially, this law states that when one has a mechanic's lien right and also a contract right, as well as an arbitration provision in his or her contract, the arbitrator cannot foreclose on a mechanic's lien and a lawsuit must be filed on a mechanic's lien very quickly. There presently is a mechanism to file suit to both foreclose on a mechanic's lien and breach of contract and other matters and ask for the lawsuit to be stayed pending the contractual arbitration.

This law revises how that is to be done by the claimant either (1) including an allegation in the Complaint that the claimant does not intend to waive any right of arbitration and intends to move within 30 days after service of the Summons and Complaint, for an Order to Stay for the proceedings in the action, or (2) files an application, at the same time the Complaint is filed that the action be stayed pending arbitration. The law would also require the claimant to file and serve a Motion to Stay the action pending the arbitration of any issue, question, or dispute that is claimed to be arbitrable under the agreement that is relevant to the action to enforce the claim of lien within 30 days after service of the Summons and Complaint. The failure of a claimant to comply with this provision would waive the claimants right to compel arbitration.

SB 134 (Figueroa)

Topic: Private Works of Improvement: Liens

After five years of trying, the American Subcontractors Association got some relief. People in the construction industry should know that they typically have 90-days from actual completion within which to record a mechanic's lien. However, if a Notice of Completion or a Notice of Cessation of Labor is recorded, then that shortens the time period from 90-days to 30-days for subcontractors. Unfortunately, subcontractors and material suppliers do not always know when that notice is recorded. This law would require that the owner, give a notice by registered or certified mail or by first class mail, evidenced by a certificate of mailing, to the original contractor and any claimant who has provided a 20-day Preliminary Notice, that a Notice of Completion or a Notice of Cessation has been recorded. It shall be sent within 10-days after recordation of the Notice of Completion or the Notice of Cessation. If it is not sent timely, then the claimants have 90-days from the date that the Notice of Completion or the Notice of Cessation has been recorded.

The law also changes the Preliminary Notice Form.

Unfortunately, this law only covers private works of improvement and also does not cover any home improvement project.

SB 146 (Escutia)

Topic: Contracts: Spanish Translation

Existing law requires that a person in a trade or business who negotiates specified contracts of agreements primarily in the Spanish language deliver to the other party prior to execution of the contract, a Spanish-language translation of the contract or agreement, with some exceptions. The aggrieved party is entitled to rescind the contract of agreement if cases of noncompliance. This law further requires that the translation is required to include a translation of every term and condition in that contract or agreement.

This law, however, is dependent on the passage of AB 309, which applies this translation to the foreign languages of Chinese, Tagalog, Vietnamese, and Korean. See also AB 309 which requires that the provisions in this law also extend to the foreign languages of Chinese, Tagalog, Vietnamese, and Korean. Thus, AB 309 and SB 146 incorporate the other.

SB 179 (Alarcon)

Topic: Contracts for labor or services

This law provides that any person or entity who enters into a labor contract for construction, farm labor, garment, janitorial, or security guard services when the person or entity knows or should know that the contract does not provide sufficient funds to allow the labor contractor to comply with all applicable laws or regulations governing the labor or services to be provided under the contract, is subject to liability and specified civil penalties.

The law also establishes a rebuttable presumption that a person or entity entering into such a contract for labor or services does not violate the law's provisions if the labor contract or material change to the labor contract meets specified requirements. The law does not apply to persons or entities who have executed certain collective bargaining agreements, or to labor or services to be performed on a person's home residence or residences, under specified conditions.

SB 228 (Alarcon)

Topic: Workers' Compensation

The following explanation of the new Workers' Compensation law (AB 227 and SB 228) is from the Governor's office.

> Governor Gray Davis signed into law a comprehensive workers' compensation legislative package that he alleges will give employers savings of more than $4 billion and protects benefits enacted last year for injured workers.
>
> "By signing this bill package, California's workers' compensation system will get a major overhaul," Gov. Davis said. "We're saving money for businesses, non-profits and cities. We're rebuilding the engines of our economy. As I've said before, our system is like a 90-year old busted-up jalopy. It's ugly. It barely runs. It needs more than tune up and a paint job, it needs a complete overhaul."
>
> The package contains a significant portion of the reforms Governor Davis and Insurance Commissioner John Garamendi jointly proposed in May of this year. It also meets the Governor's goals of preserving quality medical care for workers while reversing the rise in premium costs for employers.
>
> "By signing this bill package, our workers' compensation system gets reforms even industry analysts recognize will save more than $5 billion next year and over $4 billion each year after." Gov. Davis said. "This reform package offers relief to employers and keeps jobs in California. It will decrease expensive litigation, contain medical costs, curb fraud and support return-to-work programs."

The legislation, which emerged after hearings by a joint legislative conference committee, contains reforms lawmakers call a "first step" in righting a system that subjected employers to soaring premium increases over the last few years as medical costs skyrocketed and California-based insurance companies were forced out of the market.

Contained in the proposed package and signed by the Governor are reforms that include:

- Implementing HMO-like utilization management tools;
- Establishing a three-year pilot for an independent second opinion on recommendations for spinal surgery;
- Prohibiting doctors from referring patients to outpatient surgery clinics where the doctors have financial interests;
- Setting an outpatient surgery facility fee schedule based on the Medicare fee plus 20 percent;
- Setting a pharmaceutical fee schedule based on 100 percent of the Medi-Cal fee and requiring greater use of generic drugs;
- Increasing the penalty from 10 to 15 percent to insurance companies for late payment to health care providers;
- Reducing fraud through increased penalties, information-sharing among state programs, consistent medical billing and fraud referral protocols;
- Requiring insurance commissioner to adopt minimum standards of training, experience and skill for workers' compensation claims administrators and bill reviewers. Insurers are required to certify compliance;
- Expanding alternative workers' compensation dispute resolution processes to other unionized industries besides construction;
- Requiring listing of insurance companies and rates on the Internet.

The legislation also provides a new supplemental job displacement benefit for training, education and skill enhancement to substitute for vocational rehabilitation, estimated to save $1.2 billion per year, a cap of 24 visits to a chiropractor, and a cap of 24 visits for physical therapy for the life of a claim unless authorized by the insurance carrier;

The above is from the Governor's office. There are other opinions on the effect of this law. See our treatment of "***WORKERS' COMPENSATION AND 'PAY-OR-PLAY' HEALTH INSURANCE***" on preceding pages.

SB 364 (Figueroa)

Topic: Licensing Boards

Among other things, this law requires the Contractors' State License Board, the Structural Pest Control Board and the Bureau of Naturopathic Medicine to obtain fingerprint cards from applicants applying for licensure so that they may obtain and receive, at their discretion, criminal history information on the applicant from the Department of Justice and the United States Federal Bureau of Investigation.

This new law also extends the time within which a registered salesperson must furnish their full set of fingerprints to the Contractors Board until July 1, 2004.

SB 443 (Figueroa)

Topic: Contracting without a license: repeat offenders.

This law requires, except in unusual cases, that one who is a repeat offender of contracting without a license be confined in the county jail for not less than 90 days. The law requires the court to state on the record its reasons if the court imposed a jail sentence of less than 90 days or only a fine.

SB 523 (Escutia)

Topic: Corporate Liability

This law makes a corporation and a limited liability company liable for civil penalties up to $1,000,000 in an action brought by the Attorney General, district attorney or a city attorney if the corporation or limited liability company has knowledge of certain acts and fails to notify the Attorney General or the appropriate government agency and shareholders or investors. Acts include things like publishing or posting information that contain material statements or omissions that are false, intentionally giving shares of stock in the corporation a greater value then the apparent market value than what they really possessed, misstatements of expenditures, operations, values, etc., refusing to make entries in books, and generally misstatements or concealment. Though the law appears to be well intentioned, it could be severely mishandled by some regulators. One person's idea of value could be different than another's.

SB 777 (Escutia)

Topic: Whistleblowers.

Existing law prohibits employers from making, adopting, or enforcing a policy that prevents an employee from disclosing violations of a state or federal statute, or a violation or noncompliance with a state or federal regulation to a government or law enforcement agency, or from retaliating against an employee who makes a disclosure.

This law extends these protections to employees who report a violation of a state or federal rule, who refuse to participate in an activity that would result in a violation of state or federal statute, or a violation or noncompliance with a state or federal rule or regulation, or who exercised these rights in former employment.

SB 796 (Dunn)

Topic: Employment

This law provides that if the Labor and Workforce Development Agency does not bring a civil action for penalties for violations of the Labor Code, the aggrieved employee may do so. The law also determines to whom the penalties shall be paid. In addition, the aggrieved employee may also recover attorney's fees and costs and, in some cases, penalties.

SB 966 (Alarcon)

Topic: Public works and prevailing wages: contractor's costs.

This law authorizes a contractor to bring an action in a court of competent jurisdiction to recover from an awarding body specified labor costs, penalties, and legal fees, if certain conditions are met.

This law also authorizes a contractor to bring an action to recover from the body awarding a contract for a public work or otherwise undertaking any public work any increased cost, as defined, incurred by the contractor if certain conditions are met. This law defines "awarding body" to exclude the Department of General Services, the Department of Transportation, and the Department of Water Resources. The law defines "increased costs" to include, but not limited to, labor cost increases required to be paid to the contractor's workers and penalties for which the contractor is liable. The conditions would be that either of the following exists:

The awarding body, previously affirmatively represented to the contractor in writing, in the call for bids, <u>or</u> otherwise, that the work to be covered by the bid was not a "public work" or the awarding body received actual notice from the Department of Industrial Relations that the work to be covered by the bid or contract is a "public work" and failed to disclose that information to the contractor before the bid opening or awarding of the contract.

FIX-IT LAW CONSTRUCTION DEFECT LEGISLATION SB 800

Although this law was passed in 2002, it actually became effective January 1, 2003. We thought it was very important to highlight the law in this book.

SB 800 became law January 1, 2003, covering new homes first built and sold as of January 1, 2003. Very little is known about this law because there has not been sufficient time to have any appeals or other court interpretations. It was expected that SB 800 would be worked on by the Legislature this year. Indeed, it was expected that subcontractors would get some relief from construction defect problems. However, because of the budget crisis, the liability insurance crisis, and workers compensation crisis, nothing was done and hopefully something will happen next year. Our analysis of SB 800 is as follows:

FIX IT LAW

CONSTRUCTION DEFECT LEGISLATION

SB 800

There is always some bill moving through the Legislature dealing with construction defects. But the most "important" one to date was one that went into effect January 1, 2003, known as SB 800. For convenience of the audience, I am enclosing a copy of the legislation itself.

Commentators have had problems with some of the terminology. As an example, the word "builder" is used throughout. Section 912 defines builder as, "a builder, developer, or original seller." It is unclear whether that term includes the prime contractor as well as the owner. <u>However, it is the interpretation of the California Building Industry Association (CBIA), the trade association that negotiated the law, that the term "builder" does not include the prime contractor unless he is also the seller to the consumer</u>. No matter how you define it, there will be redundancy.

Second, there are other questions about SB 800. It went into effect January 1, 2003, dealing with homes sold after January 1, 2003. Accordingly, not too many disputes have arisen since then and as of this writing, we know of no reported cases in this short period of time. Further, different commentators have had different interpretations. Our personal feeling is that the most important thing that SB 800 has done is its attempt to delay litigation in the hope of settlement prior to the expenditure of a great deal of attorneys fees. It also sets out certain standards. If those standards are clear, then there is less likelihood of litigation over the interpretation of the standards.

CBIA states that SB 800:

- Gives homebuilders an absolute right to repair breaches of functionality standards;
- Allows homebuilders to negotiate a cash payments/liability releases on breaches;

- Limits causes of action to statutory functionality standards;
- Reduces statute of repose/limitations on several functionality standards;
- Limits homebuilder/subcontractor liability to each functionality standard;
- Imposes several duties on homeowners, including proper notification and permission to repair;
- Sets forth specific maintenance obligations for homeowners to meet;
- Sets up a mediation hurdle if disputes arise over a repair;
- Reaffirms existing homebuilder rights to establish terms of dispute resolution in sales agreements, including mandatory binding arbitration;
- Establishes statutory affirmative defenses for homebuilders; and
- Sets forth opt-out provisions for homebuilders.

The following is our analysis based on the information that we have to date:

SB 800 is rather complex and lengthy. We are only giving you a brief overview of this law. It is expected that it will be amended and refined in the future. Indeed, some such proposals are in the Legislature at this time.

The statement of legislative intent in the statute states as follows:

> "The prompt and fair resolution of construction defect claims is in the interest of consumers, homeowners, and the builders of homes, and is vital to the state's continuing growth and vitality. However, under current procedures and standards, homeowners and builders alike are not afforded the opportunity for quick and fair resolution of claims. Both need clear standards and mechanisms for the prompt resolution of claims."

A. Introduction

Governor Gray Davis signed SB 800, a law that some say will lead to increasing production of affordable condominiums and townhouses, thereby easing the state's chronic housing crisis. This law only covers new homes sold after January 1, 2003. The determination of when the home is "sold" has been said to mean the close of escrow by most commentators. This law partially reforms California's construction dispute and litigation laws by giving builders the right to fix any problems that develop before a lawsuit can be filed against them, and the law also protects homeowners by giving them recourse in the event problems are not addressed.

As contractors know, for the past decade or so there has been such a high volume of lawsuits involving construction defects, usually made up of condominiums and townhouses, that the price of insuring such housing, if available, has become sky-high. Numerous lawsuits, resulting in multimillion-dollar judgments or settlements, have caused insurers to either stop selling the insurance, exclude some work from coverage, or to raise the price of the policies that contractors need in order to build the condominiums. As a result, builders are extremely wary of such projects in California, causing what the California Building Industry Association claims is a statewide housing construction shortfall of about one million units over the past decade.

Under existing law, an owner has 10 years to sue the builder for latent defects, (ones that are not discoverable under normal inspection), such as structural problems that cause damage. Existing law also says that once owners discover a latent defect causing damage, they generally have four years to sue.

B. SB 800 Generally

SB 800, creates a process that tries to have homeowners and homebuilders working together, attempting to try to repair the problems that may arise in the home, rather than immediately jumping to litigation. First of all, before a homeowner can file a cause of action against the builder, he/she must initiate several pre-litigation procedures. The homeowner must provide notice to the builder of any problems or violations of the standards that are set out in this law regarding the functions or components of a home. The builder must then acknowledge receipt within 14 days after he/she receives notice of the claim. If the builder does not acknowledge receipt of the notice within the 14 days, the homeowner can then forego the pre-litigation requirements and go straight to litigation. In many cases, homeowner's associations are considered to be original purchasers, thereby inheriting all the rights and provisions this law sets out for homeowners.

If the builder does acknowledge receipt of the notice within 14 days, he/she can decide to schedule and carry out an inspection. The builder has an additional 14 days to carry out that inspection. All costs of this inspection and testing, including any damage caused by the builder during the inspection, are the responsibility of the builder. Within 48 hours of testing, the builder must restore the property to its pretesting condition. If the builder believes a second inspection is necessary, that second inspection would have to be completed within 40 days of the initial inspection or testing. The same requirements apply to the second inspection as to the first. Within 30 days of the initial or second inspection, the builder may offer in writing to repair the violation.

C. Right to Repair

The builder may make an offer to repair. Upon receipt of the offer to repair, the homeowner will have 30 days to authorize the repairs. The homeowner can either choose to go with the original builder or he/she can choose to request a list, supplied by the builder, of alternative contractors to complete the repairs. However, these alternative builders must not be owned or financially controlled by the original builder. The alternative contractors must also regularly conduct business in the county where the structure is located. Within 35 days after the request of the homeowner for a list of alternative contractors, the builder shall present the homeowner with the list, and within 20 days after that presentation, the homeowner shall either authorize the builder or one of the alternative contractors to perform the repair. When the chosen contractor submits the offer to repair, it should also be accompanied by an offer to mediate the dispute at the option of the owner. However, if there has been an offer to repair and the mediation has failed to solve anything, the homeowner then has to allow the repair to be performed either by the builder or the alternative contractor.

Once the offer to repair is accepted, the actual repairs have to start within 14 days. The chosen builder then has to make every effort for completion of the repairs within 120 days. If the chosen builder fails to follow these procedures, the homeowner is free to go straight to litigation.

This portion of this law is referred to as the "Right to Repair." However, in actuality this law does not give the builder the absolute right to repair. While it is true that this law offers builders the opportunity to go in and repair any alleged defect before the homeowner initiates any adversarial proceedings, the homeowner also has the choice of other contractors presented to him or her, thus taking away the original builders personal right to repair.

D. Alternative Procedures

Another option the builder has is to put in his/her contract "non-adversarial" or "non-litigation" contract clauses. These clauses would be in the contract itself. However, these alternative contractual clauses cannot provide less protection for the homeowner than what is set forth in this new law. Plus, if the builder decides to put these clauses in his/her contract, he/she must notify the homeowner at the time the contract is signed. These alternative provisions are binding even if they are not successful in resolving the ultimate dispute or if the results come out unfavorable to the builder.

An example of such a "non-adversarial" or "non-litigation" clause is one that states that should the homeowner believe there is a damage-causing defect in the construction of the home, the builder will provide a third party neutral mediator at the builder's expense to determine if there really is a damage causing defect.

E. Standards

As we said, an important part of SB 800 is the standards for what will constitute that basis of a construction defect action. These standards, as set out in the law, are intended to address every function or component of a home, such as water issues, structural issues, fire protection issues, plumbing and sewer issues, electrical plumbing issues, etc. The law also provides that if any function or component is not addressed in the law, it shall still be actionable if it causes damage.

The law also provides different statutes of limitation for different issues. For example, no action for plumbing and sewer issues may be brought more than four years after close of escrow, while an action for paints and stains may not be brought more than five years from close of escrow. The law also lists other issues, all with differing statute of limitations. For those issues not specifically given a statute of limitations, the title generally provides that no action may be brought for those claims more than 10 years from substantial completion of the improvement. For a more thorough breakdown of the standards and some statutes of limitations for actionable defects, you should review the enclosed statute.

Under this new law, the builder also has to provide the homeowner with a minimum one-year express written limited warranty covering the fit and finish of various building components, such as cabinets, mirrors, flooring, etc. If the builder does not provide for this warranty expressly, a one-year limited warrant, will be implied. The builder may also choose to offer more protection or a warranty covering a longer period of time than one-year. However, this enhanced protection agreement needs to be made in writing with the homeowner no later than the close of escrow.

F. Damages

A claim for damages by the owner made under this area of law is the reasonable value of the loss. The loss could include the reasonable cost to repair, the cost of relocation, if any, etc. There is no compensation for loss of use unless the home was used as a principal place of business.

G. Immunity

SB 800 also makes certain 'qualified' persons immune to liability. These qualified persons consist of third-party certified inspectors, registered professional engineers, licensed general contractors, or licensed architects who render "independent quality review of the work of improvement." The purpose of these third-party 'qualified' individuals is to provide an independent review in order to be certain that all State Housing Law is followed. However, should a qualifying person cause damage to the home due to either negligence or willful misconduct, that qualifying person may lose his/her immunity.

H. Subcontractors

While builders are afforded the opportunity to go in and repair the alleged damage thus providing some protection for them, subcontractors are not protected at all in this bill. Rather, the builder, once presented with a claim of damage by the homeowner, can turn around and hold his/her subcontractor liable for the damage brought by the homeowner. The only obligation the builder has towards the subcontractor, if he/she intends to hold the subcontractor liable for the damage, is to provide notice to the sub so that the sub can attend the initial or second inspection. We, along with others, believe providing some procedural protection for subcontractors will be the next step in this legislation.

In 2000, when the state Supreme Court handed down the Aas decision, builders were thrilled over the huge protection they were offered – homeowners were prevented from suing certain builders for defects unless there has been actual bodily injury or damage to property. This bill, recently signed into law, gives up some of those Aas protections. However, in turn, builders now have a "right to repair" before homeowners can bring a case in court, as well as definite standards for what constitute defects. Further, a mediation process is reestablished. Whether or not this new law will provoke a growth in the condominium market and lessen the amount of construction defect litigation remains to be seen. Remember, this new law covers only new homes sold after January 1, 2003. Also remember that this is a brief overview of a very complicated new law.

The standards set out in the law are:

With respect to water issues, the following standards apply:

(1) A door shall not allow unintended water to pass beyond, around, or through the door or its designed or actual moisture barriers, if any.

(2) Windows, patio doors, deck doors, and their systems shall not allow water to pass beyond, around, or through the window, patio door, or deck door or its designed or actual moisture barriers, including, without limitation, internal barriers within the systems themselves. For purposes of this paragraph, "systems" include, without limitation, windows, window assemblies, framing, substrate, flashings, and trim, if any.

(3) Windows, patio doors, deck doors, and their systems shall not allow excessive condensation to enter the structure and cause damage to another component. For purposes of this paragraph, "systems" include, without limitation, windows, window assemblies, framing, substrate, flashings, and trim, if any.

(4) Roofs, roofing systems, chimney caps, and ventilation components shall not allow water to enter the structure or to pass beyond, around, or through the designed or actual moisture barriers, including, without limitation, internal barriers located within the systems themselves. For purposes of this paragraph, "systems" include, without limitation, framing, substrate, and sheathing, if any.

(5) Decks, deck systems, balconies, balcony systems, exterior stairs, and stair systems shall not allow water to pass into the adjacent structure. For purposes of this paragraph, "systems" include, without limitation, framing, substrate, flashing, and sheathing, if any.

(6) Decks, deck systems, balconies, balcony systems, exterior stairs, and stair systems shall not allow unintended water to pass within the systems themselves and cause damage to the systems. For purposes of this paragraph, "systems" include, without limitation, framing, substrate, flashing, and sheathing, if any.

(7) Foundation systems and slabs shall not allow water or vapor to enter into the structure so as to cause damage to another building component.

(8) Foundation systems and slabs shall not allow water or vapor to enter into the structure so as to limit the installation of the type of flooring materials typically used for the particular application.

(9) Hardscape, including paths and patios, irrigation systems, landscaping systems, and drainage systems, that are installed as

part of the original construction, shall not be installed in such a way as to cause water or soil erosion to enter into or come in contact with the structure so as to cause damage to another building component.

(10) Stucco, exterior siding, exterior walls, including, without limitation, exterior framing, and other exterior wall finishes and fixtures and the systems of those components and fixtures, including, but not limited to, pot shelves, horizontal surfaces, columns, and plant-ons, shall be installed in such a way so as not to allow unintended water to pass into the structure or to pass beyond, around, or through the designed or actual moisture barriers of the system, including any internal barriers located within the system itself. For purposes of this paragraph, "systems" include, without limitation, framing, substrate, flashings, trim, wall assemblies, and internal wall cavities, if any.

(11) Stucco, exterior siding, and exterior walls shall not allow excessive condensation to enter the structure and cause damage to another component. For purposes of this paragraph, "systems" include, without limitation, framing, substrate, flashings, trim, wall assemblies, and internal wall cavities, if any.

(12) Retaining and site walls and their associated drainage systems shall not allow unintended water to pass beyond, around, or through its designed or actual moisture barriers including, without limitation, any internal barriers, so as to cause damage. This standard does not apply to those portions of any wall or drainage system that are designed to have water flow beyond, around, or through them.

(13) Retaining walls and site walls, and their associated drainage systems, shall only allow water to flow beyond, around, or through the areas designated by design.

(14) The lines and components of the plumbing system, sewer system, and utility systems shall not leak.

(15) Plumbing lines, sewer lines, and utility lines shall not corrode so as to impede the useful life of the systems.

(16) Sewer systems shall be installed in such a way as to allow the designated amount of sewage to flow through the system.

(17) Shower and bath enclosures shall not leak water into the interior of walls, flooring systems, or the interior of other components.

(18) Ceramic tile and tile countertops shall not allow water into the interior of walls, flooring systems, or other components so as to cause damage.

With respect to structural issues, the following standards apply:

(1) Foundations, load bearing components, and slabs, shall not contain significant cracks or significant vertical displacement.

(2) Foundations, load bearing components, and slabs shall not cause the structure, in whole or in part, to be structurally unsafe.

(3) Foundations, load bearing components, and slabs, and underlying soils shall be constructed so as to materially comply with the design criteria set by applicable government building codes, regulations, and ordinances for chemical deterioration or corrosion resistance in effect at the time of original construction.

(4) A structure shall be constructed so as to materially comply with the design criteria for earthquake and wind load resistance, as set forth in the applicable government building codes, regulations, and ordinances in effect at the time of original construction.

With respect to soil issues, the following standards apply:

(1) Soils and engineered retaining walls shall not cause, in whole or in part, damage to the structure built upon the soil or engineered retaining wall.

(2) Soils and engineered retaining walls shall not cause, in whole or in part, the structure to be structurally unsafe.

(3) Soils shall not cause, in whole or in part, the land upon which no structure is built to become unusable for the purpose represented at the time of original sale by the builder or for the purpose for which that land is commonly used.

With respect to fire protection issues, the following standards apply:

(1) A structure shall be constructed so as to materially comply with the design criteria of the applicable government building codes,

regulations, and ordinances for fire protection of the occupants in effect at the time of the original construction.

(2) Fireplaces, chimneys, chimney structures, and chimney termination caps shall be constructed and installed in such a way so as not to cause an unreasonable risk of fire outside the fireplace enclosure or chimney.

(3) Electrical and mechanical systems shall be constructed and installed in such a way so as not to cause an unreasonable risk of fire.

With respect to plumbing and sewer issues, the following standard applies:

Plumbing and sewer systems shall be installed to operate properly and shall not materially impair the use of the structure by its inhabitants. However, no action may be brought for a violation of this subdivision more than four years after close of escrow.

With respect to electrical system issues, the following standard applies:

Electrical systems shall operate properly and shall not materially impair the use of the structure by its inhabitants. However, no action shall be brought pursuant to this subdivision more than four years from close of escrow.

With respect to issues regarding other areas of construction, the following standards apply:

(1) Exterior pathways, driveways, hardscape, sidewalls, sidewalks, and patios installed by the original builder shall not contain cracks that display significant vertical displacement or that are excessive. However, no action shall be brought upon a violation of this paragraph more than four years from close of escrow.

(2) Stucco, exterior siding, and other exterior wall finishes and fixtures, including, but not limited to, pot shelves, horizontal surfaces, columns, and plant-ons, shall not contain significant cracks or separations.

(3) (A) To the extent not otherwise covered by these standards, manufactured products, including, but not limited to, windows, doors, roofs, plumbing products and fixtures, fireplaces, electrical fixtures, HVAC units, countertops, cabinets, paint, and appliances shall be installed so as not to interfere with the products' useful life, if any.

(B) For purposes of this paragraph, "useful life" means a representation of how long a product is warranted or represented, through its limited warranty or any written representations, to last by its manufacturer, including recommended or required maintenance. If there is no representation by a manufacturer, a builder shall install manufactured products so as not to interfere with the product' s utility.

(C) For purposes of this paragraph, "manufactured product" means a product that is completely manufactured offsite.

(D) If no useful life representation is made, or if the representation is less than one year, the period shall be no less than one year. If a manufactured product is damaged as a result of a violation of these standards, damage to the product is a recoverable element of damages. This subparagraph does not limit recovery if there has been damage to another building component caused by a manufactured product during the manufactured product's useful life.

(E) This title does not apply in any action seeking recovery solely for a defect in a manufactured product located within or adjacent to a structure.

(4) Heating, if any, shall be installed so as to be capable of maintaining a room temperature of 70 degrees Fahrenheit at a point three feet above the floor in any living space.

(5) Living space air-conditioning, if any, shall be provided in a manner consistent with the size and efficiency design criteria specified in Title 24 of the California Code of Regulations or its successor.

(6) Attached structures shall be constructed to comply with interunit noise transmission standards set by the applicable government building codes, ordinances, or regulations in effect at the time of

the original construction. If there is no applicable code, ordinance, or regulation, this paragraph does not apply. However, no action shall be brought pursuant to this paragraph more than one year from the original occupancy of the adjacent unit.

(7) Irrigation systems and drainage shall operate properly so as not to damage landscaping or other external improvements. However, no action shall be brought pursuant to this paragraph more than one year from close of escrow.

(8) Untreated wood posts shall not be installed in contact with soil so as to cause unreasonable decay to the wood based upon the finish grade at the time of original construction. However, no action shall be brought pursuant to this paragraph more than two years from close of escrow.

(9) Untreated steel fences and adjacent components shall be installed so as to prevent unreasonable corrosion. However, no action shall be brought pursuant to this paragraph more than four years from close of escrow.

(10) Paint and stains shall be applied in such a manner so as not to cause deterioration of the building surfaces for the length of time specified by the paint or stain manufacturers' representations, if any. However, no action shall be brought pursuant to this paragraph more than five years from close of escrow.

(11) Roofing materials shall be installed so as to avoid materials falling from the roof.

(12) The landscaping systems shall be installed in such a manner so as to survive for not less than one year. However, no action shall be brought pursuant to this paragraph more than two years from close of escrow.

(13) Ceramic tile and tile backing shall be installed in such a manner that the tile does not detach.

(14) Dryer ducts shall be installed and terminated pursuant to manufacturer installation requirements. However, no action shall be brought pursuant to this paragraph more than two years from close of escrow.

(15) Structures shall be constructed in such a manner so as not to impair the occupants' safety because they contain public health hazards as determined by a duly authorized public health official, health agency, or governmental entity having jurisdiction. This paragraph does not limit recovery for any damages caused by a violation of any other paragraph of this section on the grounds that the damages do not constitute a health hazard.

The law also provides, as a "catch all":

> **"The standards set forth in this chapter are intended to address every function or component of a structure. To the extent that a function or component of a structure is not addressed by these standards, it shall be actionable if it causes damage."**

I.
INTRODUCTION

This book is about the business of contracting in California. It does not tell you how to lay tile or follow plans and specifications. The book discusses the rules and regulations governing the contractors and how the industry is regulated and controlled. This book talks about how contractors can protect themselves and explains the Contractors' License Law and the disciplinary process utilized by the Contractors' State License Board to regulate the construction industry. The book talks about how contractors can protect themselves financially by utilizing Mechanics' Lien, Stop Notices, and Bond Rights as well as recent California laws requiring prompt payment of bills. All references in this book, unless otherwise noted, are solely to California law.

This book is a compilation from a number of other sources. We have previously published a book called California Contractors' Law. That entire book is incorporated herein. Previously, the author had included written portions of the Contractors' License Law for attorneys to utilize as a guide. That is also included in this book.

We tried to include most everything that a contractor needs to know with respect to the business of construction other than taxes, insurance and the craft of the construction. Those subjects are too voluminous to be discussed here.

Sam has been representing contractors for many years and has been following the Contractors' State License Board and its evolution for approximately 30 years.

Construction attorneys are also used to doing things differently than other attorneys. The construction process is very different than any other area of law. As an example, in some ways it is sometimes as complex to do a residential remodel, as it is to build a high-rise. Of course, a high-rise requires greater management because there are so many more people working on the project. However, from a technical or a customer relations standpoint, one may be as tough as the other.

By the same token, construction dispute resolution and litigation is also a very different process. **Construction attorneys are used to working with very short deadlines.** As an example, the time to file suit on a personal injury claim is one year from the date of the injury. The time to file suit on the breach of a written contract is four years from the date of breach. The time to file suit to foreclose on a mechanics' lien is only 90 days from the date the lien is recorded. The time to record a mechanics' lien may be as short as 30 days. Oftentimes you must serve a 20-day preliminary notice in order to have the right to record a mechanics' lien.

Further, the people involved in the construction process are very different than the typical corporate executive.

Because of all of this, choosing an attorney to handle your construction dispute is very important. You must be sure that the attorney is one who has handled construction disputes in the past. One who is used to the quick turnaround in filing documents and lawsuits and defending them. Probably the best way to find a construction attorney is to talk to other contractors who have been happy with the person who represented them. Otherwise, you may turn to your construction trade association for a referral.

With respect to construction contracts, many attorneys write very good and lengthy contracts. However, if they are not familiar with the contractor's license law, the mechanics' lien procedures, and construction requirements, they may not do a good job on a construction contract. Contractors are required by law to include many items in their contract that a non-construction related attorney would not know of. These things are not taught in law school. Further, the construction process itself requires certain language to be placed in a specific manner in a contract that another attorney may not be aware of.

Make sure that you hire a knowledgeable construction attorney. You need one to make sure your contract forms are correct and meets all statutory requirements, to advise you as you work, and to assist and advise you in the event of a dispute.

II.
SUMMARY OF THE CONTRACTORS' LICENSE LAW

It is almost impossible to write a short version of the Contractors' License Law. Contractors are required to comply with all of the federal laws as well as the laws of the State of California. Therefore, the license law is as broad as the laws of this state. However, certain areas of the license law are more important than others. Of particular importance are those areas of the law that subject a contractor to discipline (citation, suspension, or loss of license). This area is detailed in this chapter.

Another area of the law substantially affecting contractors is the "prompt pay" laws of the state of California. A detailed analysis of those laws is shown on flow charts at the end of this book in Chapter XIV.

The laws that are highlighted below are generally called the "Contractors' License Law." Those included certainly are not all-inclusive. The paragraphs are shortened versions designed to give you some familiarity with the laws that govern your industry.

Other laws of particular concern are the Civil Code dealing with Mechanics' Liens, the Labor Code dealing with compensation, citations and penalties, as well as insurance, and the Health and Safety Code. These laws are discussed in other chapters. In addition, there are rules and regulations put forth by the Contractors' State License Board, which serve to further define the Contractors' License Law. For a complete version of the license law you should obtain a book from the Contractors' Board entitled "Contractors' License Law and Reference Book." It is a good reference book.

The following represents merely shorthand versions of portions of the Business and Professions Code commonly called Contractors' License Law and is generally designed to license and regulate contractors.

7000.2 Local Business Taxes

This section clarifies that cities and counties can require local business taxes prior to issuing a building permit to a contractor.

7011.8 Filing False Claim

It is an infraction punishable by a fine not to exceed $1,000.00 for someone to knowingly file a false complaint against a licensee, alleging that he or she has been guilty of professional misconduct.

7018.5 Notice to Owner

The Legislature has prepared a lengthy form entitled "Notice to Owner." This form describes, in common everyday language, the pertinent provisions of the California Mechanics' Lien laws and the rights and responsibilities of a property owner and a contractor under these laws. Each licensed contractor must give a copy of this "Notice To Owner" to the owner, his or her agent, or the payer, before entering into a contract with an owner for work which is described as home improvement or swimming pool.

7019.1 Investigative Reports

This section became effective January 1, 1998 requiring the Board to furnish a copy of any opinion prepared by a licensed professional such as a contractor who was used as an expert to review the work of a contractor whose work is being investigated. The report prepared by this "expert" should be sent to the complainant, the licensee, and others including the bonding company. The section is relatively detailed as to what is required in that report.

7026 - 7026.3 Contractor Defined

The term "contractor" is synonymous with builder and means any person who offers or undertakes to have the capacity to or submits a bid to construct, alter, repair, add to, subtract from, improve, move, wreck or demolish any building, highway, road, parking facility, railroad, evacuation, or other structure, project, development, or improvement. This includes subcontractors as well as specialty contractors. This means that if you fall within this definition, you must be licensed unless you are somehow exempt. The erection of scaffolding or cleaning of grounds or structures in connection with the improvement requires a license.

The term contractor also includes consultants to owner/builders and includes persons who perform tree removal, tree pruning, and others who holds him or herself out as being able to construct a building or any portion thereof, stump removal or engage in tree or limb cabling or guying. The term contractor does not include a nurseryman who in the normal course of work performs incidental pruning of trees, or guying of planted trees and their limbs.

In addition, any person engaged in the business of drilling, digging, boring or otherwise constructing, deepening, repairing, re-perforating or abandoning any water well or cathodic protection well or monitoring a well is also included in the definition of a contractor.

Contractor includes a person engaged in the business of construction, installation, alteration and repair of a mobile home with certain exceptions.

Contractor also includes one who installs or contracts for the installation of carpeting when the carpeting is attached to the structure by any conventional method. However, one who holds a retail furniture dealer's license and has carpeting installed may be exempt.

7026.12 Fire Protection Systems Installation

The installation of all fire protection systems, including electrical alarm systems, can only be performed by a contractor holding a fire protection contractor classification, or by an owner/builder of an owner-occupied single family dwelling (or two single family dwellings on the same lot if they are completed within one year).

7027.1 Advertising; Penalty

It is a misdemeanor for any person to advertise for construction or for work of improvement covered by state law unless that person holds a valid license in the classification so advertised. The exemption to this rule is that a licensed building or engineering contractor may advertise as a general contractor. For the purposes of this rule, "advertise" and "advertising" are broadly interpreted.

7027.3 Willful and Fraudulent Use of License Number; Penalty

Any person who willfully and intentionally uses a contractor's license that doesn't correspond to the number on his or her current contractor's license with the intent to defraud another, is subject to a fine of $10,000.00 or imprisonment in state prison or in county jail or both.

7027.5 Landscape Contractor

A landscape contractor may design systems or facilities for work being performed and supervised by that landscape contractor if the work being performed falls within that specialty. As of January 1, 2004, a landscape contractor may take a job that includes a swimming pool so long as the swimming pool is part of a landscape project that the landscape contractor has contracted to perform. A licensed swimming pool contractor must perform that work.

7028 Contracting Without License

Contracting without a license is a misdemeanor, unless you are exempt from licensing. A second conviction is punishable by a fine of twenty (20) percent of the price of the contract under which the unlicensed person performed contracting work, or $4,500.00, whichever is greater, or imprisonment for not less than ten (10) days nor more than six (6) months, or both.

7028.1 Asbestos and Underground Storage Tanks

Any contractor who engages in asbestos related work or underground storage tank work without the proper certification is guilty of a misdemeanor. There are additional penalties as well as a fine between $1,000.00 and $3,000.00 and possible revocation or suspension of any contractor's license. In addition, a subsequent offense <u>requires</u> a fine between $3,0000.00 and $5,000.00 and a <u>mandatory</u> action to suspend or revoke any contractor's license

7028.3 Injunction Proceedings

This section allows the Registrar to obtain an injunction against one operating without a license as well as a licensee who is engaging in any act or practice which violates the license law.

7028.5 Individual License

A person who is or has been a member, officer, director or responsible managing officer of a licensed contractor cannot engage in the business or act in the capacity of a contractor without having a valid individual contractor's license.

7028.6 - 7028.13 Citations for Unlicensed Contractors

The Registrar can issue citations against unlicensed contractors as well as licensed contractors. The amount of the penalty and the citation procedure with respect to unlicensed contractors is explained in subsequent chapters as well as in the disciplinary chapter of this book. The Registrar may also issue a citation for the failure of an unlicensed contractor to provide the notice required in Section 7048.

7028.15 Bidding to Public Agency

It is a misdemeanor to submit a bid to a public agency or act as a contractor without a license (some exceptions apply). On the second and subsequent convictions, the court will impose an additional fine tied into a percentage of the contract price.

7029 Joint Venture License Defined and Suspension

A joint venture license will be issued to two or more current licensees in any classification that any of them are licensed. The joint venture license will automatically be suspended during any period of time in which any member of the entity does not hold a current active license in good standing.

7029.1 Contracting Jointly Without Joint License

Contractors eligible for a joint venture license may submit a bid as if they were licensed joint venturers but they cannot obtain a contract without first obtaining a joint venture license.

7029.5 Contractor Identification

Every plumbing contractor, electrical sign contractor and well-drilling contractor shall display their name, permanent business address, and contractor's license number on the side of each motor vehicle.

7030 Statement Required on Contracts

You must include the following statement in at least ten (10) point type on all written contracts where you are a prime contractor (not subcontractor).

Contractors are required by law to be licensed and regulated by the Contractors' State License Board, which has jurisdiction to investigate complaints against contractors if a complaint regarding a patent act, or omission is filed within four years of the date of the alleged violation. A complaint regarding a latent act or omission pertaining to structural defects must be filed within 10 years of the date of the alleged violation. Any questions concerning a contractor may be referred to the Registrar, Contractors' State License Board, and P.O. BOX 26000, SACRAMENTO, CALIFORNIA 95826.

The following disclosure and notice is required to be given to any person with whom the contractor is contracting to perform work on residential property with four or fewer units. The disclosure notice may be provided in a bid, estimate, or other document prior to entering into a contract:

"STATE LAW REQUIRES ANYONE WHO CONTRACTS TO DO CONSTRUCTION WORK TO BE LICENSED BY THE CONTRACTORS' STATE LICENSE BOARD IN THE LICENSE CATEGORY IN WHICH THE CONTRACTOR IS GOING TO BE WORKING-IF THE TOTAL PRICE OF THE JOB IS $500 OR MORE (INCLUDING LABOR AND MATERIALS).

LICENSED CONTRACTORS ARE REGULATED BY LAWS DESIGNED TO PROTECT THE PUBLIC. IF YOU CONTRACT WITH SOMEONE WHO DOES NOT HAVE A LICENSE, THE CONTRACTORS' STATE LICENSE BOARD MAY BE UNABLE TO ASSIST YOU WITH A COMPLAINT. YOUR ONLY REMEDY AGAINST AN UNLICENSED CONTRACTOR MAY BE IN CIVIL COURT, AND YOU MAY BE LIABLE FOR DAMAGES ARISING OUT OF ANY INJURIES TO THE CONTRACTOR OR HIS OR HER EMPLOYEES.

YOU MAY CONTACT THE CONTRACTORS' STATE LICENSE BOARD TO FIND OUT IF THIS CONTRACTOR HAS A VALID LICENSE. THE BOARD HAS COMPLETE INFORMATION ON THE HISTORY OF LICENSED CONTRACTORS, INCLUDING ANY POSSIBLE SUSPENSIONS, REVOCATIONS, JUDGMENTS, AND CITATIONS. THE BOARD HAS OFFICES THROUGHOUT CALIFORNIA. PLEASE CHECK THE GOVERNMENT PAGES OF THE WHITE PAGES FOR THE OFFICE NEAREST YOU OR CALL 1-800-321-CSLB FOR MORE INFORMATION."

This notice shall be set out either in capital letters in 10-point roman boldface type or in contrasting red print in at least 8- point roman boldface type.

Violation of these provisions will subject the contractor to penalties including fines for the first offense of $1,000.00, with suspension or revocation of licenses possible for further violations.

7030.1 Disclosure of License Suspension or Revocation

Any contractor who has had his or her license suspended or revoked two or more times within an eight year period must provide a disclosure in a document provided prior to entering into a contract to perform work on residential property with four or fewer units in at least ten (10) point type, all capitalized, (or eight (8) point type in contrasting red ink), of any disciplinary action, license suspension, or license revocation during the last eight (8) years.

7030.5 License Number Required on All Documents and Advertising

As a licensed contractor you must include your license number in (a) all construction contracts; (b) subcontracts and calls for bid; and (c) all forms of advertising as prescribed by the Registrar of Contractors.

7031 Compensation to Unlicensed Contractors Prohibited

No one acting in the capacity of a contractor may sue in court for damages for the performance of work for which a license is required unless that person can prove that he or she was properly licensed at the time the work was done, with certain exceptions, or in some instances, acted in good faith to maintain proper licensure, and did not know he or she was not properly licensed. This includes partnerships and corporations.

More recently the Legislature changed the law to add that one who entered into a contract with an unlicensed contractor could get back all of the money paid to the illegally unlicensed contractor.

The judicial doctrine of substantial compliance will not apply where the person engaged in the business, or acted in the capacity, of a contractor but has never been a duly licensed contractor. (Applies to contracts entered after January 1, 1992, or where litigation commenced before January 1, 1995).

7031.5 License Required for Permit

When pulling a building permit, a licensed contractor must give the number of his or her license and state that it is in full force and effect.

7034 Prohibited Clauses; Waiver of Lien Rights

A licensed contractor cannot be a party to any contract which contains a provision which indemnifies him or her against liability for any personal injury or property damage caused by his or her sole negligence, willful misconduct, or defect in design furnished by him or her or his or her agent, servant or subcontractor.

A licensed contractor cannot require any subcontractor, employee or supplier to waive his or her lien rights unless he or she gives his or her written permission on the form prescribed by law (Section 3262 of the Civil Code).

7040 - 7045.5 Exemptions From Licensure

This is a list of exemptions from the requirement for contractor's licensure. The major exemptions are public entities, governmental representatives, court officers, public utilities, except on private property where material and labor exceed $500.00, certain oil and gas operations, an owner doing work on his or her own property, work that is not a fixed part of the structure, material suppliers who do not install or contract for the installation of that material, finished products, small operations (under $500.00) and certain people such as architects, and engineers, material men or suppliers and employees.

7048 Minor Works Exemption

Business and Professions Code section 7048, provides that under certain circumstances the provisions of the Contractors' License Law do not apply to unlicensed contractors doing work where the price of the work is under $500.00. This exception is known as the "Minor Works Exception."

To qualify for the Minor Works Exception, the unlicensed person must provide to the Owner at the time of making a bid or prior to entering into a contract, a notice, a signed copy of which must be retained by the unlicensed contractor four years, that tells the owner that the Contractors' License Law does not apply on jobs under $500.00 and that the Contractors' Board will not be able to assist them if they get into a dispute. That notice also tells the owner that they may be subject to civil liability if the unlicensed contractor or his or her employees are injured on their property.

The notice, which must be in capital letters in at least 10-point roman boldface type or in contrasting red print in at least 8-point roman boldface type:

"I, ____________________ [individual's name], AM NOT LICENSED BY THE CONTRACTORS' STATE LICENSE BOARD.

STATE LAW REQUIRES ANYONE WHO CONTRACTS TO DO CONSTRUCTION WORK TO BE LICENSED BY THE CONTRACTORS' STATE LICENSE BOARD IN THE LICENSE CATEGORY IN WHICH THE CONTRACTOR IS GOING TO BE WORKING-IF THE TOTAL PRICE OF THE JOB IS $500 OR MORE (INCLUDING LABOR AND MATERIALS).

LICENSED CONTRACTORS ARE REGULATED BY LAWS DESIGNED TO PROTECT THE PUBLIC. IF YOU CONTRACT WITH SOMEONE WHO DOES NOT HAVE A LICENSE, THE CONTRACTORS' STATE LICENSE BOARD MAY BE UNABLE TO ASSIST YOU WITH A COMPLAINT. YOUR ONLY REMEDY AGAINST AN UNLICENSED CONTRACTOR MAY BE IN CIVIL COURT, AND YOU MAY BE LIABLE FOR DAMAGES ARISING OUT OF ANY INJURIES TO THE CONTRACTOR OR HIS OR HER EMPLOYEES."

If the unlicensed contractor fails to give the notice and retain its copy, he or she can be cited by the Contractors' State License Board for the failure to give the notice, plus, the Minor Works Exemption would not apply, making that unlicensed contractor working without a license subject to all penalties for contracting without a license -- which is a misdemeanor crime.

7055 - 7059.1 Licenses

These sections define the various kinds of licenses and registration such as general engineering, general building, and specialty licenses. Further, they include certification for asbestos, hazardous waste and toxic substances. These sections also state that you must utilize the name style conforming to your license.

7057 General Building Contractor (B)

As a result of the Home Depot decision, a general building contractor is now defined as a contractor whose principal contracting business is in connection with any structure being built or to be built for the support, shelter, and enclosure of persons, animals, etc.

requiring in its construction the use of at least <u>two unrelated</u> trades or crafts. However, in determining whether the project requires two or more trades, framing or carpentry cannot be included in coming up with those two trades. A general building contractor may also take a prime contract or subcontract for framing or carpentry only, or take a prime contract for any of the specialty trades provided that the general building contractor subcontracts to an appropriately licensed specialty contractor to perform the work.

In keeping with the tenor of public protection, the Board was required to set up a certification program for home improvement contractors. As of January 1, 2004, there is no requirement to certify home improvement contractors any longer. As of January 1, 2004, home improvement certification will no longer appear on the list of licenses or certifications.

7065 Qualification

This section sets out how one can qualify for a license and the examination procedure as well as the investigation of a potential licensee.

7065.4 Out of State Qualifications

This section gives the Registrar the authority to accept the qualifications of an applicant who is licensed as a contractor in a similar classification in another state if that state accepts the qualifications of a contractor licensed in this state. The Registrar may waive the trade examination for that applicant if the applicant provides written certification from the other state in which he or she was licensed.

7068.1 Responsibility of Qualifying Individual

If you are qualifying on behalf of an individual or firm, you are responsible for exercising enough direct supervision and control of the construction operations as necessary to secure full compliance with state law, and you shall not act in the capacity of a qualifying person for any other individual or firm unless one of the following conditions exits:

(a) There is a common ownership of at least twenty (20) percent of the equity of each individual or firm for which you act in a qualifying capacity;

(b) The additional firm is a subsidiary or a joint venture of the first. "Subsidiary" means any firm where at least twenty (20) percent of the equity is owned by the other firm;

(c) With respect to a partnership, limited partnership, or corporation, the majority of the partners or officers must be the same.

(d) No contractor may act as a qualifying individual for more than <u>three firms</u> in a calendar year.

7068.2 Disassociation of RMO or RME

If a responsible managing officer or employee stops being employed or associated with the firm, a notice may be given to the Registrar by the licensed contractor or firm and the responsible managing officer or employee in writing within ninety (90) days from the disassociation. The licensee shall replace the qualifier within ninety (90) days of the date of disassociation. Otherwise, the license will automatically be suspended.

If the Registrar does not receive the required notice within ninety (90) days, the license is automatically suspended. The license will be reinstated when a qualified individual takes the place of the responsible managing officer or responsible managing employee who left the firm.

To replace a responsible managing officer or employee, the firm must file an application with the Registrar. The application must state that the individual qualifying has not had a license suspended or revoked for reasons that would keep that person from personally qualifying

7068.5 Substitution of Examinee

It is a misdemeanor for anyone to take the test for anyone else. Only the examinee named in the application can take the examination.

7068.7 Providing of Examination to Another

Anyone who obtains for and provides to another any part of the examination, when not authorized to do so, is guilty of a misdemeanor.

7070 When Applicant Has Been Denied or Disciplined

An applicant for a license has to show that he or she was not previously denied a license or had a license revoked if the revocation is applicable to obtaining a license. If an application is denied, the applicant may reapply in one year.

7071.5 Contractor's Bonds; Who May Collect

This lists the people who may collect on a contractor's license bond. This bond or cash deposit is a condition to the issuance or renewal of a license.

7071.6 Contractor's Bond

Every licensed contractor, including swimming pool contractors, must have a license bond in the sum of $10,000.00.

7071.8 Bond After Suspension or Revocation

This explains the disciplinary bond that is required after one's license has been suspended or revoked (the disciplinary bond is in a sum up to ten (10) times the regular bond amount based on the Registrar's determination). This section also applies to any qualifier for a license where the licensee has been disciplined, whether or not the qualifier had knowledge or participated in the wrongful act or omission, and applies to license renewal, or changes in corporate officers after discipline.

7071.11 Action or Claim Against Bond

This is a lengthy section dealing with how to file a claim against a bond or cash deposit as well as setting out the order of preference, etc. However, this section also requires the contractor to keep the license bond or cash deposit in full force. Any judgment or admitted claim against the bond or deposit is grounds for discipline.

7071.13 Reference to Bond in Advertising Prohibited

Any reference by a contractor in advertising, solicitation, or other representation to the public to any bond required to be filed by state law is a ground for suspension of the contractor's license. (You cannot refer to your license bond in your advertising.)

7071.17 Judgment and Judgment Bond

If, when making an application, the qualifier or the licensee has an unsatisfied final judgment for failure to pay a contractor, subcontractor, consumer, material supplier or employee, the Board shall notify the applicant that he or she has ninety (90) days to satisfy the judgment or post a bond, or the application shall be void.

All licensees must notify the Registrar in writing of an entered and unsatisfied judgment within ninety (90) days of the date of judgment. Failure to do so will be grounds for automatic suspension of the contractor's license. Reinstatement of the license is conditioned upon either proof of satisfaction of the judgment or the posting of a judgment bond sufficient to guarantee payment of an amount equal to the judgment. The bond must remain on file for a minimum of one year after which it can be removed upon submitting proof of satisfaction of all debts.

Unless the judgment has been discharged in bankruptcy, failure to post the bond or satisfy the judgment in accordance with this section will be cause for immediate suspension of the license.

7075 License is Non-transferable

A contractor's license is non-transferable and must be displayed in the contractor's main office or chief place of business. A contractor must be able, upon demand, to show an up-to-date license. This is usually satisfied by carrying your pocket license with you and displaying your main license on the wall of your office.

7075.1 Transferability of License

No license, regardless of type or classification, is transferable to any other person or entity under any circumstances. However, the Legislature has now made an exception to allow a corporation to maintain the prior license number of its individuals or prior corporate entity under certain circumstances.

7076 Cancellation of License; Continuation in Business

An individual license is canceled upon the death of the person licensed as an individual. A partnership is canceled upon the death or disassociation of a partner. A joint venture license is canceled upon the cancellation, revocation, or withdrawal of any of its joint venturers. However, under certain conditions the license may continue in business for a reasonable length of time. A corporate license is canceled effective as of the date the corporation dissolves, merges out of existence or surrenders its right to do business in California.

7076.2 Doing Business as a Corporation

Contractors doing business as a corporation must at all times, be in good standing with the Secretary of State. Failure to be in good standing is cause for automatic suspension of the corporate license.

7083 Reporting Changes to Board

Contractors must report to the Registrar all changes of personnel, name style, bond exemption or addresses of record within ninety (90) days after any change is made. Failure to notify the Registrar within ninety (90) days is grounds for disciplinary action.

7085 Arbitration

These sections deal with mandatory and voluntary arbitration of complaints under specified conditions.

7090 - 7124.6 Disciplinary Proceedings

These statutes define the citation power of the Registrar, regulations regarding order of correction, appeal, etc. Some of the specific violations are listed in this section of this book.

This section also allows for discipline if the contractor violates state or local laws regarding issuance of building permits, with some exceptions.

7103 Discipline in Another State Subjects Contractor to Discipline in California

The revocation, suspension, or other disciplinary action imposed on a licensee due to actions taken against a contractor by another state are grounds for disciplinary action in this state if the individual is a licensee, or applies for a license in this state.

7108 Misuse of Funds

A contractor who diverts funds or property received for a specific construction project or operation or for a specified purpose in the same construction project is subject to disciplinary action.

7108.5 Prompt Payment of Subcontractor

Unless otherwise agreed to in writing, prime contractors or subcontractors must make payment to subcontractors within ten (10) days of receipt of each progress payment. If there is a good faith dispute over all or any portion of the amount due, then the prime contractor or the subcontractor may withhold no more than 150% of the disputed amount. A violation of this section shall be cause for disciplinary action and subject the licensee to a penalty of two percent per month payable to the subcontractor. In any action for collection of funds wrongfully withheld, the prevailing party is entitled to attorney's fees and costs.

7108.6 Prompt Payment of Dump Truck Carriers

Contractors must pay all transportation charges of any dump truck carrier, subject to the regulation of the Public Utilities

Commission, by the 20th day following the last day of the month in which the transportation was performed.

7109 Disregard of Plans or Specifications or Accepted Trade Standards

You are subject to disciplinary action if you intentionally depart from or disregard specific plans or specifications, or accepted trade standards for good and workmanlike construction and by doing so, damage another, unless such is done with the owner's consent. However, if you follow plans and specifications that are prepared by or under the supervision of an architect, you will not be violating this section.

7109.5 Violations of Safety Orders

Violation of any safety provision in the Labor Code resulting in death or serious injury to an employee is grounds for disciplinary action.

7110 Violation of Laws

Willful disregard and violation of state building laws, the building laws of any political subdivision of the state, or the state's minimum painting standards, safety laws, labor laws, compensation insurance laws, or a violation by a licensee of provisions of certain sections of the Business and Professions Code, the Health and Safety Code, Civil Code, or Water Code, relating to the digging, boring or drilling of water wells is cause for disciplinary action.

7110.1 Violation of Labor Code

A contractor cannot require the signing of a release of any claim on account of wages unless payment of the wages has been made. The release is null and void as between the employer and the employee and is cause for disciplinary action. (Labor Code Section 206.5).

7111 Preservation of Records

As a licensed contractor you must keep records showing all contracts, documents, and records, of all your transactions as a contractor, and make them available to the Registrar for inspection, under certain conditions, for up to five (5) years.

7111.1 Failure to Cooperate in Investigations

A contractor must respond to a written request of the Registrar to cooperate in an investigation or else that contractor is subject to disciplinary action.

7113 Breach of Contract

A licensed contractor's material failure to complete any construction project or operation for the price agreed is grounds for disciplinary action.

7113.5 Composition, Arrangement

If you avoid paying your lawful obligations, or settle them for less than the full amount, you are subject to discipline.

A licensed contractor will not be subject to disciplinary action for avoiding or settling obligations in bankruptcy, or by composition, arrangement or reorganization with creditors under state or federal law.

7114 Aiding Unlicensed Persons

Aiding or abetting an unlicensed person to evade the state contractors' law is cause for disciplinary action. This would include allowing someone to use your license, or acting as agent, partner, associate or otherwise, of an unlicensed person with the intent to evade the state contractors' law.

7114.1 Certifying to Falsified Experience

A contractor who falsifies a Certificate of Experience in support of someone's application is subject to disciplinary proceedings.

7116 Fraud

A licensed contractor who does any willful or fraudulent act that substantially injures another is subject to disciplinary action.

7117 Personnel Variance

You as a contractor must act in the name that is on your license and in accordance with the personnel of the license (those persons listed on your application form).

7117.5 Contracting With Inactive License

A person who acts under an inactive, suspended or expired license is subject to disciplinary action.

7117.6 Contracting Out of Classification

Acting outside the scope of your license classification is a cause for disciplinary action.

7118 Contracting With Unlicensed Contractor

Entering into a contract with an unlicensed contractor is a cause for disciplinary action.

7118.4 Asbestos Inspection and Financial Relationship

Any contractor making an inspection for the presence of asbestos must disclose, <u>both</u> orally and in writing, any financial or other relationship whatsoever, including referral fees, with an entity in the business of performing the corrective work.

7118.5 Contracting for Asbestos Related Work

You as a contractor, an applicant, or a person required to be licensed, may not enter into a contact for asbestos related work with someone who is not properly certified. If you violate this statute you subject yourself to very stiff penalties and fines.

7119 Lack of Reasonable Diligence

If you as a contractor injure another due to your willful failure or unjustified refusal to carry out a construction project or operation with reasonable diligence, you are subject to disciplinary action.

7120 Withholding Money

If you as a contractor, deliberately fail to pay money when it is due for any materials or services when you are able to pay, or when you were paid, you risk disciplinary action. Also if you falsely deny the amount due with the intent to hinder, delay or defraud the person to whom payment is due, you are subject to disciplinary action.

7121.1 & 7122.1 Disassociating Partners and Qualifier

Disassociation by officers, partners or the qualifier from firms cited will not relieve the disassociating person from responsibility for the citation if the person knew of, or participated in the acts causing the citation.

7123 Conviction as Cause For Disciplinary Action

If you are convicted of a crime related to the qualification, functions, and duties of a contractor, you are subject to disciplinary action.

7123.5 Discipline For Violating Emergency Act

If a contractor is convicted of violating section 396 of the Penal Code, which makes it a crime to take advantage of consumers in the sale, offer of sale, or contract to repair in a time of natural disaster, the contractor will be subject to disciplinary actions including at least a six-month suspension or a permanent revocation of the license.

7125 Worker's Compensation Report of Licensee

As a condition of issuance, reinstatement, reactivation, renewal or continued use of a license, all applicants who have employees, must have on file a Certificate of Workers Compensation Insurance or Certificate of Self Insurance.

The insurer must then report to the Registrar any cancellation or lapse of the policy within ten (10) days after the cancellation or lapse.

7125.1 Workers Compensation Certificate

A certificate as required by Section 7125 shall be deemed effective if received by the Registrar within ninety (90) days after the license is issued. If the certificate is received after the ninety (90) days, the Registrar will accept the certificate if the failure to file the certificate was due to circumstances beyond the control of the licensee.

7125.2 Failure to Maintain Workers Compensation Certificate

Failure to maintain Worker's Compensation Insurance shall result in an automatic suspension of licensure.

7145.5 Failure to Resolve Liabilities

After sixty (60) days notice, the Registrar may refuse to issue, reinstate, reactivate, or renew a license or may suspend a licensee for failure to resolve any outstanding final liabilities which include, taxes, additional tax, penalties, interest fees assessed by the Department of Industrial Relations, the Employment Development Department, and the Franchise Tax Board.

7151.2 Home Improvement Contract

This defines a Home Improvement Contract as an agreement, written or oral, between a contractor and the homeowner or a tenant which involves the repairing, remodeling, altering, converting or modernizing of or adding to residential real property.

7152 Home Improvement Salesperson

A home improvement salesperson is one who solicits, sells, negotiates or executes contracts for home improvement goods and services as well as swimming pools, spas or hot tubs.

7153 Registration of Salesperson for Home Improvement Contracts

It is a misdemeanor for a person to engage in the occupation of salesperson for one or more home improvement contractors without having a registration issued by the Registrar for each home improvement contractor for whom the salesperson is employed.

Any security interest taken by a contractor to secure payment pursuant to a home improvement contract is unenforceable if the salesperson soliciting the contract was not a duly registered salesperson (or exempt from registration) at the time the contract solicited by the unregistered salesperson is signed by the homeowner.

7154 Penalty for Employment of Non-Registered Salesperson

A home improvement contractor who employs an unregistered home improvement salesperson to sell home improvement contracts is subject to disciplinary action.

7155.5 Participation in Violation

A violation of the law by a home improvement salesperson constitutes cause for disciplinary action against the contractor regardless of whether the contractor has knowledge of the violation.

7156 Salesman Penalty

It is a misdemeanor for any person to use a contract form in the home improvement business or any other work of improvement if the form does not disclose the name of the principal by whom that person is employed. Further, a salesperson must account and remit to the employing contractor any payment received in connection with the construction business.

7157 "Kickbacks"

This section deals with illegal promotion or "kickbacks."

(a) A contractor cannot give compensation or reward of any kind to an owner for referral sales involving home improvement contracts;

(b) A contractor, his or her agent or salesperson can give gifts for advertising or sales promotion purposes only if the gift is not conditioned upon obtaining a contract for home improvement work, and if the gift does not exceed a value of five dollars ($5.00) and only one such gift is given in connection with any transaction;

(c) No salesperson or contractor's agent can accept any compensation of any kind, from any person other than the contractor whom he or she represents, nor shall he or she make any payment to any person other than his or her employer on account of sales;

(d) A contractor cannot make a payment or give other consideration to a contractor or salesperson for or on account of the performance of any work of improvement including home improvement work or services, unless he or she is licensed except where the person whom you are paying is exempt from licensing or where the project is exempt.

7158 False Completion Certificate

Any person who accepts or receives a false Certificate of Completion on performance of a work of improvement with knowledge that the document is false, and who uses the document in order to negotiate or obtain a payment, is guilty of a misdemeanor. If this section is violated as part of a plan to defraud an owner for the repair of damages caused by a natural disaster, the contractor must make full restitution, and may also be assessed a severe penalty which may include imprisonment.

7159 Home Improvement Contract Form

This is a long list of contractual requirements for home improvement contracts totaling more than $500.00 and all swimming pool contracts. It says that the contracts must be in writing and signed by the parties. The contract shall include the following:

(a) The name, address and license number of the contractor, and the name and registration number of any salesperson that solicited or negotiated the contract;

(b) The approximate dates when the work will begin and be substantially completed;

(c) A description of the work to be done and description of the materials to be used and the equipment to be used, or installed, and the agreed (price) consideration for the work. With respect to a pool, you have to have a plan and scale drawing showing the shape, size, dimensions and construction and equipment specifications;

(d) On home improvements, the down payment cannot be more than ten (10) percent or $1,000.00 whichever is less (excluding finance charges). With respect to swimming pools, the down payment can not exceed $200.00 or two (2) percent of the contract, whichever is less;

(e) A schedule of payments showing the amount to be paid in dollars and cents (not percentages). The schedule of payments must be referenced to work performed and any material or equipment supplied. You can never receive proportionately more money than the work performed (except for the down payment). If you fail to substantially commence work within twenty (20) days of the date specified in the contract, the next payment due will be postponed for the same period. With respect to swimming pools, the final payment may be made at the completion of the final plastering phase of construction providing that equipment, decking or fencing required by the contact is also completed;

(f) The contract must also state that upon satisfactory payment being made for any portion of the work performed, the contractor <u>shall</u> furnish the person contracting a full and unconditional lien release from any claim for the portion of the work for which payment has been made;

(g) The provisions of (d), (e) and (f) above, relating to the payment schedule, do not apply when you furnish a performance and payment bond, lien and completion bond, or use a joint control approved by the Registrar. You must also place a notice in at least ten (10) point type, within three (3) inches of the signature line, telling the tenant or owner that he or she has the right to require a performance and payment bond;

(h) No extra or change order work will be required to be performed without prior written authorization. The change order shall incorporate and become part of the contract;

(i) Any salesperson's commission can only be paid in proportion to the schedule of payments;

(j) You must give the Notice to Owner required by Section 7018.5;

(k) A statement defining what constitutes substantial commencement;

(l) A notice that failure by the contractor, without lawful excuse, to substantially commence work within twenty (20) days from the approximate date specified in the contract when work will begin is a violation of the Contractor's License Law;

(m) If the contract provides for a contractor to furnish joint control, the contractor shall not have any interest in such joint control;

(n) If this section is violated as part of a plan to defraud an owner for the repair of damages caused by a natural disaster, the contractor must make full restitution, and may also be assessed a severe penalty which may include imprisonment;

(o) (1) Criminal charges against a person who is not licensed but who is required to be licensed as a contractor must be brought within four years from the date the buyer signs the contract;

(2) Criminal charges against a person who is licensed as a contractor must be brought within one year from the date that the buyer signs the contract;

(3) The limitations on criminal charges pursuant to this section do not apply to administrative actions filed against a licensed contractor.

7160 False Representation; Penalty

If you enter into a contract based on false or fraudulent information knowingly made, the person you are contracting with may recover from you or the person soliciting the contract a penalty of $700.00 plus reasonable attorney's fees in addition to the other damages sustained as a result of those representations.

7161 False Advertising

The following acts are misdemeanors. Any licensed contractor or applicant who commits one of these acts is also subject to disciplinary actions:

(a) Using false, misleading or deceptive advertising to induce a person into any contract for a work of improvement;

(b) Making any substantial misrepresentation in obtaining a home improvement contract or other work of improvement, or making any false promise of a character likely to influence any person to enter into such a contract;

(c) Any fraud in the execution of, or material alteration of, any contract, trust deed, mortgage, promissory note or other document incident to a home improvement transaction or other transaction involving a work of improvement;

(d) Preparing or accepting any trust deed, mortgage or promissory note for any work of improvement transaction with knowledge that it is for more money than the real value of the improvement work;

(e) Publishing any advertisement, which is in any way false, deceptive or misleading. Advertising any improvement work while intending not to accept contracts for that particular work or at the price which is advertised or offered to the public;

(f) Any person who violates subdivision (b), (c), (d) or (e) as part of a plan to defraud an owner for the repair of damages caused by a natural disaster, must make full restitution, and may also be assessed a severe penalty which may include imprisonment.

7168 Action on Swimming Pool Contract

In any action on a swimming pool contract, the court will award reasonable attorney's fees to the prevailing party.

7180 - 7189.7 Asbestos Consultants

These sections deal entirely with asbestos related matters, asbestos consultants and site surveillance technicians. They address such matters as experience, requirements and the qualifications of the consultant as well as the certification by the Division of Occupational Safety and Health. These sections also address the penalties for their violation.

7190 Advertising

The name of a public official may not be used in any advertisement or any promotional material by a licensed contractor, without the written approval of the public official. Even with the approval, any advertisement using the name of the public official must contain a disclaimer as follows:

"THE NAME OF (specify name of public official) DOES NOT IMPLY THAT (specify name of public official) ENDORSES THIS PRODUCT OR SERVICE IN (his or her) OFFICIAL CAPACITY AND DOES NOT IMPLY AN ENDORSEMENT BY ANY GOVERNMENTAL ENTITY."

7191 Arbitration Clauses

(a) If a contract for work on residential property with four or fewer units contains a provision for arbitration of a dispute between the principals in this transaction, the provision shall be clearly titled "ARBITRATION OF DISPUTES."

If a provision for arbitration is included in a printed contract, it shall be set out in at least 10-point roman boldface type or in contrasting red print in at least 8-point roman boldface type, and if the provision is included in a typed contract, it shall be set out in capital letters.

(b) Immediately before the space provided for the parties to indicate their approval to the arbitration provision described in subdivision (a), and immediately following that arbitration provision, the following shall appear:

"NOTICE: BY INITIALING IN THE SPACE BELOW YOU ARE AGREEING TO HAVE ANY DISPUTE ARISING OUT OF THE MATTERS INCLUDED IN THE 'ARBITRATION OF DISPUTES' PROVISION DECIDED BY NEUTRAL ARBITRATION AS PROVIDED BY CALIFORNIA LAW AND YOU ARE GIVING UP ANY RIGHTS YOU MIGHT POSSESS TO HAVE THE DISPUTE LITIGATED IN A COURT OR JURY TRIAL. BY INITIALING IN THE SPACE BELOW YOU ARE GIVING UP YOUR JUDICIAL RIGHTS TO DISCOVERY AND APPEAL, UNLESS THOSE RIGHTS ARE SPECIFICALLY INCLUDED IN THE 'ARBITRATION OF DISPUTES' PROVISION. IF YOU REFUSE TO SUBMIT TO ARBITRATION AFTER AGREEING TO THIS PROVISION, YOU MAY BE COMPELLED TO ARBITRATE UNDER THE AUTHORITY OF THE BUSINESS AND PROFESSIONS CODE OR OTHER APPLICABLE LAWS. YOUR AGREEMENT TO THIS ARBITRATION PROVISION IS VOLUNTARY."

"WE HAVE READ AND UNDERSTAND THE FOREGOING AND AGREE TO SUBMIT DISPUTES ARISING OUT OF THE MATTERS INCLUDED IN THE 'ARBITRATION OF DISPUTES' PROVISION TO NEUTRAL ARBITRATION."

I (WE) AGREE TO ARBITRATION ______ ______

Initial Initial

If the above provision is included in a printed contract, it must be set out either in at least 10-point roman boldface type or in contrasting red print in at least 8-point roman boldface type, and if the provision is included in a typed contract, it shall be set out in capital letters.

(c) A provision for arbitration of a dispute between a principal in a contract for work on a residential property with four or fewer units that does not comply with this section may not be enforceable against any person other than the licensee.

(d) This section does not limit the Board's authority to investigate complaints or to discipline a licensee for violations of the Contractors' License Law.

The above just highlights some of the laws. If you have a specific issue, you should check with an attorney experienced in such matters.

III.
LICENSING AND REGULATION OF CONTRACTORS

A. Introduction

This chapter will discuss the licensing and regulating of a contractor, the laws dealing with licensing and regulating, and specifically how contractors doing business in California are controlled and regulated. As any contractor knows, and every potential contractor needs to know, California is very consumer oriented. Evidently the Legislature feels that the marketplace cannot effectively regulate the construction industry and that construction is a field that must be regulated in order to protect the public interest. Accordingly, this chapter will discuss the licensing and enforcement of contractors with emphasis on how those differ from normal expectations.

The Contractors Board is part of the Department of Consumer Affairs. It is not surprising that most of the Contractors' License Law deals with consumer protection. Indeed, many of the larger contractors are not really regulated by the Contractors' Board but by their bonding companies, the marketplace, and other forces. That is to say, it is not hard for a large contractor to obtain a bond. It's not hard for large contractors, who may have lost their qualifier, to obtain another qualifier. It is merely a matter of money. It is much harder for contractors who do business with consumers to comply with the maze of laws that are discussed in this book. The Contractors' Board is part of the Department of Consumer Affairs and it is the purpose of the Board, as well as this state's laws, to protect those consumers.

A "B," General Building Contractor, can contract to take a project that requires in its construction two or more unrelated trades; however, in counting those two or more trades, one cannot count framing or carpentry. That is to say that a "B" cannot take a contract for only framing and plumbing because in counting the number of trades, you would only count plumbing. You would not count framing to determine whether the "B" can do the work.

Despite what is stated above, a "B" can take a contract to do any single trade if the "B" subcontracts it to a properly licensed subcontractor.

Some history on this matter is appropriate. In 1996 the Court of Appeals invalidated the requirement that a "B" contractor could only take a contract that required three or more unrelated trades. This was the result of a legal interpretation of a Board rule. ("Board rules" are regulations passed by the Contractors' Board. They do not have the same weight as legislation. The "law" is legislation that is passed by the Legislature.) The Board rule stated that a "B" could only take contracts for construction of a project that required in its construction, three or more unrelated trades. The court threw that out because the law passed by the Legislature stated that a "B's" principal business was with respect to a project requiring in its construction three or more unrelated trades. It did not say that the "B's" only business was with projects requiring three or more unrelated trades or that a "B" could not take a project that required in its construction less than three unrelated trades. The principal business of the "B" had to be with respect to projects requiring three or more unrelated trades. Further at that time, a "B" could not take a contract that the "B" was not licensed to do. As an example, a "B" could not enter a single trade contract, even if the "B" contractor subcontracted it to a properly licensed contractor.

What the Home Depot decision did was to allow a "B" contractor to take almost any single trade contract and do it him or herself, or subcontract it.

As a result of the Home Depot case, one surety company and the Contractors' State License Board, sponsored legislation that would have put the law back to where it was prior to the Home Depot case.

In 1997 the Governor vetoed that proposed legislation out of hand.

The construction industry stood up and fought for the legislation discussed above that has now been the law since January 1, 1998.

B. Definition of Contractor

This book applies to people acting as contractors only. A good rule of thumb to follow is if one is doing some physical work that alters or adds to a structure, and that work becomes part of the real estate, or the person is building something, then that person is defined as a contractor. Also, those working on fixed works, such as bridges, dams, roadways, etc. require contractors' licenses. However, you should be very careful in using this "rule of thumb" definition. It should be noted that a painter is considered a contractor, interior decorators who do painting and carpeting have been held to be contractors, as are people doing construction clean up.

The definition is important. Section 7026 of the Business and Professions Code defines "contractor" as being synonymous with "builder." It is one who undertakes to, or offers to undertake to, or purports to have the capacity to undertake to, or submits a bid to construct, alter, repair, add to, subtract from, improve, move, wreck or demolish any building, highway, road, parking facility, railroad, excavation or other structure, project, development or improvement. The term "contractor" includes subcontractor and specialty contractor as well. As you can see, this is a rather broad definition.

The maintenance and service of air conditioning, heating or refrigeration equipment that is a fixed part of the structure to which it is attached requires a contractor's license. A person drilling water wells is also a contractor.

A tree trimmer or mover may be treated as a contractor. A tree trimmer who is employed by a contractor, needs a contractor's license but when employed by an owner may not need a contractor's license.

C. Importance of Proper License

There are two very important reasons why one must be properly licensed. First, doing work for which a license is required while not being licensed is a criminal violation. Secondly, one cannot collect payment for work for which a license is required unless that person is properly licensed. More recently the Legislature increased the penalty for unlicensed contracting by stating that one who contracts with an unlicensed contractor may actually get the money that he/she paid to the unlicensed contractor. Previously, not having a contractors license would only keep you from collecting your money and could result in a criminal violation. Now, an unlicensed contractor will have to give the money back that he or she obtained as an unlicensed contractor.

D. Regulations in General

Contractors, like others who are in business, are regulated by numerous agencies. Contractors are regulated by local building departments, federal and CAL OSHA, and taxing authorities, among others. However, the agency that regulates and licenses contractors is the Contractors' State License Board (CSLB).

E. California Government

The California government, like the Federal government, is made up of three branches: the executive, legislative and judicial. This means basically a split into three different powers: the Governor, the Legislature, and the courts. All three branches work in a system of checks and balances. That is, each branch jealously guards its own power and in this way no one branch can become all-powerful or dictatorial. The executive branch executes the laws and has control of the military as its ultimate weapon. The legislative branch makes the laws and has as its ultimate weapon control of the purse strings. The judicial branch interprets the laws and ensures that they are consistent with the Constitution and are fairly applied. Its ultimate weapon is the ability to overrule any law passed by Congress and the President.

The California Constitution is the highest law in the state of California, as the U.S. Constitution is the highest law in the nation. The laws of California must first conform to the U.S. Constitution and then the California Constitution. The Constitution in California may be changed in three different ways. The most popular way is by amendment. There are two ways to amend the Constitution. The one with which most of us are familiar is by having an amendment put on the ballot by the initiative process (having the required number of signatures on a petition). The other way to amend is where the California Legislature acquires a two-thirds vote of the members of both the Assembly and the Senate.

Another way the Constitution can be changed is via a Constitutional Convention. This is done by the Legislature passing a two-thirds vote to hold a convention. If this is approved by the voters, the convention must be held within six months of the passage of the vote. The last way the California Constitution may be changed is by having the Legislature propose revisions.

The laws that the legislative branch makes are governed by some restrictions. The California laws must conform to the U.S. Constitution and when they conflict with federal laws the federal laws win, that is they take precedence. Similarly the state laws prevail over local governments such as counties and cities.

As mentioned earlier the various branches perform various functions. The executive branch administers and enforces the law. But in reality the legislative and executive branches work together on legislation since the executive branch implements the legislation. The Governor is in charge of the executive branch. He or she is chief executive and has appointing authority for most state department heads and officials in key policy-making positions. The Governor also acts as legislative leader by keeping the Legislature up to date on the affairs of state.

Another aspect of the Governor's job is to nominate judges to the highest courts of the state. He or she is also the leader of his or her political party. The Governor is also the ceremonial head of state performing such duties as ribbon-cutting ceremonies and appearing at parades, etc. As you can see, the Governor has a lot of power, which is why the State Constitution states, "The supreme executive power of this State is vested in the Governor. The Governor shall see that the law is faithfully executed."

The legislative process can be divided into distinct stages. First the proposed law is drafted and then introduced into one of the Houses (Senate or Assembly). The process is the same for each House at this point. The rules committee assigns the bill to the appropriate policy committee based on its subject matter. The policy committee then hears the pros and cons of the bill and can basically either pass or fail the bill. If the bill passes the policy committee, it is then sent to the fiscal committee where the process can start over again. If the bill reaches this point, a floor vote is then taken of all members of the Legislature (Senate and Assembly). If the bill passes, it is then sent to the second house where the entire process starts over again. If the second house passes the bill without changing it, the bill then goes to the Governor's desk where he or she either signs it into law or vetoes it. If vetoed, a two-thirds vote of both houses can override the veto. If the second house amends the bill, it is sent back to the original house which in turn can either concur and send it to the Governor or reject it and send it to conference committees for a compromise of the bill, which in turn will be sent to the Governor.

The judicial branch applies the laws and therefore its power lies within the various court systems. There are essentially two types of courts: the trial and appellate. Decisions are made based on an application of the law to the facts of the case in a trial court. If the decision is appealed then the case goes to the appellate court to be reviewed. All cases are tried in either municipal, superior, or justice courts. Municipal courts are created when there is a district with a population of 40,000 or more. Districts with fewer than 40,000 people have justice courts.

Within the municipal and justice courts there are small claims courts for hearing claims where the amount in dispute is $5,000.00 or less. If you as plaintiff (the person suing) choose to sue in small claims court you give up your right of a possible appeal and you cannot have an attorney represent you in court. Therefore, you act as your own attorney, but your costs of going to court are much less. Consequently, it is sometimes wise for plaintiffs to take their case to small claims court even if their real amount is over $5,000.00 because they will save on court costs, attorneys fees, and their cases will be tried much faster.

In each district there is also a superior court. The superior courts handle all felony cases, wills, estates, domestic, mental competency, custody of children and adults, real property, and probate as well as appeal cases from the municipal and justice courts. If a case is appealed in superior court, it goes to the court of appeal for that area. However, this is not so for death penalty cases, in which case it goes straight to the California Supreme Court. When a party wants to appeal a case from the court of appeal, it may ask for review by the Supreme Court, but this review is often denied.

The Contractors State License Board like other boards and bureaus is part of the Executive Branch which executes the laws. One would think that the Legislature has very little to say in that arena. This is untrue. As an example, the Board members are set out in the statute as being eight public members out of fifteen. The Governor appoints four of the public members and five contractor members, which leaves six to be appointed by the Legislature. This gives the Legislature substantial input into the operation of the License Board.

More importantly, the budget process as well as the "Sunset Review" process is with the Legislature. The Sunset Review process is where each board and bureau justifies its own reason for existence to the Legislature. The Legislature also provides a budget that can be signed or vetoed by the Governor. However, the budget is first prepared by the Legislature. In Utah, at one point in time, the Legislature deleted the budget for the Contractors Board except for the Director and Deputy Director. That made the Board inoperable. That shows some power over an executive branch.

In California, when the Contractors Board's Sunset Review process was going through the Legislature, the Board was told that if they did not "do the right thing" the Bill that would have kept the Board in existence as a Board, would not be signed. It turns out that the "right thing" was to force the Board's then Registrar to resign.

F. Department of Consumer Affairs

The original purpose of the Contractors' Board was to protect the public against poor construction practices. The original Board was part of the Department of Professional and Vocational Standards and the Director of that Department was the Registrar of Contractors. At its origin there were only four reasons for disciplinary action. At present this number has increased by roughly five fold.

In 1970, the Department of Professional Vocational Standards was changed to the Department of Consumer Affairs. The Contractors' State License Board is one of the 38 boards and bureaus (known as licensing bodies) that are part of the Department of Consumer Affairs. There have been numerous failed attempts to remove the Contractors' Board from the Department of Consumer Affairs, or to join the CSLB with other construction related boards in a separate "construction" department. However, as part of the "Sunset Review" process, boards and bureaus including the CSLB have to justify their existence to the Legislature. As a result of the

Legislature's perceived ineptness of the Contractors' Board, there has been little or no recent discussion whatsoever as to removing the Contractors' Board from the Department of Consumer Affairs.

Many of the decisions dealing with whether the agency should be a Board, Bureau or Department, have been based on politics rather than what is good for either the construction industry or the consumers dealing with the industry. For example, the CSLB is the largest board under the Department of Consumer Affairs. It contributes a substantial portion of the Department's budget. Moreover, contributions by the CSLB help defray the cost of running the Department of Consumer Affairs. If the CSLB were to move from the Department of Consumer Affairs, then the CSLB's contribution to the Department's budget would no longer exist. Since the CSLB regulates over 300,000 contractors, it is a nice plum to have under your wing.

The direction of the Department of Consumer Affairs is controlled by the Chief Executive Officer, who is known as the Director. The Director is appointed by the Governor and holds the office at the Governor's pleasure.

The stated intent of the Legislature in forming the Department, and the purpose of its laws, is to promote and protect the interests of the people of the State as consumers. The Legislature feels that vigorous representation and protection of consumer interests are essential to the fair and efficient functioning of a free enterprise market economy. The Legislature believes that government can (a) educate and inform the consumer to ensure rational consumer choice in the marketplace; (b) protect the consumer from deceptive methods, acts, or practices used in the sale of goods and services, which are detrimental to the general welfare of consumers; (c) foster competition; and (d) promote effective representation of consumers' interest in all branches and levels of government.

G. How the Contractors' State License Board Operates

The California Contractors' State License Board (CSLB) was originally established in 1929 as the Contractors' License Bureau. It has since had a name change to the Contractors' State License Board.

1. Membership

The CSLB is made up of fifteen (15) members. Eight of those members are to be public members. A public member can not be a current or former contractor of the Board, or a close family member of a licensee, or be currently or formerly connected with the construction industry, or have any financial interest in the business of a licensee of the Board. The eight public members must meet all of the requirements for membership of a public member on a Board. One of the public members must be a representative of a statewide senior organization. A representative of a labor organization is eligible for appointment to serve as a public member.

One contractor member must be a general engineering contractor, two members must be general building contractors, two members must be specialty contractors, and one member must be a member of a labor organization representing the building trades. The last member of the Contractor's Board must be an active local building official.

The Governor appoints four of the public members (including the one from a statewide senior organization), the local building official, the member of a labor organization representing the building trades, and the five contractor members. The Senate Rules Committee and the Speaker of the Assembly appoints two public members.

Nominally the Board hires their Chief Executive Officer who is known as the Registrar of Contractors. The Board has broad policy power over the day-to-day functioning carried out by the Registrar.

2. Meetings

The Contractors' State License Board must hold at least four (4) regular meetings each fiscal year. There are mandatory meetings in January, April, July and October. In addition, the Board can have any additional meetings that it wishes. Typically, full Board meetings are held either quarterly, or once every two months, as necessary. This is usually left to the discretion of the Board's Chair. In order to obtain more public and industry involvement, Board meetings are usually held alternately in the northern and southern parts of the State. Meetings are <u>open</u>.

Anyone can address the Board. The public may also be present when the Board discusses or votes on matters.

In addition to its regular Board meetings, the Contractors' State License Board often works through committees, and committee meetings are where much of the Board's business takes place. Committee meetings are also open to the public.

The Contractors' State License Board states its intent as being to objectively promote the health, safety and general welfare of the public in matters relating to building construction by:

(a) insuring that all construction is performed in a safe, competent and professional manner;

(b) providing resolution to disputes which arise from building construction activities; and

(c) providing information so that the public can make informed choices. The courts have stated that the purpose of the Contractors' License Law is to protect the public from incompetent and dishonest contractors.

For various reasons, including budgetary restraints, the Contractors' State License Board has not been able to accomplish all of its stated goals. What the Board actually does is license and regulate contractors. Its public education effort has now substantially picked up with a commitment to educate consumers. At the urging of the Board, the Legislature has funded a large public awareness campaign. Its contractor education is still relatively non-existent.

As a result of California's budget problems, the staff and expenditures have both been severely curtailed. Backlogs in the licensing function have grown.

One of the Board's primary functions is to interpret license requirements. It is not unusual for the CSLB to determine which license category, if any, is required to do certain work. Public agencies frequently ask for such interpretations. However, recently the courts have gotten more deeply involved in the licensing area and some of the Board's decisions have not been upheld.

The CSLB has become more involved in the legislative arena by sponsoring legislation relating to licensing and enforcement.

3. Staff

The Chief Executive Officer is the Registrar of Contractors who oversees less than 300 employees. Note that this is a drop from approximately 450 employees as a result of California's budget problems. Those employees are divided between the field and administrative staffs.

a. Field

The Contractors' State License Board is now made up of two regions (Northern and Southern). These regions contain various offices that employ clerical personnel, consumer services representatives, and Enforcement Representatives who investigate and sometimes mediate complaints. Each region also includes an Intake and Mediation Center, as well as various investigative centers. The location of the various offices is based upon workload.

b. Administrative

The headquarters of the Contractors' State License Board is in Sacramento. The headquarters' operation is involved in the administrative function, budget, personnel, of the CSLB etc., as well as its licensing function. It should be noted that some of the licensing function is passed on to Deputy Registrars in the field, who investigate and verify license applications.

Recently enforcement staff has been redirected to the licensing area as a result of the backlog in the licensing function.

4. The Budget

Historically, approximately two-thirds of the Contractors' Licensing Board budget has been spent on enforcement, while licensing and administration split the remaining one-third (1/3).

Goals of the CSLB are to license qualified contractors, enforce its rules and regulations, conduct consumer and contractor education, resolve disputes, and streamline its regulations.

Recently, with California's budget woes, the Contractors Board has not been able to utilize all of the budget that had been appropriated to it by the Legislature. Further, the Contractors Board like other governmental entities had to cut its staff. This was true even though the cutting of the staff came at a time when the Contractors Board was not fully staffed. Therefore, the budget woes left the Contractors State License Board with very few personnel.

However, sometimes out of adversity comes something good. In this case, although the licensing function at the Contractor's Board was slowed significantly, the investigative and enforcement people started to do appropriate things rather than jumping through hoops for every complainant. The enforcement section started to conduct a real "triage" in prioritizing its complaint handling. Health and Safety issues and elder abuse have taken the top spot in priority. The Contractors Board has suggested that it will not handle all of the complaints that come in.

H. How Contractors are Regulated

1. Statutes

Generally, the Contractors' State License Law is found in Business and Professions Code sections 7000 through 7199. These laws deal with the Board, as well as its functions. They also deal with licensing, discipline and regulation.

2. Regulations

In addition to the laws passed by the Legislature, the CSLB has the power to pass regulations that further define and implement the laws enacted by the Legislature. The regulations must be reasonably necessary to carry out the law. They must be adopted in accordance with strict administrative procedures.

Courts have held that the regulations which the CSLB adopts cannot enlarge or restrict the scope of a statute which the Legislature passes.

3. Procedural Requirements

The CSLB has the authority to classify and limit the operations of licensed contractors. All the rules and regulations in this regard are passed according to the Administrative Procedures Act. However, as stated previously, the rules and regulations cannot enlarge or restrict the scope of the law itself. For example, the courts have struck down portions of the Contractors' Board's interpretation of some statutory licensing dealing with interpretation of portions of the licensing scheme relating to the "A" license "General Engineering," and the "B" license "General Building," as will be discussed below.

4. The Licensing Requirement

The need to be licensed is found in the Business and Professions Code. Section 7031 states, among other things, that one cannot collect for work for which a contractor's license is required unless that person is duly licensed. Recently the law has been changed to allow someone who contracted with an unlicensed contractor to get his or her money back. Duly licensed means more than just being licensed. That is to say, a contractor must be licensed for the specific craft or trade that is required for that task. As stated previously, it is not uncommon for CSLB deputies to interpret which license is required in order to even allow bidding on a particular project.

In addition to the inability to collect, the Business and Professions Code also contains a section (Section 7028) which makes it a misdemeanor to engage in the business of contracting without having a license. More recently the Legislature increased the penalty for unlicensed contracting by stating that one who contracts with an unlicensed contractor may actually get the money that he/she paid to the unlicensed contractor. Previously, not having a contractors license would only keep you from collecting your money and could result in a criminal violation. Now, an unlicensed contractor would have to give the money back that he or she obtained as an unlicensed contractor.

5. Exemptions from Licensure

The major exemptions from licensure can be found in the statute that defines a contractor. If one does not fall within that statute, then that person or entity does not need a license. But beware, additional exemptions exist. A contractor is defined as being synonymous with builder (see chapter III B).

a. Minor Work

The Contractors' License Law does not apply when the entire project is under $500 in value. If the project is to build a house but a subcontractor's portion of the work is less than $500, that subcontractor still needs to be licensed. For this exemption to apply, the entire project must be less than $500. It should be noted that this amount used to be $300, but it was changed by the Legislature to $500 and was effective January 1, 1999.

b. Independent Contractor and Employee

An employee working for wages does not require a contractor's license. There is a great deal of litigation involving the determination of when one is an independent contractor or employee. The definition turns on whether the "master" or "principal" has the right to control the manner or means by which an end result is reached. This is easy to state but hard to determine in practice. The gist is, who controls how the work is done. Under the same set of facts, you may have a completely different answer making it even more difficult to determine the definition. That is to say that for Workers' Compensation purposes, a person may be deemed an employee so as to recover compensation if he or she is hurt. But in the same situation, that same person may be deemed an independent contractor for purposes of recovery under a Mechanics' Lien statute. Otherwise the owner might have to pay twice.

This is a very hazy area of the law and it appears that the distinguishing factors are based on the interests to be protected by the specific legislation. There may be specific statutes that will help in this determination.

c. Owner Doing Own Work

This exemption is broken up into three categories:

(1) Work Done by Owner's Employees

An owner need not have a license if the work is done through the owner's employees, so long as the structures are not intended for sale. The statute also contains various presumptions regarding the "intention for sale."

(2) Work Done by Licensed Contractors

An owner need not have a license if the owner contracts with licensed contractors.

(3) Homeowner Repairs Prior to Sale

A homeowner improving his or her principal place of residence need not have a license if the work is done prior to sale, <u>and</u> the owner has resided there twelve (12) months prior to completion, <u>and</u> the owner has not used this exception on more than two structures more than once during any three (3) year period.

d. Miscellaneous Exemptions

There are other miscellaneous exemptions listed below which should be checked. Some of the exemptions are based on the fact that the work is regulated by another agency. One example is that an architect working as an architect need not have a contractor's license.

e. Work and People Not Requiring a License:

(1) Finished products which do not become a fixed part of the structure (this exemption does not apply to carpeting or home improvement goods);

(2) Repairing personal property;

(3) Construction or repair of irrigation and drainage ditches of irrigation or reclamation districts as well as some fire clearing work, some farming <u>except</u> when the work is done by a licensed contractor;

(4) Architects, engineers, and pest control operators;

(5) Material suppliers;

(6) Alarm company operators if they are licensed under other sections of the law;

(7) Public employees or representatives;

(8) Court officers (while working under the control of the court);

(9) Public utilities, to a certain extent;

(10) Gas, heating or electric companies regulated as public utilities under certain situations;

(11) Oil and gas operations by owner or lessee; and

(12) Federal work, such as work done on Federal property.

Although California does not have a law exempting Federal work from contractors licensing requirements, we believe that no state can impose its licensing requirements upon the Federal government. Therefore, unless the Federal government requires it, you do not need a contractors' license to do Federal work.

6. Qualification for a License

Every entity must qualify through a natural person (human being). Therefore, a sole proprietorship must qualify as a contractor either by its owner or by an employee. A partnership must qualify by a qualifying partner or its employee. A corporation must qualify by a responsible managing officer or a responsible managing employee.

The qualifying individual is responsible for controlling the construction operation of the business so as to secure full compliance with the license law.

a. Responsible Managing Employee (RME)

This is a person who is a bona fide employee and is actively engaged in the classification of the work for which the new license is applied. In order to be a bona fide employee, the person must work at least 32 hours per week or at least 80 percent of the time that the employer is in operation, whichever is less.

b. Responsible Managing Officer (RMO)

This is an officer (not necessarily an employee) of the corporation.

c. Qualification

No person can qualify for more than one license unless one of the following exists:

(1) Common ownership of at least 20 percent of the equity; or

(2) The additional firm is a subsidiary; or

(3) The majority of the partners or officers is the same.

If an RME or RMO disassociates from the licensed entity, the licensee or the qualifier must inform the Registrar in writing and the qualifier must be replaced within ninety (90) days or the license is automatically suspended.

It should be noted that the qualifying individual must possess the following qualifications:

(4) Experience

At least four years experience as a journey person, foreman/forewoman, supervising employee, or contractor within the last ten years in the <u>specific classification</u> applied for.

(5) Examination

The qualifying individual of each entity must pass a written examination covering both the specific trade as well as a law and business portion. There are certain circumstances under which a written examination can be waived.

7. In addition to the qualifications, every contracting entity must have a license bond.

All licensed contractors, including swimming pool contractors, must have a license bond in the amount of $10,000.00. The bond is for the benefit of anyone who is injured as a result of a violation of the license law. These types of bonds are rather easy to obtain and really do not require any underwriting on the part of the bonding company. This bond must be distinguished from a performance and payment bond. The license bond is for the benefit of:

a. Any homeowner contracting for home improvement on his or her personal residence;

b. Any person damaged as a result of a willful and deliberate violation;

c. Any employee of a licensee damaged by the failure to pay wages.

Since all licensed contractors are required to have this license bond, and since this bond is not a performance and payment bond, it is illegal for one to advertise that they are "bonded." This is because it could lead people to believe that the advertising contractor might have something that other licensed contractors do not.

8. Renewal

A contractor's license is valid for two years unless suspended or revoked. Therefore, contractors' licenses are up for renewal every two years. There has been some talk of increasing the license period so that the license need not be renewed as often. A license may be renewed after its expiration date, if within three years of the expiration the applicant files for a renewal and pays the appropriate fees. This is important in that the applicant need not take another examination if the renewal is within three years.

9. Denial of License

A license may be denied for various reasons. If the license application is denied, the applicant has a right to a hearing. The hearing is required to be heard within 90 days. However, if the matter is not heard within 90 days, nothing ever happens. This is really a wrong without a remedy.

The hearing with respect to the license application is called a Statement of Issues. In the disciplinary section, we will be discussing Accusations. The hearings are almost identical. However, the significant difference between a Statement of Issues and an Accusation is that during the Accusation the burden of proof is upon the Registrar in suspending or revoking a license. The opposite is true when one is seeking licensure, through a Statement of Issues, where the burden is on the applicant.

10. Classifications of Licensing

Contractors' licenses are classified according to the kind of work that is done. The authority to classify the license has already been discussed. However, the courts have sometimes questioned and overruled the Board's regulations and interpretations. Essentially, licenses are classified as follows:

a. General Engineering Contractor ("A")

General Engineering Contractors do fixed work requiring specialized engineering knowledge and skill. They do work such as irrigation, drainage, water power, flood control, docks, shipyards, railroads, highways, etc. It should be noted that the word "persons" is not included in the description of the structures built by a general engineering contractor. The word "persons" is included under the definitions of structures built by a general building contractor. Therefore, the Contractors' State License Board has held that the structures being built by general engineering contractors cannot be structures that are intended to house persons.

An appellate court did not agree with this interpretation, stating that whether the structure houses persons is immaterial. The issue was whether the structure required specialized engineering skill and knowledge.

b. General Building Contractor ("B")

A "B", general building contractor, <u>can</u> contract to take a project that requires in its construction two or more unrelated trades; however, in counting those two or more trades, one cannot count framing or carpentry. That is to say that a "B" cannot take a contract for only framing and plumbing. That is because in counting the number of trades, you would only count plumbing.

Despite what is stated above, a "B" can take a contract to do any single trade if the "B" subcontracts it to a properly licensed subcontractor.

c. Specialty Contractor ("C")

A specialty contractor is a contractor whose operation requires specific skill and knowledge in a particular craft or trade. A listing of the specialty contractors is as follows:

Rule #	Specialty Contractors Classified	
832.02	**Class C-2**	Insulation and Acoustical Contractor
832.04	**Class C-4**	Boiler, Hot Water Heating and Steam Fitting Contractor
832.05	**Class C-5**	Carpentry, Cabinet and Millwork Contractor
832.07	**Class C-7**	Low Voltage Systems Contractor
832.08	**Class C-8**	Concrete Contractor
832.09	**Class C-9**	Drywall Contractor
832.10	**Class C-10**	Electrical Contractor
832.11	**Class C-11**	Elevator Contractor
832.12	**Class C-12**	Earthwork and Paving Contractor
832.13	**Class C-13**	Fencing Contractor
832.15	**Class C-15**	Flooring and Floor Covering Contractor
832.16	**Class C-16**	Fire Protection Contractor
832.17	**Class C-17**	Glazing Contractor
832.20	**Class C-20**	Warm-Air Heating, Ventilating and Air-Conditioning Contractor
832.21	**Class C-21**	Building Moving/Demolition Contractor
832.23	**Class C-23**	Ornamental Metal Contractor
832.27	**Class C-27**	Landscaping Contractor
832.28	**Class C-28**	Lock and Security Equipment Contractor
832.29	**Class C-29**	Masonry Contractor
832.31	**Class C-31**	Construction Zone Traffic Control Contractor
832.32	**Class C-32**	Parking and Highway Improvement Contractor

832.33	**Class C-33**	Painting and Decorating Contractor
832.34	**Class C-34**	Pipeline Contractor
832.35	**Class C-35**	Lathing and Plastering Contractor
832.36	**Class C-36**	Plumbing Contractor
832.38	**Class C-38**	Refrigeration Contractor
832.39	**Class C-39**	Roofing Contractor
832.42	**Class C-42**	Sanitation System Contractor
832.43	**Class C-43**	Sheet Metal Contractor
832.45	**Class C-45**	Electrical Sign Contractor
832.46	**Class C-46**	Solar Contractor
832.47	**Class C-47**	General Manufactured Housing Contractor
832.50	**Class C-50**	Reinforcing Steel Contractor
832.51	**Class C-51**	Structural Steel Contractor
832.53	**Class C-53**	Swimming Pool Contractor
832.54	**Class C-54**	Tile Contractor (Ceramic & Mosaic)
832.55	**Class C-55**	Water Conditioning Contractor
832.57	**Class C-57**	Well Drilling Contractor
832.60	**Class C-60**	Welding Contractor
832.61	**Class C-61**	Limited Specialty Contractor

Contractors are prohibited from working in a classification unless they are licensed in that classification, or unless that work is incidental and supplemental to the work they are licensed to do. The definition of what is "incidental" and "supplemental" work has been an area of much confusion, and has been heavily litigated. The Board has determined that "incidental" and "supplemental" means that the work must be essential to the specialty of the contractor's license rather than the specialty of the project itself. This interpretation seems ludicrous. It means that a swimming pool contractor is not allowed to build a fence even though it is necessary to the project. This is because it is not necessary to the craft.

As of this writing, the issue of classification and regulation is being studied by the CSLB. Stay tuned.

11. Probationary License

Every original license, except an additional classification, is a probationary license. The significance here is that the Registrar may issue an Order to Show Cause why the probationary license should not be revoked. This is different from filing an Accusation to suspend or revoke a license. Further, a probationary license may not be renewed while a proceeding is pending. This is not true with respect to a license that is not a probationary license, which is the subject of an Accusation.

The next two items, although not technically licenses, deal with another requirement in order to do work.

12. Home Improvement Salesperson Registration

A Home Improvement Salesperson is one who is employed by a contractor to solicit, sell, negotiate or execute home improvement contracts or swimming pool contracts. In order to work as a Home Improvement Salesperson, a Home Improvement Salesperson must be registered and the registration must list the name of the contractor who employs the salesperson. A Home Improvement Salesperson can be employed by more than one contractor, so long as he or she is registered with each one.

An officer of a corporation, or the owner of any contracting company who is licensed, need not register as a Home Improvement Salesperson. Further, anyone whose sales are made pursuant to prior negotiation or buyer initiated service repair or emergency repair, need not be registered as a Home Improvement Salesperson.

13. Certification

Again, this is technically not a license. In 1986, the Legislature passed statutes that required anyone who disturbed asbestos of 100 square feet or more, to be registered and pass an examination. Since then, the Board added a certification requirement for working with hazardous substances and removing of underground storage tanks.

This method of "licensure" is unique in that it crosses crafts or trades. The reasoning is that different crafts could run into the disturbance of asbestos and hazardous substances, etc. How else would you classify which trade would do that? The answer was that any trade could continue to do the same work that they were already doing. However, they would require an additional certification. In order to obtain certification, one must take an examination showing competence in the area.

It should be remembered that the certification does not allow one to perform work that he or she was not licensed to do before. However, it does allow people to continue work that they were doing previously, and in conjunction with that work, do work requiring a certification.

IV.
ENFORCEMENT

One of the two major functions of the Contractors' State License Board is enforcement of the State's contracting laws. Indeed, approximately two thirds of the CSLB budget is spent on enforcement.

The Contractors Board was entirely restructured in the year 2001 under the administration of then Registrar of Contractors, Dr. C. Lance Barnett. This was referred to as "re-engineering." The Board established two Intake and Mediation Centers. One was for Northern California and one for Southern California. Deputy registrars no longer existed; they became Enforcement Representatives. The various district offices were closed and eight Investigative Centers were opened.

SB 2029 (Figueroa) requested that the Contractors Board hire an outside enforcement monitor to make recommendations as to enforcement as well as an outside consultant to review the re-engineering. Both agreed in their reports to the Legislature that additional offices were necessary.

The CSLB has a number of ways to handle enforcement. The severity of the violation is probably the most important factor in determining which alternative is used.

A. Complaint Handling

The manner in which complaints are handled is really within the discretion of "the powers that be" at the Contractors' State License Board. At times, it may slough off certain violations while at other times, it will jump on technical violations. As will be discussed later, technical violations are rather easy to prove and can make a very good report card for an overzealous Enforcement Representative. Yet, because of the complaint disclosure laws, technical violations can be deadly to service and repair contractors. There is no consistency on how complaints are handled.

Recently, with California's budget woes, the Contractors Board has not been able to utilize all of the budget that had been appropriated to it by the Legislature. Further, the Contractors Board like other governmental entities had to cut its staff. This was true even though the cutting of the staff came at a time when the Contractors Board was not fully staffed. Therefore, the budget woes left the Contractors State License Board with very few personnel.

However, sometimes out of adversity comes something good. In this case, although the licensing function at the Contractor's Board was slowed significantly, the investigative and enforcement people started to do appropriate things rather than jumping through hoops for every complainant. The enforcement section started to conduct a real "triage" in prioritizing its complaint handling. Health and Safety issues and elder abuse have taken the top spot in priority. The Contractors Board has suggested that it will not handle all of the complaints that come in.

Although a complaint can be received in a number of ways, typically it is handled by an Intake and Mediation Center. At the Intake and Mediation Center, a representative of the Contractors Board will screen the complaint and will conduct a more detailed type of "triage" which will determine where that complaint would be placed in the pecking order of complaint handling. As a result of California's budget crisis, hiring freezes and various spending reductions, the triage has substantially reduced the number of complaints the Contractor's Board actually investigates. During this screening process, in addition to attempting to mediate the complaint, the Consumer Services Representative attempts to obtain all of the necessary documentation and to determine whether a license violation has in fact even been sufficiently alleged.

Many complaints involve failure of a licensed contractor to fulfill the terms of an agreement, including work quality. Anyone may file a complaint, including a homeowner, other contractors or suppliers.

If a violation is alleged, the Board will usually send the contractor a letter. In addition, during this process, the complaint is <u>prioritized</u>. Complaints dealing with health and safety generally receive the <u>highest</u> priority. Most recently, complaints by the elderly are receiving very high priority. Complaints against multiple offenders also receive a high priority. Other factors that enter into prioritizing complaint handling are dollar value, and whether or not there is an arbitration provision in the contract.

At some point in the process, the complaint is either referred for investigation or closed. It can be closed for a number of reasons, such as settlement, lack of jurisdiction or failure of the owner to produce records. If it is not closed, it may be referred to an Investigative Center where it will be assigned to an Enforcement Representative for further investigation.

It should be remembered that the ultimate weapon within the disciplinary power of the Registrar is revocation of a license. However, the Registrar can use court procedures to go beyond that, up to and including criminal penalties.

Civil penalties can also be imposed by the CSLB. The decision of the Registrar will be in writing and shall contain findings of fact and conclusions of law. Once the Registrar's decision becomes final, the only remedy is administrative mandamus through the court system. This appellate process and judicial review is discussed elsewhere.

B. Enforcement

1. Injunction

The Board, through the civil court system, can obtain temporary restraining orders, injunctive relief, as well as court ordered restitution.

2. Criminal

In addition to the injunctive relief, there are a number of violations that might be pursued in the criminal courts, such as criminal diversion of funds or contracting without a license. In this regard, the Board may seek criminal sanctions.

3. Interim Suspension Order

In addition to a civil injunction or restraining order, the Board can also obtain an Interim Suspension Order through the Office of Administrative Hearings. This is similar to an injunction for a short period of time.

4. Accusation

One method of handling violations of the license law is through the Administrative Procedures Act. This may be done by filing an Accusation. The Board is represented by the Attorney General's Office. The specific laws and rules are explained in more detail in other areas of this book. However, it is less formal than criminal or civil proceedings, and more formal than the citation systems. An Accusation seeks to suspend or revoke a license.

5. Citation

In 1980, the Legislature enacted section 7099 of the Business and Professions Code as part of the Contractors' License Law. The law authorized the Contractors' State License Board to issue citations, correction orders and civil penalties for violations of laws pertaining to contractors. The CSLB passed Board rules implementing the citation procedures.

The citation procedures implemented by the CSLB are an alternative to the more formalized procedures that the Board has used in the past. Under the Accusation procedure of complaint handling, the contractor and the Board hire attorneys and proceed to an administrative hearing in order to try the matter. This procedure is costly, and in numerous instances, wasteful.

The citation procedure allows the Contractors' State License Board to issue a citation requiring the contractor to do various things. It may require the contractor to correct a deficiency in the construction project, it may require the contractor to pay a penalty up to $5,000, or the citation may require the contractor to do both. In no event can the citation for a single construction project have a fine in excess of $5,000. However, a penalty of $15,000 may be assessed for one who is aiding and abetting an unlicensed contractor to evade the law or contracting with an unlicensed contractor.

Issuing citations is a much simpler process than the more formal Accusation process. If a contractor is issued a citation, the contractor has various alternatives. The contractor may choose to pay the civil penalty and correct any deficiencies alleged in the citation. In the alternative, the contractor may wish to appeal all or any portion of the citation. This is done simply by checking off boxes on the citation form. **See the Appendix for copies of the forms. The appeal**

must be filed within fifteen (15) days after service of the citation. Don't delay.

In addition to citations against licensed contractors, there is a possibility of citing unlicensed contractors. However, they would not require an unlicensed contractor to complete the project, but rather to cease and desist doing the work, and to make restitution and pay civil penalties.

C. Arbitration

If a contract does not have an arbitration provision in it, and the contract deals with workmanship, and the contractor is not a habitual criminal or repeated violator, then the Contractors' State License Board could suggest that the parties arbitrate their dispute rather than pursue the matter through the administrative system. The Contractors' State License Board will choose an arbitration tribunal and the decision of the arbitrator will become the decision of the Registrar. Failure to comply with the arbitration ruling will be grounds for discipline. Arbitration is a good tool for everyone. For the CSLB it closes complaints relatively quickly. For the contractor and owner, it lends finality to the dispute quickly. Importantly for the contractor, the arbitration will not be disclosed unless the contractor does not timely comply with the Award.

D. Complaint Disclosure

Under the contractor's law, certain items in a contractor's file are matters of public record, such as license history, bonding information, and names of qualifying individuals. These can usually be obtained both formally and informally. In addition to the public record information, which one may usually obtain by telephone or the Internet, certain complaints against contractors can also be disclosed.

As of July 1, 2002, the Board will continue to disclose matters of public record as well as make available to the public the nature and status of complaints against a licensee that have been referred for Accusation or complaints that have been reviewed by a supervisor who has determined that the charges, if proven, would result in suspension or revocation of the license or criminal prosecution, and that the acts present a risk of harm to the public.

Citations shall only be disclosed for five years after the contractor has complied with everything in the citation if the contractor has been active for that period. Accusations that result in either suspension or stayed revocation shall be disclosed for seven years after the term of the probation and any corrective order has been completed if the contractor was active for that period. Accusations where there has been a revocation that was not stayed will be disclosed forever.

In addition to what the CSLB will disclose, if a contractor is disciplined, the contractor may be required to make certain disclosures. As an example, see Business and Professions Code section 7030.1.

E. Disciplinary Bonds

Every active licensed contractor must have a license bond. In addition, if one has been disciplined, the Registrar will order a disciplinary bond. The amount of the bond is based upon the seriousness of the violation. However, the sum of the bond must be between $15,000 and up to ten times the normal amount of the license bond required.

F. Judgment Bonds/Suspensions

If a contractor has an unsatisfied judgment related to his or her construction activity, the contractor must post a bond to ensure payment of the judgment, otherwise the license will be suspended.

G. Non-licensee Enforcement

The CSLB has a number of actions that they can take against a non-licensee. The most obvious is proceeding through the criminal courts under Business and Professions Code section 7028 (contracting without a license). In addition, the CSLB may obtain an injunction through the civil courts. However, more and more, the Registrar is issuing citations against unlicensed contractors, requiring either a civil penalty, an order of abatement, or both.

The entity or person cited has 15 working days after service of the citation to appeal, and if no appeal is filed, it becomes a final order and can be the subject of a civil action.

Sometimes the procedure dealing with non-licensees does not work as well as expected. That is because many of them do not stay in one place. However, if one is a repeat violator, after a number of such citations, the CSLB stands a good chance of obtaining severe criminal sanctions against the unlicensed contractor.

V.
HOME IMPROVEMENT AND SWIMMING POOL CONTRACTING

A. Introduction

Home improvement work is different than any other type of construction. The residential contractor, in addition to being proficient, must be able to adapt to conditions which he or she may not possibly know about until demolition begins. Further, there are many regulations and laws which only affect residential construction and more specifically remodeling.

Because of the present make up of the Board, which is heavily weighted towards signatory contractors and others with organized labor contacts, much of the enforcement deals with employee protection.

Also, as a result of recent trends, the Board deals with elder abuse issues more quickly and more often.

Recognizing this, the Contractors' Board was required to institute a certification program for home improvement contractors. On January 1, 1999, the Contractors' Board established its certification program. That program is no longer in effect as of January 1, 2004.

In addition, some problems that we see quite often in home improvement work are not always based on "construction practices" but rather on business practices. Indeed, home improvement contractors are probably some of the better "contractors" in the construction industry because they have to continually adapt to existing conditions. However, unlike other construction work, home improvement contracting is almost a separate industry.

One might also think that a plumber, merely putting in a water heater or even a faucet, would not have to comply with all of the requirements of home improvement contracts. However, if the work is in excess of $500.00, and is defined as home improvement, the contract must have all of the provisions of a contract for a second story room addition.

Discussed below are some differences in the law dealing with residential remodeling and swimming pool work. We also thought it would be a good idea to take a moment to discuss some non-legal differences as well.

We have written a number of articles dealing with home improvement contracting and the laws required by our Legislature for people that are involved in that industry. Those laws are discussed further in this chapter. However, there are other practicalities with respect to home improvement contracting.

When you are doing work in someone's home, you are disturbing their life style. It is not unusual to have an entire family living in one room for a couple of weeks. Clearly, no matter how careful you are, the house will be full of dust. Life will not be the same. The owners will be uptight and on edge.

You should remind your employees and subcontractors of this and keep these realities in mind yourself during your involvement with your customer. Also keep in mind that the customer is not a sophisticated purchaser for your services. Chances are, this is the first and last time the homeowner will be purchasing services such as yours. Although this may be the largest single purchase your customer makes in his or her lifetime (other than the purchase of the home), quite often your customer has spent little time planning the project. Your customer will have little understanding of the problems that he or she might run into. Therefore a significant part of the construction process in home improvement is education and hand-holding. Make sure you cover these bases.

Make sure that your subcontractors, your employees and your customers know that communication with each other must go through a representative of your company. That is the only way you can be responsible for the entire job. In return, make sure that you are sensitive to the problems of the homeowner at this time. Keep them informed. Try to anticipate problems. Let them know when problems might come up. This is their home, it is something that they will have to live with during remodeling and for the balance of their lives. It is this lifestyle that you are disturbing.

To the greatest extent possible, the owners should be made aware of potential problems.

If, for some reason, someone leaves a circuit breaker off or leaves the refrigerator unplugged, it would be good practical sense to offer to pay for any spoilage. Regardless of right or wrong, it is good marketing to have satisfied customers. Just as important, that satisfied customer will not be looking at each and every item for problems.

The information given to the owners is even more important if they remain in their home while construction is undertaken. If you are doing roofing and there is a likelihood of rain, be sure they want you to commence then. In the summer, if no air conditioning will be operating, tell them. The same is true for heat in the winter.

In essence, a significant portion of the work that a home improvement contractor will ever do is keeping the customer informed and happy.

Although it might seem that home improvement and swimming pool contracting should be included in other areas of the license law, it is our opinion that the home improvement and swimming pool fields have been the target of very specific legislation. It should be noted that the Contractors' State License Board's estimates indicate that approximately one third of its complaints are a result of home improvement or swimming pool work. Here the buyer is less sophisticated than the commercial buyer. Consequently, the Legislature has regulated the home improvement and swimming pool business to a much greater degree than any other.

B. Portions of the Law

SB 2029 which became law effective January 1, 2001, required the Contractors Board to provide a statement that emphasizes the value of commercial general liability insurance and encourages the owner or tenant to verify the contractor's insurance coverage and status as well as a check box indicating whether or not the contractor carries commercial general liability insurance, and if that is the case, the name and telephone number of the insurer.

The Contractors Board was also required to prepare a checklist through regulation, setting forth the items that an owner contracting for home improvement should consider when reviewing a proposed home improvement contract.

C. Home Improvement Defined

The term "home improvement" is defined in various ways and in various places of the Business and Professions Code. A home improvement contractor is defined as a contractor who is engaged in the business of home improvement. Home improvement means the repairing, remodeling, altering, converting, or modernizing of, or adding to, residential property including swimming pools, etc. Given this broad definition, almost anything done to an existing residence could be home improvement.

A home improvement contract means an agreement between a contractor and an owner, or a contractor and a tenant for home improvement work. As discussed previously, anyone who sells home improvement goods and services and is not an officer, partner or owner of the business must be a registered Home Improvement Salesperson.

D. The regulation on home improvement and swimming pool work contains the following requirements:

1. Contract requirements

You should review Business and Professions Code section 7159. This is a long list of contractual requirements for use in home improvement and swimming pool contracts totaling more than $500. The section states that these contracts must be in writing and signed by the parties, and shall include all of the following:

a. The name, address and license number of the contractor, and the name and registration number of any salesperson who solicited or negotiated the contract;

b. The approximate dates when the work will begin and be substantially completed;

c. A plan and scale drawing showing the shape, size, dimensions and construction and equipment specifications for a swimming pool, and for other home improvements, a description of the work to be done and a description of the materials to be used or installed and the agreed price or consideration for the work;

d. If there is a down payment, the down payment shall not <u>exceed</u> $200 or two percent (2%) of the contract for swimming pools, or $1000 or ten percent (10%) of the contract for home improvements, ***<u>whichever is less</u>*** (as an example, a $1000 contract for a home improvement can have a $100 deposit, and a $50,000 contract can have a $1,000 deposit);

e. A schedule of payments showing the amount to be paid in dollars and cents (not just percentages). The schedule of payments must be referenced to work performed and any material or equipment supplied. A contractor can never receive proportionately more money than the work performed (except for the down payment). On swimming pool contracts, the final payment may be made at the completion of the final plastering phase, so long as any installation of equipment, decking or fencing required under the contract is also completed. If the contractor fails to substantially commence work within 20 days of the date specified in the contract, the next payment due will be postponed for the same period;

f. The contract shall also state that upon satisfactory payment being made for any portion of the work, the contractor, before receiving any further payment, shall give to the person contracting for the work, a full and unconditional release from any claim or mechanics' lien for that portion for which payment has been made;

g. The down payment or payment schedule provisions of (d) and (e) do not apply when a contractor furnishes a payment and performance bond, lien and completion bond, or a joint control approved by the Registrar. A contractor must also place a notice in at least 10-point type, within three inches of the signature line, telling the tenant or owner that he/she has the right to require a performance and payment bond;

h. No extra or change order work shall be required to be performed without the prior written agreement of the person contracting for the construction. Any change order forms shall be incorporated in and shall become a part of the contract.

No change order is enforceable against the person contracting for the home improvement work or swimming pool construction unless it clearly sets forth the scope of work encompassed by the change order, and the price to be charged for the changes. However, the contractor who fails to have a written change order may still be able to recover on a "quantum meruit" basis for the reasonable value of the work they performed;

i. Any salesperson's commission can only be paid in proportion to the schedule of payments;

j. A contractor must give the notice required by Business and Professions Code section 7018.5. (See section 2 below.)

k. A statement defining what constitutes substantial commencement;

l. A notice that failure by the contractor without lawful excuse to substantially commence work within twenty (20) days from the approximate date specified in the contract when work will begin is a violation of the Contractors' License Law.

If the contract provides for a contractor to furnish a joint control, the contractor shall not have any financial or other interest in such joint control.

A contractor must give a signed copy of the contract to the owner.

m. SB 2029, which became effective January 1, 2001, required the Contractors' Board to provide a statement that emphasizes the value of commercial general liability insurance and encourage the owner or tenant to verify the contractor's insurance coverage and status as well as a checkbox indicating whether or not the contractor carries general liability insurance, and if that is the case, the name and telephone number of the insurer. The Contractors Board prepared two such questionnaires. One for home improvement and one for residential.

The Home Improvement Commercial General Liability Insurance form is as follows. The form dealing with Single-Family Residence Commercial General Liability follows right after.

CSLB
CALIFORNIA CONTRACTORS STATE LICENSE BOARD

Information About Commercial General Liability Insurance

Home Improvement

Pursuant to California Business & Professions Code §7159.3 (SB 2029), home improvement contractors must provide this notice and disclose whether or not they carry commercial general liability insurance.

☐ **Did your contractor tell you whether he or she carries Commercial General Liability Insurance?**

Home improvement contractors are required by law to tell you whether or not they carry Commercial General Liability Insurance. This written statement must accompany the bid, if there is one, and the contract.

☐ **What does this insurance cover?**

Commercial General Liability Insurance can protect against third-party bodily injury and accidental property damage. It is not intended to cover the work the contractor performs.

☐ **Is this insurance required?**

No. But the Contractors State License Board strongly recommends that all contractors carry it. The Board cautions you to evaluate the risk to your family and property when you hire a contractor who is not insured. Ask yourself, if something went wrong, would this contractor be able to cover losses ordinarily covered by insurance?

☐ **How can you make sure the contractor is insured?**

If he or she is insured, your contractor is required to provide you with the name and telephone number of the insurance company. Check with the insurance company to verify that the contractor's insurance coverage will cover your project.

☐ **What about a contractor who is self-insured?**

A self-insured contractor has made a business decision to be personally responsible for losses that would ordinarily be covered by insurance. Before contracting with a self-insured contractor, ask yourself, if something went wrong, would this contractor be able to cover losses ordinarily covered by insurance?

☐ ______________________________ does not carry Commercial General Liability Insurance.
(CONTRACTOR'S NAME)

☐ ______________________________ carries Commercial General Liability Insurance.
(CONTRACTOR'S NAME)

The insurance company is ____
(COMPANY NAME)

You may call the insurance company at ______________________ to verify coverage.
(TELEPHONE NUMBER)

For more information about Commercial General Liability Insurance, contact the Contractors State License Board at *www.cslb.ca.gov* or call 800-321-CSLB (2752).

CALIFORNIA CONTRACTORS STATE LICENSE BOARD

Information About Commercial General Liability Insurance

Single Family Home

Pursuant to California Business & Professions Code §7164 (SB 2029), contractors building single-family residences for owners who intend to occupy the home for at least a year must provide this notice and disclose whether or not they carry commercial general liability insurance.

☐ **Did your contractor tell you whether he or she carries Commercial General Liability Insurance?**

Contractors building single-family residences for owners who intend to occupy the home for at least a year are required by law to tell you whether or not they carry Commercial General Liability Insurance. This written statement must accompany the contract.

☐ **What does this insurance cover?**

Commercial General Liability Insurance can protect against third-party bodily injury and accidental property damage. It is not intended to cover the work the contractor performs.

☐ **Is this insurance required?**

No. But the Contractors State License Board strongly recommends that all contractors carry it. The Board cautions you to evaluate the risk to your family and property when you hire a contractor who is not insured. Ask yourself, if something went wrong, would this contractor be able to cover losses ordinarily covered by insurance?

☐ **How can you make sure the contractor is insured?**

If he or she is insured, your contractor is required to provide you with the name and telephone number of the insurance company. Check with the insurance company to verify that the contractor's insurance coverage will cover your project.

☐ **What about a contractor who is self-insured?**

A self-insured contractor has made a business decision to be personally responsible for losses that would ordinarily be covered by insurance. Before contracting with a self-insured contractor, ask yourself, if something went wrong, would this contractor be able to cover losses ordinarily covered by insurance?

☐ ______________________________ does not carry Commercial General Liability Insurance.
(CONTRACTOR'S NAME)

☐ ______________________________ carries Commercial General Liability Insurance.
(CONTRACTOR'S NAME)

The insurance company is ______________________________.
(COMPANY NAME)

You may call the insurance company at ____________________ to verify coverage.
(TELEPHONE NUMBER)

For more information about Commercial General Liability Insurance, contact the Contractors State License Board at *www.cslb.ca.gov* or call 800-321-CSLB (2752).

The Contractors' Board was also required to prepare a checklist setting forth items that an owner contracting for home improvement work should consider when reviewing a proposed home improvement contract. Instead, the Contractors' Board provided two such checklists. One for home improvement and one for swimming pools.

The checklist for home improvement is as follows. The checklist for swimming pools follows right after.

CALIFORNIA CONTRACTORS STATE LICENSE BOARD

Checklist for Homeowners

Home Improvement

Pursuant to California Business & Professions Code §7159.3 (SB 2029), home improvement contractors must provide this notice.

✓ Check Out Your Contractor

- ☐ Did you contact the Contractors State License Board (CSLB) to check the status of the contractor's license?

  *Contact the **CSLB at 1-800-321-CSLB (2752) or** visit our **web site: www.cslb.ca.gov**.*

- ☐ Did you get at least 3 local references from the contractors you are considering?

  Did you call them?

- ☐ Building Permits—will the contractor get a permit before the work starts?

✓ Check Out the Contract

- ☐ Did you read and do you understand your contract?
- ☐ Does the 3-day right to cancel a contract apply to you?

  Contact the CSLB if you don't know.

- ☐ Does the contract tell you when work will start and end?
- ☐ Does the contract include a detailed description of the work to be done, the material to be used, and equipment to be installed?

  This description should include brand names, model numbers, quantities and colors. Specific descriptions now will prevent disputes later.

- ☐ Are you required to pay a down payment?

  If you are, the down payment should never be more than 10% of the contract price or $1,000, whichever is less.

- ☐ Is there a schedule of payments?

  If there is a schedule of payments, you should pay only as work is completed and not before. There are some exceptions—contact the CSLB to find out what they are.

- ☐ Did your contractor give you a "Notice to Owner," a warning notice describing liens and ways to prevent them?

  Even if you pay your contractor, a lien can be placed on your home by unpaid laborers, subcontractors, or material suppliers. A lien can result in you paying twice or, in some cases, losing your home in a foreclosure. Check the "Notice to Owner" for ways to protect yourself.

- ☐ Did you know changes or additions to your contract **must** all be in writing?

  Putting changes in writing reduces the possibility of a later dispute.

1/02

CALIFORNIA CONTRACTORS STATE LICENSE BOARD

Checklist for Homeowners

Swimming Pool

Pursuant to California Business & Professions Code §7159.3 (SB 2029), home improvement contractors building swimming pools must provide this notice.

✓ Check Out Your Contractor

- ☐ Did you contact the Contractors State License Board (CSLB) to check the status of the contractor's license?

  Contact the ***CSLB at 1-800-321-CSLB (2752) or*** *visit our* ***web site: www.cslb.ca.gov.***

- ☐ Did you get at least 3 local references from the contractors you are considering?

  Did you call them?

- ☐ Building Permits—will the contractor get a permit before the work starts?

✓ Check Out the Contract

- ☐ Did you read and do you understand your contract?
- ☐ Does the 3-day right to cancel a contract apply to you?

  Contact the CSLB if you don't know.

- ☐ Does the contract tell you when work will start and end?
- ☐ Does the contract include a detailed description of the work to be done, the material that will be used and equipment to be installed?

  This description should include a plan and scale drawing showing the shape, size, dimensions and specifications. It should include brand names, model numbers, quantities and colors. Specific descriptions now will prevent disputes later.

- ☐ Are you required to pay a down payment?

  The down payment for swimming pools should never be more than 2% of the contract price or $200, whichever is less.

- ☐ Is there a schedule of payments?

  If there is a schedule of payments, you should pay only as work is completed and not before. There are some exceptions—contact the CSLB to find out what they are.

- ☐ Did your contractor give you a "Notice to Owner," a warning notice describing liens and ways to prevent them?

  Even if you pay your contractor, a lien can be placed on your home by unpaid laborers, subcontractors, or material suppliers. A lien can result in you paying twice or, in some cases, losing your home in a foreclosure. Check the "Notice to Owner" for ways to protect yourself.

- ☐ Did you know changes or additions to your contract **must** all be in writing?

  Putting changes in writing reduces the possibility of a later dispute.

2. Notice to Owner

The following is the language required to be given in a document to a homeowner prior to commencing work:

"Notice to Owner"

Under the California Mechanics' Lien Law, any contractor, subcontractor, laborer, supplier, or other person or entity who helps to improve your property, but is not paid for his or her work or supplies, has a right to place a lien on your home, land, or property where the work was performed and to sue you in court to obtain payment.

This means that after a court hearing, your home, land, and property could be sold by a court officer and the proceeds of the sale used to satisfy what you owe. This can happen even if you have paid your contractor in full if the contractor's subcontractors, laborers, or suppliers remain unpaid.

To preserve their rights to file a claim or lien against your property, certain claimants such as subcontractors or material suppliers are each required to provide you with a document called a "Preliminary Notice." Contractors and laborers who contract with owners directly do not have to provide such notice since you are aware of their existence as an owner. A preliminary notice is not a lien against your property. Its purpose is to notify you of persons or entities that may have a right to file a lien against your property if they are not paid. In order to perfect their lien rights, a contractor, subcontractor, supplier, or laborer must file a mechanics' lien with the county recorder which then becomes a recorded lien against your property. Generally, the maximum time allowed for filing a mechanics' lien against your property is 90 days after substantial completion of your project.

To insure extra protection for yourself and your property, you may wish to take one or more of the following steps:

(1) Require that your contractor supply you with a payment and performance bond (not a license bond), which provides that the bonding company will either complete the project or pay damages up to the amount of the bond. This payment and performance bond as well as a copy of the construction

contract should be filed with the county recorder for your further protection. The payment and performance bond will usually cost from 1 to 5 percent of the contract amount depending on the contractor's bonding ability. If a contractor cannot obtain such bonding, it may indicate his or her financial incapacity.

(2) Require that payments be made directly to subcontractors and material suppliers through a joint control. Funding services may be available, for a fee, in your area which will establish voucher or other means of payment to your contractor. These services may also provide you with lien waivers and other forms of protection. Any joint control agreement should include the addendum approved by the registrar.

(3) Issue joint checks for payment, made out to both your contractor and subcontractors or material suppliers involved in the project. The joint checks should be made payable to the persons or entities which send preliminary notices to you. Those persons or entities have indicated that they may have lien rights on your property, therefore you need to protect yourself. This will help to insure that all persons due payment are actually paid.

(4) Upon making payment on any completed phase of the project, and before making any further payments, require your contractor to provide you with unconditional "Waiver and Release" forms signed by each material supplier, subcontractor, and laborer involved in that portion of the work for which payment was made. The statutory lien releases are set forth in exact language in Section 3262 of the Civil Code. Most stationery stores will sell the "Waiver and Release" forms if your contractor does not have them. The material suppliers, subcontractors, and laborers that you obtain releases from are those persons or entities who have filed preliminary notices with you. If you are not certain of the material suppliers, subcontractors, and laborers working on your project, you may obtain a list from your contractor. On projects involving improvements to a single-family residence or a duplex owned by individuals, the persons

signing these releases lose the right to file a mechanics' lien claim against your property. In other types of construction, this protection may still be important, but may not be as complete.

To protect yourself under this option, you must be certain that all material suppliers, subcontractors, and laborers have signed the "Waiver and Release" form. If a mechanics' lien has been filed against your property, it can only be voluntarily released by a recorded "Release of Mechanics' Lien" signed by the person or entity that filed the mechanics' lien against your property unless the lawsuit to enforce the lien was not timely filed. You should not make any final payments until any and all such liens are removed. You should consult an attorney if a lien is filed against your property.

3. Notice of Cancellation

On every job entered into between a contractor and a residential homeowner that is not made at the contractor's place of business, the contract must contain a notice that the owner has a three day right to cancel, and a **separate** "Notice of Cancellation" must be given that allows the homeowner three days to cancel the transaction without any liability to the contractor. That period is extended to seven days following a declaration of a disaster (such as a flood or earthquake.)

In addition to the "Notice of Cancellation," the Home Improvement Contract itself must have language explaining this right to the owner. This language must be in the following format, and as discussed above, must be given to every homeowner prior to commencing work, if the contract is not made at appropriate trade premises:

a. Language Required to be Used in the Home Improvement Contract

The Home Improvement Contract, in close proximity to the signature line, must contain the following language printed in at least 10 point **bold** roman style type:

"You, the buyer, may cancel this transaction at any time prior to midnight of the third business day after the

date of this transaction. See the attached notice of cancellation form for an explanation of this right."

Note that if the agreement is following the Declaration of a Disaster, the language must read in least 10 point **bold** roman style type:

"You, the buyer, may cancel this transaction at any time prior to midnight of the seventh business day after the date of this transaction. See the attached notice of cancellation form for an explanation of this right."

On occasion, clients tell us they do not want to use two contracts. In that case, we suggest the following dual purpose language above the signature line of the contract:

"YOU, THE BUYER, MAY CANCEL THIS TRANSACTION AT ANY TIME PRIOR TO MIDNIGHT OF THE THIRD BUSINESS DAY AFTER THE DATE OF THIS TRANSACTION. OR IF THIS IS A CONTRACT FOR THE REPAIR OF DAMAGES RESULTING FROM AN EARTHQUAKE, FLOOD, FIRE, HURRICANE, RIOT, STORM, TIDAL WAVE, OR OTHER SIMILAR CATASTROPHIC OCCURRENCE FOR WHICH A STATE OF EMERGENCY HAS BEEN DECLARED, YOU THE BUYER MAY CANCEL THIS TRANSACTION AT ANY TIME PRIOR TO MIDNIGHT OF THE SEVENTH BUSINESS DAY AFTER THE DATE OF THIS TRANSACTION. SEE THE ATTACHED NOTICE OF CANCELLATION FORM FOR AN EXPLANATION OF THIS RIGHT."

If the contract is in a foreign language, e.g., Spanish, this clause must be in that language as well.

b. "Notice of Cancellation"

The "Notice of Cancellation" must be in the following format, and, must be given to every homeowner prior to commencing work if the contract is not made at appropriate trade premises:

"Notice of Cancellation

____

Date

You may cancel this transaction, without any penalty or obligation, within three business days from the above date.

If you cancel, any property traded in, any payments made by you under the contract or sale, and any negotiable instrument executed by you will be returned within 10 days following receipt by the seller of your cancellation notice, and any security interest arising out of the transaction will be canceled.

If you cancel, you must make available to the seller at your residence, in substantially as good condition as when received, any goods delivered to you under this contract or sale, or you may, if you wish, comply with the instructions of the seller regarding the return shipment of the goods at the seller's expense and risk.

If you do make the goods available to the seller and the seller does not pick them up within 20 days of the date of your notice of cancellation, you may retain or dispose of the goods without any further obligation. If you fail to make the goods available to the seller, or if you agree to return the goods to the seller and fail to do so, then you remain liable for performance of all obligations under the contract.

To cancel this transaction, mail or deliver a signed and dated copy of this cancellation notice, or any other written notice, or send a telegram to, _______________________________,

/name of seller/

at____

____

/address of seller's place of business/

not later than midnight of_______________.

(date)

I hereby cancel this transaction _______________.

(date)

________________________________"

(Buyer's signature)

Note: that as stated above, work done as a result of a natural disaster, such as an earthquake, requires seven (7) days notice as opposed to three (3).

c. Emergency Repair Exception to Notice of Cancellation

There is an exception to the right to cancel for emergency repair work. That exception provides that the three day period for cancellation (or seven days after a disaster) shall not apply to a contract that is initiated by the buyer (homeowner) or his agent, including an insurance agent, where the contract is for emergency or necessary repairs or services that are necessary for the immediate protection of persons or their property, provided that the buyer signs a separate dated and signed personal statement describing the situation requiring the immediate repair and expressly acknowledging and waiving the right to cancel the sale within three or seven days, whichever applies. **This exception is most important to service and repair contractors.**

The law states that no pre-printed form is allowed to be used for such a waiver. The waiver must be in the handwriting of your customer. The following is language that may be used:

"I, Jane Doe, homeowner of the property located at 1234 Main Street, Anytown, California hereby declare that I have requested that 123 Plumbing make the repairs to my water heater now because my family and I need hot water and can not wait for three days for that repair. 123 Plumbing has provided me with a Notice of Cancellation giving me a three day period to cancel this contract; however, because of this necessity, for the protection of my family and myself, I expressly waive the cancellation period that has been explained to me.

Signed, Jane Doe."

d. Problems With Some Pre-printed Forms

A word of caution. Some stationery stores and mail order forms businesses sell a "Home Improvement Contract" with the "Notice of Cancellation" printed on the back of the contract. To use that notice would require the physical tearing or destruction of the contract. The language of the statute requires the form to be **separate** from the contract.

4. Other Notice Requirements

A contractor must include the following statement in at least 10-point type on all written contracts where he or she is a prime contractor (***not subcontractor***).

"Contractors are required by law to be licensed and regulated by the Contractors' State License Board which has jurisdiction to investigate complaints against contractors if a complaint regarding a patent act or omission is filed within four years of the date of the alleged violation. A complaint regarding a latent act or omission pertaining to structural defects must be filed within 10 years of the date of the alleged violation. Any questions concerning a contractor may be referred to the Registrar, Contractors' State License Board, P.O. Box 26000, Sacramento, California 95826."

This statement must be reprinted "word for word."

In addition, ***prior*** to entering into a contract to perform work on residential property of four (4) or fewer units, a contractor who has his or her license suspended or revoked two or more times within an eight year period, must disclose any disciplinary license suspension or revocation during the last eight years as a result of a violation of the Contractors' License Law, in either 10-point roman boldface type, or in contrasting red print of at least 8-point roman boldface type.

In addition to the above, any contractor, ***at the time of making a bid or prior to entering into a contract*** to perform work on residential property with four (4) or fewer units, whichever occurs first, must provide the following notice in writing:

"STATE LAW REQUIRES ANYONE WHO CONTRACTS TO DO CONSTRUCTION WORK TO BE LICENSED BY THE CONTRACTORS' STATE LICENSE BOARD IN THE LICENSE CATEGORY IN WHICH THE CONTRACTOR IS GOING TO BE WORKING--IF THE TOTAL PRICE OF THE JOB IS $500 OR MORE (INCLUDING LABOR AND MATERIALS).

LICENSED CONTRACTORS ARE REGULATED BY LAWS DESIGNED TO PROTECT THE PUBLIC. IF YOU CONTRACT WITH SOMEONE WHO DOES NOT HAVE A LICENSE, THE CONTRACTORS' STATE LICENSE BOARD MAY BE UNABLE TO ASSIST YOU WITH A COMPLAINT. YOUR ONLY REMEDY AGAINST AN UNLICENSED CONTRACTOR MAY BE IN CIVIL COURT, AND YOU MAY BE LIABLE FOR DAMAGES ARISING OUT OF ANY INJURIES TO THE CONTRACTOR OR HIS OR HER EMPLOYEES.

YOU MAY CONTACT THE CONTRACTORS' STATE LICENSE BOARD TO FIND OUT IF THIS CONTRACTOR HAS A VALID LICENSE. THE BOARD HAS COMPLETE INFORMATION ON THE HISTORY OF LICENSED CONTRACTORS, INCLUDING ANY POSSIBLE SUSPENSIONS, REVOCATIONS, JUDGMENTS, AND CITATIONS. THE BOARD HAS OFFICES THROUGHOUT CALIFORNIA. PLEASE CHECK THE GOVERNMENT PAGES OF THE WHITE PAGES FOR THE OFFICE NEAREST YOU OR CALL 1-800-321-CSLB FOR MORE INFORMATION."

This notice must be in either capital letters in 10-point roman boldface type or in contrasting red print in at least 8-point roman boldface type.

A contractor must disclose any disciplinary license suspension, or license revocation during the last eight (8) years resulting from any violation of this chapter by the contractor, whether or not the suspension or revocation was stayed. This disclosure applies only to any contractor who has had his or her license suspended or revoked two or more times within an eight year period. The disclosure must be in either capital letters in 10-point roman boldface type or in contrasting red print in at least 8-point roman boldface type, in a document provided prior to entering into a contract to perform work on residential property with four or fewer units.

SB 2029, which became effective January 1, 2001, required the Contractors' Board to provide a statement that emphasizes the value of commercial general liability insurance and encourage the owner or tenant to verify the contractor's insurance coverage and status as well as a checkbox indicating whether or not the contractor carries general liability insurance, and if that is the case, the name and telephone number of the insurer. The Contractors Board prepared two such questionnaires. One for home improvement and one for residential.

The Home Improvement Commercial General Liability Insurance form is as follows. The form dealing with Single-Family Residence Commercial General Liability follows right after.

CSLB
CALIFORNIA CONTRACTORS STATE LICENSE BOARD

Information About Commercial General Liability Insurance

Home Improvement

Pursuant to California Business & Professions Code §7159.3 (SB 2029), home improvement contractors must provide this notice and disclose whether or not they carry commercial general liability insurance.

Did your contractor tell you whether he or she carries Commercial General Liability Insurance?

Home improvement contractors are required by law to tell you whether or not they carry Commercial General Liability Insurance. This written statement must accompany the bid, if there is one, and the contract.

What does this insurance cover?

Commercial General Liability Insurance can protect against third-party bodily injury and accidental property damage. It is not intended to cover the work the contractor performs.

Is this insurance required?

No. But the Contractors State License Board strongly recommends that all contractors carry it. The Board cautions you to evaluate the risk to your family and property when you hire a contractor who is not insured. Ask yourself, if something went wrong, would this contractor be able to cover losses ordinarily covered by insurance?

How can you make sure the contractor is insured?

If he or she is insured, your contractor is required to provide you with the name and telephone number of the insurance company. Check with the insurance company to verify that the contractor's insurance coverage will cover your project.

What about a contractor who is self-insured?

A self-insured contractor has made a business decision to be personally responsible for losses that would ordinarily be covered by insurance. Before contracting with a self-insured contractor, ask yourself, if something went wrong, would this contractor be able to cover losses ordinarily covered by insurance?

☐ ______________________________ does not carry Commercial General Liability Insurance.
(CONTRACTOR'S NAME)

☐ ______________________________ carries Commercial General Liability Insurance.
(CONTRACTOR'S NAME)

The insurance company is ____.
(COMPANY NAME)

You may call the insurance company at ______________________ to verify coverage.
(TELEPHONE NUMBER)

For more information about Commercial General Liability Insurance, contact the Contractors State License Board at *www.cslb.ca.gov* or call 800-321-CSLB (2752).

CALIFORNIA CONTRACTORS STATE LICENSE BOARD

Information About Commercial General Liability Insurance

Single Family Home

Pursuant to California Business & Professions Code §7164 (SB 2029), contractors building single-family residences for owners who intend to occupy the home for at least a year must provide this notice and disclose whether or not they carry commercial general liability insurance.

Did your contractor tell you whether he or she carries Commercial General Liability Insurance?

Contractors building single-family residences for owners who intend to occupy the home for at least a year are required by law to tell you whether or not they carry Commercial General Liability Insurance. This written statement must accompany the contract.

What does this insurance cover?

Commercial General Liability Insurance can protect against third-party bodily injury and accidental property damage. It is not intended to cover the work the contractor performs.

Is this insurance required?

No. But the Contractors State License Board strongly recommends that all contractors carry it. The Board cautions you to evaluate the risk to your family and property when you hire a contractor who is not insured. Ask yourself, if something went wrong, would this contractor be able to cover losses ordinarily covered by insurance?

How can you make sure the contractor is insured?

If he or she is insured, your contractor is required to provide you with the name and telephone number of the insurance company. Check with the insurance company to verify that the contractor's insurance coverage will cover your project.

What about a contractor who is self-insured?

A self-insured contractor has made a business decision to be personally responsible for losses that would ordinarily be covered by insurance. Before contracting with a self-insured contractor, ask yourself, if something went wrong, would this contractor be able to cover losses ordinarily covered by insurance?

☐ ______________________________ does not carry Commercial General Liability Insurance.
(CONTRACTOR'S NAME)

☐ ______________________________ carries Commercial General Liability Insurance.
(CONTRACTOR'S NAME)

The insurance company is ______________________________.
(COMPANY NAME)

You may call the insurance company at ____________________ to verify coverage.
(TELEPHONE NUMBER)

For more information about Commercial General Liability Insurance, contact the Contractors State License Board at *www.cslb.ca.gov* or call 800-321-CSLB (2752).

The Contractors' Board was also required to prepare a checklist setting forth items that an owner contracting for home improvement work should consider when reviewing a proposed home improvement contract. Instead, the Contractors' Board provided two such checklists. One for home improvement and one for swimming pools.

The checklist for home improvement is as follows. The checklist for swimming pools follows right after.

CALIFORNIA CONTRACTORS STATE LICENSE BOARD

Checklist for Homeowners

Home Improvement

Pursuant to California Business & Professions Code §7159.3 (SB 2029), home improvement contractors must provide this notice.

✓ **Check Out Your Contractor**

- Did you contact the Contractors State License Board (CSLB) to check the status of the contractor's license?

  Contact the ***CSLB at 1-800-321-CSLB (2752) or*** *visit our* ***web site: www.cslb.ca.gov****.*

- Did you get at least 3 local references from the contractors you are considering?

  Did you call them?

- Building Permits—will the contractor get a permit before the work starts?

✓ **Check Out the Contract**

- Did you read and do you understand your contract?
- Does the 3-day right to cancel a contract apply to you?

  Contact the CSLB if you don't know.

- Does the contract tell you when work will start and end?
- Does the contract include a detailed description of the work to be done, the material to be used, and equipment to be installed?

  This description should include brand names, model numbers, quantities and colors. Specific descriptions now will prevent disputes later.

- Are you required to pay a down payment?

  If you are, the down payment should never be more than 10% of the contract price or $1,000, whichever is less.

- Is there a schedule of payments?

  If there is a schedule of payments, you should pay only as work is completed and not before. There are some exceptions—contact the CSLB to find out what they are.

- Did your contractor give you a "Notice to Owner," a warning notice describing liens and ways to prevent them?

  Even if you pay your contractor, a lien can be placed on your home by unpaid laborers, subcontractors, or material suppliers. A lien can result in you paying twice or, in some cases, losing your home in a foreclosure. Check the "Notice to Owner" for ways to protect yourself.

- Did you know changes or additions to your contract **must** all be in writing?

  Putting changes in writing reduces the possibility of a later dispute.

1/02

CALIFORNIA CONTRACTORS STATE LICENSE BOARD

Checklist for Homeowners

Swimming Pool

Pursuant to California Business & Professions Code §7159.3 (SB 2029), home improvement contractors building swimming pools must provide this notice.

✓ Check Out Your Contractor

- ☐ Did you contact the Contractors State License Board (CSLB) to check the status of the contractor's license?

  Contact the ***CSLB at 1-800-321-CSLB (2752) or*** *visit our* ***web site: www.cslb.ca.gov***.

- ☐ Did you get at least 3 local references from the contractors you are considering?

  Did you call them?

- ☐ Building Permits—will the contractor get a permit before the work starts?

✓ Check Out the Contract

- ☐ Did you read and do you understand your contract?
- ☐ Does the 3-day right to cancel a contract apply to you?

  Contact the CSLB if you don't know.

- ☐ Does the contract tell you when work will start and end?
- ☐ Does the contract include a detailed description of the work to be done, the material that will be used and equipment to be installed?

  This description should include a plan and scale drawing showing the shape, size, dimensions and specifications. It should include brand names, model numbers, quantities and colors. Specific descriptions now will prevent disputes later.

- ☐ Are you required to pay a down payment?

  The down payment for swimming pools should never be more than 2% of the contract price or $200, whichever is less.

- ☐ Is there a schedule of payments?

  If there is a schedule of payments, you should pay only as work is completed and not before. There are some exceptions—contact the CSLB to find out what they are.

- ☐ Did your contractor give you a "Notice to Owner," a warning notice describing liens and ways to prevent them?

  Even if you pay your contractor, a lien can be placed on your home by unpaid laborers, subcontractors, or material suppliers. A lien can result in you paying twice or, in some cases, losing your home in a foreclosure. Check the "Notice to Owner" for ways to protect yourself.

- ☐ Did you know changes or additions to your contract **must** all be in writing?

  Putting changes in writing reduces the possibility of a later dispute.

1/02

5. Referrals/Kickbacks
   a. No rebate or kickback for "referrals."
   b. No gift of tangible items in excess of $5.00 that is conditioned upon the obtaining of a home improvement contract.
   c. No compensation to salesperson or agent except from employing contractor.

E. Home Improvement Salespersons' Registration

For a number of years, Home Improvement Salespeople have had to be registered. This requirement continues even though under recent legislation a Home Improvement Contractor must be certified. This section will discuss the registration of Home Improvement Salespersons.

1. Home Improvement Salesperson

The definition of a Home Improvement Salesperson is one who is employed by a licensed contractor, and is a person who sells, negotiates or signs for that licensed contractor, contracts involving Home Improvement goods and services, including swimming pools.

Anyone who solicits, sells, negotiates or signs a Home Improvement Contracts for a licensed contractor outside of the contractor's normal place of business must be registered with the Contractors' State License Board. However, a salesperson who sells any such items in a place of business where those items are normally sold is not required to be registered with the Contractors' Board. This is true whether the sale is initiated by the contractor, the salesperson or the owner. However, as long as the sale is made somewhere other than the "appropriate trade premises of the contractor," the salesperson must be registered.

2. Exemption

Those persons listed on the Contractors' State License Board's records for that license (e.g. partners, officers of the corporation or the responsible managing officer or employee) are not required to be registered as Home Improvement

Salespeople.

There are no residential or experience requirements for a Home Improvement Salesperson. The registration is good for two years. The salesperson must keep his or her address information current.

A Home Improvement Salesperson may work for any number of contractors, but must register separately for each contractor for whom that Salesperson is working.

3. Utilizing Your "Salesperson"

Up until mid 2003, the Contractors' Board took the position that one could not employ a revoked contractor as a home improvement salesperson. This was in direct violation of the California constitution as pointed out in an Attorney General's Opinion, which came about in mid-2003. It should be noted that our firm argued that and submitted our argument to the Attorney General's office.

F. What Happens When a Contractor Fails to Comply With the Requirements of the Home Improvement Act

Frankly, most contractors violate the Home Improvement Act in at least one way. Either their contract doesn't comply, they take too large of a deposit, or they commence work prior to waiting the three-day waiting period.

The question of what happens if the contractor fails to comply is twofold. First, the contractor will be subject to discipline by the Contractors' Board. The Contractors' Board rarely will issue a citation against a contractor simply for using the wrong form. However, the Contractors' Board will issue a citation for taking too large of a down payment, or when it is investigating a contractor for other violations, and that violation is also noted.

That is unfortunately not the end of the story. When a contractor enters into a home improvement contract with an owner and fails to comply with the Home Improvement Act, nothing may happen unless the contractor and owner get into a dispute. Then what often happens is the contractor will be unpaid and sue the owner or the owner will be unhappy with the contractor's performance and sue the contractor. An attorney knowledgeable in construction law will notice that the Home Improvement Act has been violated, and argue to the court that the entire transaction may be voided by the owner.

In essence, there are two legal theories for voiding a contract for residential work where the contractor has violated the law. Under the Home Improvement Act, a Supreme Court case has held that an "unsophisticated" home owner may void the contract between it and the contractor if that contract violates the Home Improvement Act. There, of course, is a question of fact as to whether an owner is "sophisticated." In the cases that have held homeowners to be sophisticated, they were either real estate developers, real estate brokers, persons who owned commercial real property, and in one case, a homeowner who had a social relationship with the contractor. In those cases, the court did not declare the contract void between the owner and contractor, and the contractor was entitled to be paid.

If the contract is void, there is a question of whether or not any payment can still be received by the contractor. The same question as to whether the contractor gets anything also applies to the Home Solicitation Act, which requires the "Notice of Cancellation" that is also discussed in this chapter. If the contractor fails to give the "Notice of Cancellation" in the form required by the law, the owner may cancel the transaction at any time before the contractor complies, even if that is a year or more after the work is completed. However, the effect of the cancellation is in dispute in the courts. An examination of the contractor's conduct will be required.

At the outset, upon the cancellation of the contract using the Notice of Cancellation, in a perfect world, the owner is supposed to return to the contractor all of the "goods" that the contractor has provided, and the contractor must return all money paid by the owner. However, once those goods are attached to the home, the argument is that it is "waste" to tear the house apart to return those goods. There have been three Court of Appeal cases interpreting the right to cancel in residential construction. The first of those cases was a boon to owners, in that it held that the contractor will receive nothing if it failed to comply with the Notice of Right to Cancel provisions.

The second case, was far more lenient to contractors. It stated that on a long term contract, where the contractor has performed substantial work for the owner, it would be unfair to give an enrichment to the owner to the detriment of the contractor. Therefore, the Court of Appeal allowed the contractor to recover, not on the contract, but the value of the work that was done. This is called "quantum meruit." The difference is that rather than getting your contract price, the contractor will only get the value of that work. Experts will have to testify as to the value.

While there has been no case on point regarding the Home Improvement Act and a voidable home improvement contract, many believe that the same quantum meruit valuation could be allowed to the contractor where that contract is voided.

There is, however, a later case with another view on the same subject. It is unfortunate that construction cases rarely get to the Court of Appeal because of the cost to get there, thus the issue has not been tested in the courts for more than thirteen years. In the latest case regarding the "Right to Cancel," a plumbing contractor answered a service call relating to sewer line work at a residential home that was not occupied by the owner. The contractor gave the owner a price, and the owner stated they wanted a couple of days to think about it. Indeed the first service call visit came on the weekend. Without their knowledge that work was commencing, the contractor began tearing up the driveway to install new sewer lines on Sunday.

Once the owner discovered that the contractor had started work before he finished getting other bids, and before the three day period had passed, the contractor was kicked off the job by the owner. The contractor sued the owner alleging that it was entitled to the value of the work that was done. The Court of Appeal disagreed. The Court of Appeal stated that the intent of the Legislature was to prevent this type of conduct and that contractors can inexpensively protect themselves by complying with the requirements of the Home Solicitation Act. Therefore, the Court of Appeal allowed no recovery. Many people examining this case, limit it to cases where the contractor "spikes" the job. That term has come to describe situations like the factual scenario above -- where the contractor starts immediately on the job, putting pressure on the owner not to cancel the contract. Some attorneys argue that the language of the Court of Appeal in the latest case means that contractors should not recover for any violation of either the Home Solicitation Act or the Home Improvement Act, as truly the contractor can inexpensively protect itself by using the right forms and waiting three days. This has not been tested in the Court of Appeal and is not stated in the statutes.

Our recommendation is that you comply with the law and avoid any controversy yourself.

G. Summary

It should be noted that in reality the Contractors' License Law generally governs home improvement and swimming pool work to a much greater degree than commercial or public works. The Contractors' State License Board is so bogged down in minutia that the customers in a larger construction contract who are sophisticated will not turn to the Contractors' State License Board for help. Nor will a mere $10,000 bond make them whole. The rules and regulations of the Contractors' State License Board really serve to regulate the home improvement and swimming pool contractor.

VI.
CONTRACTING WITH PUBLIC ENTITIES IN CALIFORNIA

It has been said that California Public Works projects drive the California economy. Clearly it is a substantial portion of the construction work that goes on in the state of California. It is important to note that when the owner is a public entity, the manner in which contracting is handled can be very different from bidding and doing work in the private sector. There can even be a substantial difference between the various public entities.

State agencies are governed by the State Contract Act which is found in the Public Contract Code. However, local agencies may have different requirements that are usually specific to the type of local agency involved. Further, how one deals with a public entity may also be found in city charters and ordinances as well as the California Code of Regulations. These various statutes, regulations, and ordinances create a patchwork of laws that may create contractual provisions that are not found in the Public Contract Code or other places. Indeed, they may even have special claims procedures and statutes of limitations (see the chapter on Mechanics' Liens, Stop Notices and Bonds).

Public Agencies enter into contracts in a manner similar to private companies. However, the exact mechanism of how one enters into a contract may be different for public agencies. The similarity is that one enters into a contract by an agreement. However, some remedies available to contractors dealing with other individuals or corporations that are not public entities, may not be available. As an example, "quantum meruit" claims or claims seeking the value of work performed, are not allowed against a public agency. Claims of "abandonment of contract," which in the private sector would allow claims for the value of all work performed where the contract was abandoned by a <u>major</u> change in scope, are also not allowed against a public entity.

A. How the Contract is Formed

Typically, a contract is formed by people agreeing to do something. However, with respect to public contracts, typically those contracts are awarded under competitive bidding laws. That requires a bid and an award. A contract is formed when the award is made. Further, public construction contracts generally require the prime contractor to obtain a bond for any contracts in excess of $25,000. Performance and payment bonds are the rule rather than the exception as they are in commercial contracts. Prime contractors will also be required to post a guaranty (such as a bond) to insure that they will enter into a contract if it is awarded to them. In addition, prime contractors are required to list in their bid all of the their subcontractors who will perform more than one half of one percent of the amount of work to be done.

Lastly, a public entity has the right to specify the type of license required. This is unlike commercial contracts wherein the licensing law determines what type of license is necessary to do the work.

B. The Bidding Process

Unlike commercial contracts, there is a complicated set of rules for bidding public contracts. This complex set of rules also provides a lot of work for lawyers in that the rules tend to be violated and misinterpreted, thereby requiring litigation involving bid disputes.

1. Prequalification

Many public entities are now prequalifying contractors so that they do not have to qualify the contractor during the bidding process. The basis for awarding the bid is that the contractor be the lowest responsible and responsive bidder. A responsible bidder is one who has demonstrated the attributes of trustworthiness as well as quality, fitness, capacity and experience to perform the public works contract. This area is the area that is most used during the prequalification procedures (however, see the area dealing with design/build contracting discussed later).

2. Bidding

In order to submit a bid, unless the prime contractor is doing all the work him or herself, the prime contractor must receive bids from its subcontractors. Previously subcontractors would call in their bid, or have someone standing by to insert a number at the last minute so that the prime contractor would not use one bid against another subcontractor. That is called "bid shopping." With the advent of faxes and email this procedure has lessened substantially.

The law presumes the contractor is doing any portion of the work (greater than 1/2 of the one percent of the contract price) where a subcontractor is not listed. Typically, the bid will require a "bid bond," which essentially guarantees that the bidder will enter into a contract if the bidder is awarded the contract. Note that some public entities are not required to follow all of the competitive bidding requirements, such as charter cities and the University of California.

Competitive bidding may not be required if it will not produce any advantage such as ordering off the shelf items.

C. Design/Build Procurement

Recently, the Legislature has seen fit to allow public entities to enter into design/build contracts. This means that one entity will contract for both the design and building the project. The rationale is that this will be less costly and quicker than having one entity design the project and another one build it.

This may be true but the design/build manner of contracting requires much more effort on the part of the public entity to put together a bid package that includes the desired criteria.

D. The Bid Process

As indicated above, there are laws commonly known as the Subcontractor's Listing Law, which is intended to provide the public entity with the lowest responsible and responsive bid, but keep the prime contractor from bid shopping or bid peddling. That is to say that the prime contractor should not be able to use one bid against another <u>after</u> accepting and utilizing that bid in its bid to the public entity. In that the prime contractor must list every subcontractor that will perform work in excess of one-half of one percent of the prime contractor's total bid, if the prime contractor doesn't list someone the public entity will assume that the prime contractor will be doing that work him or herself. The prime contractor may require subcontractors to also provide payment and performance bonds.

E. Substituting Listed Contractors

As stated above, the prime contractor cannot use a listed subcontractor's bid to get others to reduce their price. There is a complex manner in which one can substitute a listed subcontractor, and the process requires a hearing before the public entity to allow the substitution. This is one area of the law that becomes very problematic. Many public entities are not as large or capable of making these kinds of decisions and thereby end up making erroneous decisions or decisions that would unfairly favor one contractor over the other.

With that said, the list of matters in which one can substitute one subcontractor for another is finite and is only when:

- The listed subcontractor fails or refuses to execute a contract;
- The listed subcontractor becomes bankrupt or insolvent;
- The listed subcontractor refuses to perform its contract;
- The listed subcontractor fails to post payment and performance bonds in accordance with the law (<u>if the request for bid required the potential subcontractor to provide a payment and performance bond</u>);
- The subcontractor was listed because of an inadvertent clerical error;
- The listed subcontractor is unlicensed;
- The listed subcontractor performs work unsatisfactorily;
- The listed subcontractor is ineligible to work on public works projects pursuant to the Labor Code; or
- The awarding authority determines that the listed subcontractor is not a responsible subcontractor.

In order to make that substitution, the public entity must give notice of the requested substitution and the reasons for it to the listed subcontractor, and a hearing will be held.

Significantly, the subcontractor who becomes substituted for the listed subcontractor does not inherit the rights of a listed subcontractor.

F. Mistakes

It is not uncommon for one who submits a bid to allege that it has made a mistake. As explained above, prime contractors may be required to provide bid security or a bond that the contractor will enter into a contract if one is awarded to him. What happens if there is a mistake? The one who submits a bid by mistake might be relieved from going forward if the awarding authority allows it to do so. However, if the public entity does not so allow, then the matter goes to the Superior court. The bidder has to state that he made a mistake, that he gave written notice to the public entity within five days after bid opening specifying how the mistake occurred, and lastly that the mistake was material and not due to an error in judgment or carelessness in inspecting the site or reading the plans and specifications. In essence, if it is a material error in calculation, then the bidder may be relieved.

G. Subcontractor Bidding

The California Supreme Court has stated that by a subcontractor submitting a bid, the subcontractor is binding himself to enter into a contract if: (1) the prime's bid was accepted, and (2) the subcontractor's bid was used by the prime contractor in obtaining the award. In essence, the contractor is entitled to <u>rely</u> on the bid in providing its bid to the owner. The primary defense to the "reliance" theory is that the contractor should not have relied on the subcontractor's bid because it was unreasonably low or that the prime contractor had knowledge that the subcontractor did not.

H. Awarding of the Project

The public entity usually has the right to reject all bids. Quite often the public entity is given the right to reject the low bid. If the low bid is rejected, generally the agency or the public entity must give notice and right to be heard to the low bidder. There are generally two reasons that the low bid may be rejected --either the bid is "non-responsive," or the bidder is "non-responsible."

As discussed in the introduction to this section, a responsible bidder is one who has demonstrated the attributes of trustworthiness, quality, fitness, capacity and experience to perform the public works contract. The public agency may use a prequalification questionnaire to determine responsibility. The relative responsibility of one bidder versus another bidder is not allowed as a basis to reject a bidder. If that were the case, the largest contractors would get all of the jobs. If the public agency is going to deem a bidder to be non-responsible, that bidder is entitled to an opportunity to hear the evidence of its non-responsibility and to put on evidence rebutting the evidence of its non-responsibility as well as evidence proving its responsibility. The courts do not require a formal hearing, but typically a hearing is held before the awarding agency.

The other reason for the rejection of a bid is that the bid is deemed to be "non-responsive." A responsive bid is one that responds to the Request for Bid in all material respects. No hearing is required if a bid is to be rejected for responsiveness reasons. It is very common that one bidder will complain to the public agency that another's bid is non-responsive, and must be rejected. Often, a deficiency in a bid is deemed to be material, and cannot be ignored or overlooked by an agency, if it gave that bidder an advantage over other bidders such that they would get their bid bond back if they were to back out of the bid. In either case, the issues become very complicated, and an attorney should be consulted. Indeed, the fact of a declaration of non-responsibility could be used against you in the future based upon prequalification questionnaires which ask if you have ever been deemed non-responsible.

I. Differences in the Laws Governing Public Works Contracts

There are some areas of the law in which suing a public agency is different than a private owner. As discussed briefly above, there are theories of law that apply only to private contracts, such as "quantum meruit" (the value of the work), which is commonly plead to obtain the value of the work where there is no specific written contract for that work - - very common is the instance of change orders; where there is a large number of change orders such that the entire character of the contract has been changed. That has been alleged in the private works sector to be an "abandonment of the contract." In the private sector, such a theory would allow the entire contract to be ignored, and allow the contractor to receive the value of all of its work on a quantum meruit basis. This could result in a significantly greater recovery for the contractor than merely the fixed price of the contract plus any change orders. In a rather recent Supreme Court case, more than 240 changes to the electrical plans of a civic center were requested by the city. The electrical contractor contended that there were so many change orders that the changes could not take into account all of their additional overhead expenses. The contractor sued the city for additional money, alleging an abandonment of contract. The Supreme Court held that such a recovery is not allowed on public works projects.

The reason for that is that this violates the Public Contract Act. What ends up happening in an abandonment is that when the job is abandoned, the parties would have entered into a new contract. They have not done this through the competitive bidding process, therefore, it is a violation of law.

Another area where the law differs is with regard to how a complaint is filed. In order to sue a public entity, one may need to comply with certain claims procedures. The claims procedures generally do not apply to those who are seeking to enforce stop notice claims against a public agency. You should refer to the chapter entitled "Mechanics' Liens, Stop Notices and Bonds" for a discussion of those rights. However, the prime contractor who has a contract with the owner does not have such remedies on public works. Instead, they must file a Government Code claim, and then sue the public entity for breach of contract. This again is a very complicated area of the law, with short statutes of limitations. If in doubt, an attorney should be consulted.

Other areas where public contracting is very different is with regard to prevailing wage laws and liquidated damages. On virtually every public works project, the contractor and all of its subcontractors are required to pay what is known as the prevailing wage. These wages may be significantly higher than paid in the private sector (unless the contractor is a union shop). This could have grave impacts on the profit margin of the contractor if it did not realize that they had to comply with the prevailing wage laws. Further, the way the Labor Code is written, the prime contractor is responsible to make sure its subcontractors comply with the prevailing wage laws. The prime contractor's payment bond will also be implicated if prevailing wages are not paid by any other persons below the prime contractor.

Liquidated damages, which is another way of describing fixed delay damages are common on public works projects. There are many reasons why a project may be delayed. In some cases, the contractor will contend that the owner is partially or completely responsible for the delay. However, the liquidated damages are sometimes rather substantial, and the general contractor will likely try to pass those on to its subcontractors or anyone else it blames for the imposition of delay damages.

Another common problem with public works projects is that change orders are usually only allowed if approved by the owner. There are two issues in this regard. If the prime contractor directs the subcontractor to perform work, generally the prime contractor may be indebted to the subcontractor even if the owner has not authorized that work to be performed. However, it is more typically that the owner will direct the prime to perform work, even where the price hasn't been agreed upon, and then the prime contractor will direct the subcontractor to perform that work. Both the prime contractor and subcontractor will thereafter each seek compensation for the work. The work is typically priced using the same schedule as in the original bid. The mark up is usually limited by the project specifications to a set sum. Sometimes, there is an additional markup allowed because of the labor burden. However, again, this is a very complicated area of the law, and contractors should be aware of all of the intricacies before they bid on public works projects.

For claims against the public entity, please see the chapter called Mechanics' Liens, Stop Notices and Bonds.

VII. CONSTRUCTION CONTRACTS

A. Introduction

Many contractors do not understand the concept of contracts. Although there are specific contractual requirements for home improvements, swimming pool and other contractors, a contractor should also become knowledgeable of the general rules of contracts. This chapter will discuss the general rules of contracts as well as some rules specific for contractors. In many instances they will be identical. However, the contractor's contracts will have to have additional requirements as indicated in other portions of this book.

It should be noted that much of what will be discussed in this chapter may differ based upon whether your contract is for the sale of goods or for the sale of services. Because most construction contracts consist of both, they are placed in one category or the other based upon which (goods or services) makes up the majority of the contract. Most of the law which is discussed in this chapter applies to both situations. However, there are some differences between the two in certain instances. For example, if the contract is for the sale of goods, a counter-offer to an offer serves as an acceptance of the agreed upon terms, with a proposal for modification by the additional terms. In a contract for services, however, a counter-offer to an offer serves as a rejection of the entire original offer. Note that this chapter has been written with sales of services in mind, as most construction contracts are for services. Therefore, if your contract is primarily for the sale of goods, you should consult an attorney or the Uniform Commercial Code (UCC) for the specific rules that govern such contracts.

Generally, except under certain circumstances, a contract need not be in writing. Although it is very important to have the terms written down, the rules of contracts do not require a writing. A "contract" is merely an agreement between two or more people that the law will enforce.

This chapter is divided into two sub-sections. One deals with the rules of contracts and the other with what should be included in a contract.

B. The Rules of Contracts

1. Offer and Acceptance

Most contracts are formed by an offer and acceptance. That means that someone offers to do something and then if you accept, a binding agreement is formed. A different way for a contract to be formed is by a request for "proposal" which is a request to have you make an offer, and then that offer is accepted by the person who actually asked for a proposal. In order to determine whether a communication is an offer, or a request to receive an offer, the surrounding circumstances need to be determined including the standard in the industry.

a. Offer

In order for something to be an offer, it must contain two (2) essential elements. The first is an indication that the person intends to get into a contractual relationship immediately. The second is that the terms of the offer be sufficiently certain, so that a legal and binding agreement can be made.

The legal significance of an offer is that it gives the person who receives the offer, the "offeree," the power to enter into a contract. No one can require you to enter into a contract. Therefore, when one sends you an offer, by accepting that offer, you are the one creating the contract. It puts the offeree in the position of having power to accept the contract and create a binding agreement.

Another thing that an offer does, is that it puts the "offeror" in a position where he should be very careful in how he frames the offer. Because an offer that is accepted can create a contract, the offeror must be sure he or she wants to be bound in the manner in which he tenders the offer.

(1) Termination of an Offer

An offer can be terminated before it is accepted (however, see below with respect to Detrimental Reliance). Further, the offer can have a "limited life." For example, in your offer you may state that the offer can only be accepted within the next 48 hours. Therefore, an acceptance after 48 hours is not binding since the acceptance did not comply with the offer.

In addition, an offer will be terminated after the passage of reasonable time even if no time is specified. This again will be based on the circumstances surrounding the offer, including industry standards.

The offer can also be terminated if the offeree rejects the offer. If the offeree says "no," he cannot thereafter accept the offer.

A counter-offer is deemed to be a rejection. If I offer to sell you something for $5,000, you come back with "I'll buy it for $2,000," you have made a "counter-offer," and the original $5,000 offer is no longer subject to acceptance. However, if the counter-offer, which is actually a new offer is accepted, a contract is formed based on the terms of the counter-offer.

(2) Revocation of an Offer

Generally, an offer can be revoked (called back) by the offeror as long as it has not yet been accepted. This is not a hard and fast rule. There are certain situations where the offer may not be revoked.

b. Option

An option, even though it has to qualify under the rules of Offer and Acceptance, cannot be revoked during the option period. The reason for this is that the option itself is a contract. Under an option contract, one person agrees to hold the offer open for a specific period of time. The option must have all of the elements of a contract itself. As an example, one may pay $1,000 for an option to buy a piece of property for a specific time. That means that piece of property can be bought by that person, at anytime during the period of option.

c. Acceptance

Assuming that the offer is found to be a valid offer, then it may be accepted, and a contract will be formed, based on the offer itself. Acceptance can be done by way of an act or another promise. The statement "I accept your offer," if that is what the offeror intended, will be deemed to form a contract. If you are sent a purchase order, and then you start to perform by delivering goods, etc., it will probably be deemed that you have accepted the purchase order, as an offer, and you are now bound by the terms of that purchase order.

Acceptance is effective upon transmittal by the same means as the offer was transmitted. If you receive an offer by mail, and accept it by mail, it is accepted when placed in the mailbox, even if not yet known to the offeror. The offer cannot then be revoked!

Sometimes the question comes up as to what exactly are the terms of the contract formed when, upon receiving a Request for Quote, you send in your bid. Here again, the standards of the industry and the prior relationship of the parties will be very helpful in determining what the terms of the contract are. If the offer includes terms and conditions, and you submit your bid, you are probably agreeing to be bound by all of the terms and conditions. This is also true if past dealings between you indicate that you have been receiving the terms and conditions, and therefore expect that a contract will be formed utilizing the same terms and conditions. In order to protect yourself, you might include in the offer that you are submitting this bid with the understanding that the terms and conditions will be those of a specific form contract or contract that is enclosed, etc. As an example, your bid might state that you agree to be bound by your bid assuming that an AIA sub-contract agreement is negotiated or that the AIA terms and conditions will be incorporated in the sub-contract agreement. If you do not wish to do this you may wish to leave out certain "killer clauses," such as "Our Bid Does not Include a Pay if Paid Clause," "Conduit Clause," etc. That means that an acceptance by the person who sent you the RFP would not include those clauses.

d. Drennan v. Star Paving

There is a case that many contractors do not know of and therefore it bites them where it hurts. This is a case called Drennan v. Star Paving. In Drennan, the prime contractor sent out a "Request for Quotation" to various sub-contractors. One sub-contractor submitted a sealed bid. The prime contractor utilized the subcontractor's bid in its bid to the owner. The prime contractor was awarded the contract.

Unfortunately, the sub-contractor found it had made a mistake in its bid. Prior to the time that the prime contractor accepted the sub-contractor's bid, the sub-contractor "withdrew" its bid. The argument was, since that bid (offer) was never accepted, no valid contract was formed.

The California Supreme Court held otherwise. The theory is that when one submits a bid to a prime contractor, he can assume that if it is low, the prime contractor will utilize his bid in presenting the prime contractor's bid to the owner. It would be unfair to have the prime contractor utilize that bid, and then not be able to require the sub-contractor to be bound. In essence, what the Supreme Court did was to turn a revocable offer into an irrevocable offer for a reasonable period of time.

The acceptance by the prime contractor has to be reasonable however. The prime contractor has to reasonably rely on the offer. If a mistake is obvious, there is likely no reasonable reliance by the prime contractor. Therefore, if a sub-contractor submits an offer that is 1/4 of the price of all the other offers, unless you get some verification that there was no mistake, it might be unreasonable to rely on the offer.

e. Mistake

As stated in the previous section, once a bid is made, it is very difficult to withdraw. This partially conflicts with the previously stated principles of law that an offer may be withdrawn anytime before its acceptance.

If the court determines that a mistake was made in submitting a bid, the party making the bid may not be held to it. The essential fact necessary to allow a retraction of a bid after acceptance is that the mistake was one in calculations, rather than a mistake that arose from the failure to read instructions, or the failure to understand the instructions or plans. Thus, for example, if a bid is low because of a mistake in calculations, where the accepting party should have realized a mistake was made, the subcontractor's bid will not be enforced.

Sometimes these situations are protected, as on certain types of projects a bidding subcontractor or contractor is required to post a bond along with his bid, assuring that the bidder will sign a contract if the contract is awarded.

f. Bid Shopping, Bid Peddling, and Bid Chiseling

These three practices have been viewed as unethical in the construction industry.

"Bid Shopping" is the practice of a prime contractor who solicits subcontractors before the award of the prime contract in an attempt to obtain lower sub-bids by revealing existing sub-bids.

"Bid Peddling" is the term that describes a subcontractor's actions towards undercutting the bids of other subcontractors in order to obtain the job from the prime contractor.

"Bid Chiseling" describes the attempts of the prime contractor to obtain lower sub-bids after the prime contract has been awarded. "Bid Chiseling" is prohibited by the Public Contracts Code, and is made difficult by the requirement that the bid include the names of subcontractors who will perform more than one half of one percent (0.5%) of the prime contract. However, this prohibition applies only to public works projects.

These three practices impede on the competitive aspects of the construction industry, and although they may benefit one party, i.e. the owner, it is usually the honest subcontractor who loses out. These practices allow a subcontractor to gain a job without taking the time and expense of estimating the job.

The California Supreme Court has implied its approval of pre-award "Bid Shopping," as "open price competition in its purest form." While it is true the owner benefits from "Bid Shopping," the rest of the construction industry loses from this practice.

2. Performance Under the Contract

The contract will require certain people to do certain things. In many cases, the contract will merely require payment from one side, while the other side has a myriad of things that have to be performed. A number of questions must be asked in order to determine whether one actually performed, and if not, whether the performance was excused.

a. Express Conditions

Many of the things that have to be done under the contract (many times called conditions by attorneys) are essentially things that one has to perform before the other has an obligation to perform. For example, if there is a draw schedule that states that a certain draw will be paid upon completion of framing, then the owner's obligation to make the payment does not occur until the framing is completed. Certain conditions are expressed in the contract itself. A condition will not be enforced unless it is clear. For example, the framing draw is a condition that is clear.

b. Implied Conditions

In addition to the express conditions, there are certain conditions that are either implied by law or implied under the rules of construction, i.e. relationship of the parties or industry itself. An example of an implied condition is that work will be done in accordance with accepted trade standards, unless stated otherwise.

c. Excuse

Sometimes a condition is excused. As an example, the contractor in the framing draw case could not sue the owner for not paying the framing draw, if the framing was not completed. That is to say, since the framing was not completed, the owner's requirement to pay for that framing draw never arose and therefore was excused.

d. Damages

There are different types of damages that can be assessed against the party failing to perform (i.e. breaching party) in a construction case. Generally, the types of damages are compensatory damages, liquidated damages, and punitive damages. Not all will be assessed.

(1) Compensatory Damages

Compensatory damages means those damages that actually flow from the contract. Too often, when an owner does not pay the contractor in full, the contractor believes that he or she is entitled to be paid the actual dollar amount in the contract, less what he has been paid to date. That is not always the case.

Compensatory damages are intended to put the parties in the place they would have been, had the contract not been breached. For instance, if you have done all of the work and you have not been paid at all, you should be entitled to be paid everything that you would have been paid (the contract amount). However, all too often, you have only done a portion of the work. At that point, you are not entitled to be paid the entire contract amount, even though many contractors believe that would be the case. You should be put in the position where you would have been had the contract not been breached. Accordingly, you are entitled to all of the costs incurred to date, plus the profit that you would have earned on the entire job, less any amounts that you have been paid to date. However, if you would have lost money on the project, there will be some deduction, because you are not to be put in a better position by performing less than you would have been had you performed the entire contract. Therefore, if you made a contract that was a "loser," you will not be excused or put in a better position because of a breach.

(2) Liquidated Damages

Liquidated damages are damages that are written into the contract at the time that it is negotiated. Sometimes liquidated damages are called a "penalty." If a court decides that the liquidated damages are a penalty, the courts will not enforce that provision. The breach of contract should not result in punishment, unless the acts are so bad that they are to be exemplary. Therefore, liquidated damages are damages for the loss of something, rather than punishment. Thus, it is not uncommon to have liquidated damages in a specific sum for delay. If the contract stated that work would be completed on a specific date, the contract could also state that the contractor would have to pay damages in the sum of $200 per day for every day that the project is delayed. This is a typical and enforceable liquidated damages provision, if it is properly written. The amount of damages should be a reasonable amount as contemplated at the time the contract was made.

(3) Punitive Damages

Punitive damages are intended to punish someone for a violation. First, you should understand that a breach of contract would not normally lead to punishment and therefore, punitive damages. It will have to be such a bad act that the judge or jury wants to punish you for doing that act. The purpose of punitive damages is to set an example, to keep others from doing a similar act. Punitive damages are rarely assessed in contract cases and are based on the amount of money that it would take to "punish you." Therefore, punitive damages against someone who earns very little would be less than punitive damages against someone who makes more money. Punitive damages are usually assessed in cases of fraud or other extreme cases of intentional wrongdoing.

3. Modification

Construction contracts are almost always modified to some degree. Usually, the owner will have a change of heart, or the work is not as originally contemplated, and therefore the parties enter into a "change order" or "extra work." Unfortunately, many contractors do not negotiate changes at the time that they occur.

It is very important that the contractor immediately negotiate the effect of a change. There are a number of reasons for that. First, if you are going to have an argument, you'd better know it early on rather than at the tail-end of a project, when you are negotiating from a weaker position. At that point the contractor has already performed the work and is usually left "holding the bag" debating whether to let the money go or to gamble on litigation. Secondly, you will never be in a better negotiating position than when you are asked to do something "different." Change orders should be issued, negotiated, and written. Do not forget to add into your change orders <u>all</u> of the effects of the change including the delay, cost, etc.

Quite often a situation arises where a change order is not written down. Although this is not a good thing, it does happen. We <u>urge</u> contractors to immediately document a change, by either having a change order executed, or at a minimum, by sending a confirming letter to the person initiating the change indicating that a change has been made and that there may be other factors involved, such as cost and delay.

C. Contract Requirements

In negotiating a contract, you have to assume that there is going to be a dispute sometime during your performance. If you have no dispute you don't have to worry about a written contract. A well written contract tends to minimize such disputes. If there is a dispute, however, the court is supposed to interpret what your intent was in forming a contract or agreement. If you <u>don't</u> want the <u>court</u> to determine your intent for you, then set out specifically what it is that you agree to, so that there is very little left to interpret. Therefore, you want to put down everything that is important to you. Here are some general items which your contract should include.

D. General Items

1. Price

   Clearly price is important.

2. Time

   Time is very important and you need to know how much time you have to do that which you promised to do. You need to know how much time it's going to take from the time that you are required to start work. You don't want to be caught between a rock and a hard place. If it takes thirty days to do your portion of the work, then you don't want a date certain for completion. Rather, you want the agreement to say that your work will be completed thirty days from your required start date. Be wary of clauses such as "Time is of the essence." Such clauses may be interpreted by courts to substantially limit your ability to collect even if you are just a day or two late.

3. Arbitration

   Do you or don't you want arbitration? Under California law, arbitration provisions are totally different from litigation.

4. Mechanics' Lien and Stop Notice Information

   If something goes wrong, you may wish to record a Mechanics' Lien or pursue a Stop Notice. In this regard you should obtain the following:

   a. The name and address of the owner;
   b. If you are a sub-contractor, the name and address of the prime contractor;
   c. The name and address of the construction lender;
   d. A description of the job site sufficient for identification.

5. Payment Schedule

   How and when are you going to be paid. Under the home improvement laws there are limitations which you need to be aware of.

6. Scope of Work

This should be very well defined. How can you determine what a change order is if you don't know the scope of work that was originally required?

7. Bad Contract Clauses For Sub-Contractors and Good Contract Clauses for Prime Contractors

a. Conduit Clauses

These clauses incorporate information or requirements from the prime contract to the sub-contract. The worst conduit clause for sub-contractors is one that merely incorporates by reference everything from the prime contract to the sub-contract. The corollary is that what's best for prime contractors is worst for sub-contractors.

b. "Pay if Paid" or "Pay when Paid" Clauses

A "Pay if Paid" clause is a clause that basically says that the sub-contractor will only be paid if the prime contractor is paid. Therefore, if the owner does not pay the prime contractor even though all work may be perfect, the sub-contractor will not be paid. This has been a heavily litigated area of the law. In 1997, the California Supreme Court struck down such a clause as being against public policy.

A "Pay When Paid" clause defers payment for a reasonable period of time. No case has yet determined what a reasonable period of time means.

c. No Damages for Delay

This clause says that if the sub is delayed through no fault of its own, it will not be entitled to any damages. The sub will only be entitled to adjust its date of completion. This clause has been upheld in California. However, clever attorneys have at times been able to phrase the damages in something other than delay. In addition, in public works projects, the "no damages for delays" clause will not be upheld.

d. Changes

Read the changes clause very carefully to see how it effects your work. Must the subcontractor immediately notify the prime contractor of the impact of the change? Does the sub waive its right if it doesn't do so? What does it say about who is authorized to make the change?

e. Protection of Equipment

Who is responsible to protect the equipment or work in place? Does the owner or prime contractor provide the sub with a secured place?

f. Indemnification

These clauses between primes and subs are very tough and the clause should be read very carefully. Typically, between large primes and large subs, the indemnification clause merely determines whose insurance company will cover a loss. Therefore, it is strictly a matter of insurability and the courts will leave the prime and the sub to their own devices. This may not be quite so true with respect to a large prime and a small sub. A court might say that the indemnification clauses are unconscionable and that it will not uphold the indemnification clause. However, in all cases, no one can be indemnified for his sole negligence or willful misconduct. This is illegal.

g. Termination

There are two (2) types of termination clauses, one is called a "Termination for Convenience" and the other is called a "Termination for Default" clause. Termination means that the contract is over.

(1) Termination for Convenience

This clause allows the owner or prime contractor in a subcontract to terminate an agreement <u>without</u> cause. Therefore, anytime an owner or a prime contractor wishes, he can terminate the job. Further, there must be some compensation for the work that was done, plus a reasonable allowance for profit. However, under a termination for convenience, the prime contractor or the owner does not have to pay for lost profits, unless the clause specifies that he does.

(2) Termination for Default

Anytime someone breaches a contract, the other party may be able to terminate it because of the default. This is proper. The real problem comes in how one enforces that termination clause. As an example, in one case, the notice that is required to be given is a Three (3) Day Notice and you must correct the work within those three days. This may be very tough and it may be very hard to actually complete all of the corrected work. The AIA contract, for example, allows for a Three (3) Day Notice. However, all you must do with respect to that Three (3) Day Notice is to commence or begin the corrective work, but need not complete it within that time.

In conclusion keep in mind that the general requirements of a contract are that it be sufficiently certain so that it can be enforced. This means that the essential terms are set out, or somehow otherwise determinable.

E. Specific Requirements

Under the Contractors' License Law there are specific requirements for various kinds of contracts.

1. Notice Regarding State License Board

All construction contracts require a notice explaining that the Contractors' State License Board has jurisdiction, etc. The notice is as follows:

Contractors must include the following statement in at least 10-point type on all written contracts where he or she is a prime contractor ***(not subcontractor).***

"Contractors are required by law to be licensed and regulated by the Contractors' State License Board which has jurisdiction to investigate complaints against contractors if a complaint regarding a patent act or omission is filed within four years of the date of the alleged violation. A complaint regarding a latent act or omission pertaining to structural defects must be filed within

10 years of the date of the alleged violation. Any questions concerning a contractor may be referred to the Registrar, Contractors' State License Board, P.O. Box 26000, Sacramento, California 95826."

This statement must be reprinted "word for word."

2. Specific Contractual Requirements For Specific Types of Contracts

a. Home Improvement and Swimming Pool Contracts

Home Improvement and Swimming Pool Contracts have specific contractual requirements as follows:

<u>Business and Professions Code</u> Section 7159

This is a long list of contractual requirements in one or more Home Improvement and Swimming Pool contracts totaling more than $500.00. It says that these contracts must be in writing and signed by the parties, and shall include all of the following:

(1) The name, address and license number of the contractor, and the name and registration number of any salesman who solicited or negotiated the contract.

(2) The approximate dates when the work will begin and be substantially completed.

(3) A plan and scale drawing showing the shape, size, dimensions and construction equipment specifications for a swimming pool and for other home improvements, a description of the work to be done and a description of the materials to be used or installed and the agreed consideration for the work.

(4) If there is a down payment, the down payment shall not <u>exceed</u> $200 or two percent (2%) of the contract for *swimming pools*, or $1000 or ten percent (10%) of the contract for home improvements, <u>***whichever is less***</u>.

(5) A schedule of payments showing the amount to be paid in dollars and cents (not just percentages). The schedule of payments shall be referenced to work performed and any material or equipment supplied. You can never receive proportionately more money than the work performed (except for the down payment). On swimming pool

contracts, the final payment may be made at the completion of the final plastering phase, so long as any installation of equipment, decking or fencing required under the contract is also completed. If you fail to substantially commence work within 20 days of the date specified in the contract, the next payment due will be postponed for the same period.

(6) The contract shall also state that upon satisfactory payment being made for any portion of the work, the contractor, before receiving any further payment, shall give to the person contracting for the work, a full and unconditional release from any claim or mechanics' lien for that portion for which payment has been made.

(7) The down payment or payment schedule provisions of (4) and (5) do not apply when you furnish a payment and performance bond, lien and completion bond, or a joint control approved by the Registrar. You must also place a notice in at least 10-point type, within three inches of the signature line, telling the tenant or owner that he has the right to require a performance and payment bond.

(8) No extra or change order work shall be required to be performed without the prior written agreement of the person contracting for the construction. Any change order forms shall be incorporated in and shall become a part of the contract.

(9) Any salespersons commission can only be paid in proportion to the schedule of payments.

(10) You must give the notice required by Section 7018.5 (Notice to Owner which is printed in full in this book).

(11) A statement defining what constitutes substantial commencement.

(12) A notice that failure by the contractor without lawful excuse to substantially commence work within twenty (20) days from the approximate date specified in the contract when work will begin is a violation of the Contractors' License Law.

(13) If the contract provides for a contractor to furnish a joint control, the contractor shall not have any financial or other interest in such joint control.

(14) You must give a signed copy of the contract to the owner.

Business and Professions Code Section 7030

In addition to information regarding licensing as explained in other portions of this book, **prior** to entering into a contract to perform work on residential property of four (4) or fewer units, a contractor who has his or her license suspended or revoked *two or more times* within an eight year period, must disclose any disciplinary, license suspension, or revocation during the last eight years as a result of a violation of the Contractors' License Law, in either 10-point roman boldface type, or in contrasting red print of at least 8-point roman boldface type.

In addition to the above, any contractor, ***before making a bid, or prior to entering into a contract*** to perform work on residential property with four (4) or fewer units, whichever occurs first, must provide the following notice in writing:

"STATE LAW REQUIRES ANYONE WHO CONTRACTS TO DO CONSTRUCTION WORK TO BE LICENSED BY THE CONTRACTORS' STATE LICENSE BOARD IN THE LICENSE CATEGORY IN WHICH THE CONTRACTOR IS GOING TO BE WORKING--IF THE TOTAL PRICE OF THE JOB IS $500 OR MORE (INCLUDING LABOR AND MATERIALS).

LICENSED CONTRACTORS ARE REGULATED BY LAWS DESIGNED TO PROTECT THE PUBLIC. IF YOU CONTRACT WITH SOMEONE WHO DOES NOT HAVE A LICENSE, THE CONTRACTORS' STATE LICENSE BOARD MAY BE UNABLE TO ASSIST YOU WITH A COMPLAINT. YOUR ONLY REMEDY AGAINST AN UNLICENSED CONTRACTOR MAY BE IN CIVIL COURT, AND YOU MAY BE LIABLE FOR DAMAGES ARISING OUT OF ANY INJURIES TO THE CONTRACTOR OR HIS OR HER EMPLOYEES.

YOU MAY CONTACT THE CONTRACTORS' STATE LICENSE BOARD TO FIND OUT IF THIS CONTRACTOR HAS A VALID LICENSE. THE BOARD HAS COMPLETE INFORMATION ON THE HISTORY OF LICENSED CONTRACTORS, INCLUDING ANY POSSIBLE SUSPENSIONS, REVOCATIONS, JUDGMENTS, AND CITATIONS. THE BOARD HAS OFFICES THROUGHOUT CALIFORNIA. PLEASE CHECK THE GOVERNMENT PAGES OF THE WHITE PAGES FOR THE OFFICE NEAREST YOU OR CALL 1-800-321-CSLB FOR MORE INFORMATION."

This notice must be in either capital letters in 10-point roman boldface type or in contrasting red print in at least 8-point roman boldface type.

b. Notice to Owner

The following is the language required to be given in a document to a homeowner prior to commencing work:

"Notice to Owner

Under the California Mechanics' Lien Law, any contractor, subcontractor, laborer, supplier, or other person or entity who helps to improve your property, but is not paid for his or her work or supplies, has a right to place a lien on your home, land, or property where the work was performed and to sue you in court to obtain payment.

This means that after a court hearing, your home, land, and property could be sold by a court officer and the proceeds of the sale used to satisfy what you owe. This can happen even if you have paid your contractor in full if the contractor's subcontractors, laborers, or suppliers remain unpaid.

To preserve their rights to file a claim or lien against your property, certain claimants such as subcontractors or material suppliers are each required to provide you with a document called a "Preliminary Notice." Contractors and laborers who contract with owners directly do not have to provide such notice since you are aware of their existence as an owner. A preliminary notice is not a lien against your property. Its purpose is to notify you of persons or entities that may have a right to file a lien against your property if they are not paid. In order to perfect their lien rights, a contractor, subcontractor, supplier, or laborer must file a mechanics' lien with the county recorder which then becomes a recorded lien against your property. Generally, the maximum time allowed for filing a mechanics' lien against your property is 90 days after substantial completion of your project.

To insure extra protection for yourself and your property, you may wish to take one or more of the following steps:

1. Require that your contractor supply you with a payment and performance bond (not a license bond), which provides that the bonding company will either complete the project or pay damages up to the amount of the bond. This payment and performance bond as well as a copy of the construction contract should be filed with the county recorder for your further protection. The payment and performance bond will usually cost from 1 to 5 percent of the contract amount depending on the contractor's bonding ability. If a contractor cannot obtain such bonding, it may indicate his or her financial incapacity.
2. Require that payments be made directly to subcontractors and material suppliers through a joint control. Funding services may be available, for a fee, in your area which will establish voucher or other means of payment to your contractor. These services may also provide you with lien waivers and other forms of protection. Any joint control agreement should include the addendum approved by the registrar.
3. Issue joint checks for payment, made out to both your contractor and subcontractors or material suppliers involved in the project. The joint checks should be made payable to the persons or entities which send preliminary notices to you. Those persons or entities have indicated that they may have lien rights on your property, therefore you need to protect yourself. This will help to insure that all persons due payment are actually paid.

4. Upon making payment on any completed phase of the project, and before making any further payments, require your contractor to provide you with unconditional "Waiver and Release" forms signed by each material supplier, subcontractor, and laborer involved in that portion of the work for which payment was made. The statutory lien releases are set forth in exact language in Section 3262 of the Civil Code. Most stationery stores will sell the "Waiver and Release" forms if your contractor does not have them. The material suppliers, subcontractors, and laborers that you obtain releases from are those persons or entities who have filed preliminary notices with you. If you are not certain of the material suppliers, subcontractors, and laborers working on your project, you may obtain a list from your contractor. On projects involving improvements to a single-family residence or a duplex owned by individuals, the persons signing these releases lose the right to file a mechanics' lien claim against your property. In other types of construction, this protection may still be important, but may not be as complete.

   To protect yourself under this option, you must be certain that all material suppliers, subcontractors, and laborers have signed the "Waiver and Release" form. If a mechanics' lien has been filed against your property, it can only be voluntarily released by a recorded "Release of Mechanics' Lien" signed by the person or entity that filed the mechanics' lien against your property unless the lawsuit to enforce the lien was not timely filed. You should not make any final payments until any and all such liens are removed. You should consult an attorney if a lien is filed against your property."

3. Notice of Cancellation

On every job entered into between a contractor and a residential homeowner that is not made at <u>the contractor's place of business</u>, a **<u>separate</u>** "Notice of Cancellation" must be given that allows the homeowner three days to cancel the transaction without any liability to the contractor. That period is extended to seven days following a declaration of a disaster (such as a flood or earthquake.)

In addition to the "Notice of Cancellation," the Home Improvement Contract itself must have language explaining this right to the owner. This language must be in the following format, and as discussed above, must be given to every homeowner prior to commencing work, if the contract is not made at appropriate trade premises:

a. Language Required to be Used in the Home Improvement Contract

The Home Improvement Contract, in close proximity to the signature line, must contain the following language printed in at least 10 point **bold** roman style type:

"You, the buyer, may cancel this transaction at any time prior to midnight of the third business day after the date of this transaction. See the attached notice of cancellation form for an explanation of this right."

Note that if the agreement is following the Declaration of a Disaster, the language must read in least 10 point **bold** roman style type:

"You, the buyer, may cancel this transaction at any time prior to midnight of the seventh business day after the date of this transaction. See the attached notice of cancellation form for an explanation of this right."

On occasion, clients tell us they do not want to use two contracts. In that case, we suggest the following dual purpose language above the signature line of the contract:

"YOU, THE BUYER, MAY CANCEL THIS TRANSACTION AT ANY TIME PRIOR TO MIDNIGHT OF THE THIRD BUSINESS DAY AFTER THE DATE OF THIS TRANSACTION. OR IF THIS IS A CONTRACT FOR THE REPAIR OF DAMAGES RESULTING FROM AN EARTHQUAKE, FLOOD, FIRE, HURRICANE, RIOT, STORM, TIDAL WAVE, OR OTHER SIMILAR CATASTROPHIC OCCURRENCE FOR WHICH A STATE OF EMERGENCY HAS BEEN DECLARED, YOU THE BUYER MAY CANCEL THIS

TRANSACTION AT ANY TIME PRIOR TO MIDNIGHT OF THE SEVENTH BUSINESS DAY AFTER THE DATE OF THIS TRANSACTION. SEE THE ATTACHED NOTICE OF CANCELLATION FORM FOR AN EXPLANATION OF THIS RIGHT."

If the contract is in a foreign language, e.g., Spanish, this clause must be in that language as well.

b. "Notice of Cancellation"

The "Notice of Cancellation" must be in the following format, and, must be given to every homeowner prior to commencing work if the contract is not made at appropriate trade premises:

"Notice of Cancellation

____

Date

You may cancel this transaction, without any penalty or obligation, within three business days from the above date.

If you cancel, any property traded in, any payments made by you under the contract or sale, and any negotiable instrument executed by you will be returned within 10 days following receipt by the seller of your cancellation notice, and any security interest arising out of the transaction will be canceled.

If you cancel, you must make available to the seller at your residence, in substantially as good condition as when received, any goods delivered to you under this contract or sale, or you may, if you wish, comply with the instructions of the seller regarding the return shipment of the goods at the seller's expense and risk.

If you do make the goods available to the seller and the seller does not pick them up within 20 days of the date of your notice of cancellation, you may retain or dispose of the goods without any further obligation. If you fail to make the goods available to the seller, or if you agree to return the goods to the seller and fail to do so, then you remain liable for performance of all obligations under the contract.

To cancel this transaction, mail or deliver a signed and dated copy of this cancellation notice, or any other written notice, or send a telegram to, ______________________________,

/name of seller/

at____

____

/address of seller's place of business/

not later than midnight of ______________.

(date)

I hereby cancel this transaction. ______________.

(date)

______________________________"

(Buyer's signature)

Note: that as stated above, work done as a result of a natural disaster, such as an earthquake, requires seven (7) days notice as opposed to three (3).

c. Emergency Repair Exception to Notice of Cancellation

There is an exception to the right to cancel for emergency repair work. That exception provides that the three day period for cancellation (or seven days after a disaster) shall not apply to a contract that is initiated by the buyer (homeowner) or his agent, including an insurance agent, where the contract is for emergency or necessary repairs or services that are necessary for the immediate protection of persons or their property, provided that the buyer signs a separate dated and signed personal statement describing the situation requiring the immediate repair and expressly acknowledging and waiving the right to cancel the sale within three or seven days, whichever applies. **This exception is most important to service and repair contractors.**

The law states that no pre-printed form is allowed to be used for such a waiver. The waiver must be in the handwriting of your customer. The following is language that may be used:

"I, Jane Doe, homeowner of the property located at 1234 Main Street, Anytown, California hereby declare that I have requested that 123 Plumbing make the repairs to my water heater now because my family and I need hot water and can not wait for three days for that repair. 123 Plumbing has provided me with a Notice of Cancellation giving me a three day period to cancel this contract, however, because of this necessity, for the protection of my family and myself, I expressly waive the cancellation period that has been explained to me.

Signed, Jane Doe."

d. Problems With Some Pre-printed Forms

A word of caution. Some stationery stores and mail order forms businesses sell a "Home Improvement Contract" with the "Notice of Cancellation" printed on the back of the contract. To use that notice would require the physical tearing or destruction of the contract. The language of the statute requires the form to be **separate** from the contract.

F. Contract Provisions Applicable to Unlicensed Contractors

The provisions of the Contractors' License Law require that persons or entities performing work that adds to or subtracts from real property be licensed. The Contractors' License Law, specifically Business and Professions Code section 7048, provides that under certain circumstances the provisions of the Contractors' License Law do not apply to unlicensed contractors doing work where the price of the work is under $500.00. This exception is known as the "Minor Works Exception."

To qualify for the Minor Works Exception, the unlicensed person must provide to the Owner at the time of making a bid or prior to entering into a contract, a notice, a signed copy of which must be retained by the unlicensed contractor four years, that tells the owner that the Contractors' License Law does not apply on jobs under $500.00 and that the Contractors' Board will not be able to assist them if they get into a dispute. That notice also tells the owner that they may be subject to civil liability if the unlicensed contractor or his or her employees are injured on their property.

The notice, which must be in capital letters in at least 10-point roman boldface type or in contrasting red print in at least 8-point roman boldface type is as follows:

> "I, ____________________[individual's name], AM NOT LICENSED BY THE CONTRACTORS' STATE LICENSE BOARD.
>
> STATE LAW REQUIRES ANYONE WHO CONTRACTS TO DO CONSTRUCTION WORK TO BE LICENSED BY THE CONTRACTORS' STATE LICENSE BOARD IN THE LICENSE CATEGORY IN WHICH THE CONTRACTOR IS GOING TO BE WORKING-IF THE TOTAL PRICE OF THE JOB IS $500 OR MORE (INCLUDING LABOR AND MATERIALS).
>
> LICENSED CONTRACTORS ARE REGULATED BY LAWS DESIGNED TO PROTECT THE PUBLIC. IF YOU CONTRACT WITH SOMEONE WHO DOES NOT HAVE A LICENSE, THE CONTRACTORS' STATE LICENSE BOARD MAY BE UNABLE TO ASSIST YOU WITH A COMPLAINT. YOUR ONLY REMEDY AGAINST AN UNLICENSED CONTRACTOR MAY BE IN CIVIL COURT, AND YOU MAY BE LIABLE FOR DAMAGES ARISING OUT OF ANY INJURIES TO THE CONTRACTOR OR HIS OR HER EMPLOYEES."

If the unlicensed contractor fails to give the notice and retain its copy, he or she can be cited by the Contractors' State License Board for the failure to give the notice, plus, the Minor Works Exemption would not apply, making that unlicensed contractor working without a license subject to all penalties for contracting without a license -- which is a misdemeanor crime.

In addition to this notice, unlicensed contractors must also comply with the provisions of the Home Solicitation Act, which as discussed above, require the Notice of Cancellation form and cancellation language in the contract with the buyer.

G. Conclusion

The law of contracts is very confusing. It can be very confusing what rule you are supposed to apply because depending on the different type of contract, different rules apply. Therefore, while the information above is an excellent starting point for contractors who want to learn about the law of contracts and how it applies to them, nothing can take the place of an experienced attorney.

VIII.
INDEMNIFICATION

Indemnity is a very important issue in construction. This chapter explains the concept and law dealing with indemnity. In a later section in this chapter dealing with Express Indemnity in Construction Cases, we discuss a recent case that shows how important it is to have a properly drafted indemnity clause.

A. Definition: Background

The legal definition of the term "indemnify" in accordance with Black's Law Dictionary is "to save harmless; to secure against loss or damages; to give security for the reimbursement of a person in case of an anticipated loss falling upon him." The layman's definition of "indemnify" as defined in the American Heritage College Dictionary is "security against damage, loss, or injury. A legal exemption from liability for damages. Compensation for damage, loss or injuries suffered." What this means is if someone suffers a loss and there is an agreement to indemnify, another person will pay for that loss.

At first blush indemnification appears to be similar to an insurance policy. Although in some respects it is similar, it should not be confused with an insurance policy because in the technical sense it does not insure against a loss.

When one purchases insurance, he/she is purchasing a policy that protects him/her against his/her own wrongdoing. For example, many people carry automobile insurance. If you are driving your automobile and cause an accident where you are found to be at fault, you can then "tender" (submit) the claim to your insurance company, who, in turn, will defend the claim against you and, furthermore, will pay damages the other party incurred as a result of that automobile accident. However, the insurance company will not come after you for reimbursement.

With indemnification, essentially what is being talked about is the difference between the primary and secondary liability of two persons, each of whom may be held responsible to the party who was injured even though one of the parties is primarily responsible for the actions which caused the injury.

For example, a general contractor enters into a contract with an owner of property to perform a certain phase of construction work. The general contractor then hires a series of subcontractors, i.e. plumber, electrician, etc. During the course of the construction work a subcontractor performs unsatisfactory construction work and the owner is damaged. The owner, who is certainly not at fault for the damage, wants compensation. The owner, who is under a contractual relationship with the general contractor, turns to the general contractor and makes demand upon the general contractor for compensation for the damage caused by the subcontractor. Although the general contractor is primarily responsible to the owner by way of contract, the general contractor may not be the <u>cause</u> of the damage. In this instance, the main person responsible for the damage is the subcontractor, and the secondary person liable for the damage is the general contractor. On these facts, the concept of indemnification plays an extremely important role. The general contractor is going to look to the subcontractor to indemnify him/her for the potential loss that the general contractor will have to absorb because of his/her contractual relationship between his/her company and the owner. In this case, the general contractor will look to the subcontractor to defend the general contractor against the potential loss that the general contractor is subject to as a result of the claims being made against him/her by the owner. Furthermore, the general contractor will look to the subcontractor to indemnify (pay) him/her for any damages that the general contractor suffers.

The concept of indemnification is a right which is given to the person who may be without active fault on his/her part, but for some reason has been put in a position by virtue of his/her legal obligation to pay damages that occur as the result of the action or fault of another person.

B. Express/Implied Indemnity

The concept of indemnity is very common in the construction industry. It's not unusual to find an indemnification clause in any written contract. An indemnification clause in a contract defines how indemnification is to be treated between the parties. A contract containing a clause addressing the issue of indemnity is typically called "express indemnity." A written contract with no indemnity clause, or alternatively if the parties have entered into an oral contract, the concept of indemnity still and often does apply. That form of indemnity is called "implied indemnity."

In the above example of the owner, prime contractor, subcontractor situation, the owner will look to the prime contractor for his/her damages. The prime contractor will have a right to be indemnified by the subcontractor who actually caused the damages. This is true even if there is no indemnification agreement. The law will imply an agreement to indemnify.

Express indemnity is an express agreement between the parties to indemnify each other as set out by the language of the indemnification clause.

Implied indemnity is an agreement implied by law between the parties to indemnify the other for damages. Because there is no specific language between the parties addressing how the indemnification should occur, courts will typically determine the scope of implied indemnity on a case-by-case basis and apply what the courts believe is equitable (fair). The reasoning behind implied indemnity is that a person should be held responsible for things resulting from his or her own fault.

One of the biggest problems that occurs with respect to any form of indemnity is that the person and/or entity seeking indemnification protection often believes that he or she is adequately protected from claims if he or she signs a contract containing an indemnification clause which in turn requires the other contracting party to defend and hold him or her harmless should any claim arise. Additionally, people also feel that they are adequately protected if they require the other party to list them as an additional insured on their general liability policy. Often times these two forms of protection do not do what one might expect.

The effect of an indemnification clause and how it is going to be applied in any given set of facts will turn on the specific language of the indemnification clause. Remember that any time you have language that specifically sets forth the type of indemnification, you are then dealing with the concept of express indemnity. That language will generally control what the courts will order.

C. Active/Passive Conduct

When discussing express and implied indemnity, you must also consider two other concepts: one who is actively involved in the loss and one who is passively involved in the loss.

Active negligence is conduct where one party participates with another party to commit either (1) an act of negligence, or (2) a failure to act by knowledge or information, or (3) an agreement not to perform which causes injury or damage. To put it more in perspective, using our examples from above, where an owner enters into a contract with a general contractor and then the general contractor enters into a series of subcontracts with sub-contractors, an active negligence situation arises for the general contractor if, even though the subcontractor is the one who performed the work, the general contractor participated with the subcontractor in performing the work and/or participated or had knowledge of the negligent work or the failure to perform that work which later turned out to be negligent in nature. On these facts, the general contractor actually did something negligently and therefore the general was "actively" negligent.

Passive negligence is conduct where someone could be held to answer for another's action where his or her conduct had nothing to do with the act of negligence. Using the same example above, if the general contractor entered into a subcontract agreement with a plumber and the plumber, during the course of his work, caused injury or damage and that work was done without the participation or knowledge of the general contractor, then the general contractor could be held to be passively negligent.

Whether negligence is to be characterized as active or passive is typically based upon the circumstances of each case and will generally present a question of fact to be decided by a judge or a jury. In some situations, the evidence is so clear and indisputable that reasonable minds will not differ; thus, the negligent act can be immediately determined to be active or passive. California Law has generally established that maintaining a dangerous condition is considered to be active negligence. This is important from the standpoint of construction since many construction sites can and often are deemed to be dangerous conditions and therefore the concept of active negligence could be imputed to the general contractor even though his subcontractors are performing the work.

The typical problems that arise from indemnification clauses are that people often think that they have a certain amount of protection when in fact they do not. As mentioned above, many of the indemnification clauses that are contained within contracts do not provide enough protection.

D. Types of Indemnity

A real life example addressing this issue is a good illustration of the problems that can occur with regards to indemnification and how a situation could have been avoided. Although this example is not construction-related, the same law applies in a construction-related contract.

A community college made its track and field facilities available to a local high school to run its track meet. A track meet was entirely organized and run by the local high school. During the track meet an individual who was participating in the pole vault event failed on one of his attempts, missed the landing mat, and fatally struck the concrete apron. The high school had requested the college pole vault coach to participate in the track meet. In fact the college pole vault coach was officiating the pole vault event at the time of the fatal injury.

The college was sued on the theory that the concrete apron surrounding the pole vault pit created a dangerous situation and furthermore that the college's pole vault coach was negligent in that he failed to properly supervise the event. The high school was also sued on the theory that the high school negligently supervised the track meet and its coaching staff was unqualified to teach pole vaulting.

The college, as part of the agreement to allow the high school to use its facilities, attempted to protect itself by having an "application for use" prepared between the parties, and included in that application was an indemnification clause. The application also required that the college be listed as an additional insured under the sponsoring high school's general liability policy.

The application for use of the college facilities included indemnification language which required the high school to "indemnify, hold harmless, and provide legal defense... for any and all claims, expenses, liability, loss or injury regardless of their nature or character, in any manner whatsoever, arising out of, or relating to the use of facilities." At first blush, this would seem to protect the college. However, first impressions are not always correct.

After the filing of the lawsuit, the college demanded the high school defend and indemnify the college in accordance with the indemnity agreement and also pursuant to the general liability policy in which the college was named as an additional insured. With regard to the indemnity clause, the tender of defense was denied based upon the language of the agreement itself. The attorneys for the high school took the position that the language of the clause did not require the high school to indemnify the college in this instance. Specifically, the indemnity agreement did not address whether the high school was required to indemnify the college for the college's own negligence. If you remember from the facts of this case, the complaint filed by the decedent's family alleged that the college was negligent for the dangerous condition of the concrete apron in close proximity to the pole vault pit and further that the college pole vault coach was negligent in his supervision. Both of these allegations are describing conduct that can be defined as "active negligence." The high school took the position that there is no language in the indemnification clause requiring the high school to indemnify the college for the college's own active negligence. Therefore, the high school did not defend the college for the college's active negligence.

As you can see, the concept of indemnification becomes tricky and the language of the indemnification clause is all important. Because of these issues, the California courts have developed a rather complex set of rules categorizing indemnification agreements. A full and detailed discussion of indemnification is found in the case of *MacDonald & Kruse, Inc. v. San Jose Steel Company, Inc., etc., et al., 29 Cal App 3d 413 (1972).*

The MacDonald case essentially broke down indemnification into three separate categories.

The first type of indemnity provides expressly and unequivocally that the "indemnitor" (the party required to indemnify another) is to indemnify the "indemnitee" (the party who is being indemnified) for any reason whatsoever. Under this type of indemnification agreement, the indemnitor would be required to indemnify the indemnitee even if the liability arose as a result of the active negligence of the indemnitee along with the co-negligence of the indemnitor. If this form of indemnity agreement had been contained in the application between the high school and the college, the high school would have been required to indemnify the college even if the college was actively negligent. This is sometimes called a Type 1 indemnity clause.

The second type of indemnity agreement provides that the indemnitor (party agreeing to indemnify another) is to indemnify the indemnitee (party being indemnified) for the indemnitee's liability resulting from its passive, but not active, negligence. This second type of indemnity language was used in the application between the high school and the college. Therefore, the high school was required to indemnify the college for its passive negligence but not from the college's active negligence. Since the allegations of the decedent's family was that the college was actively negligent, this type of indemnity clause contained in the application did not require the high school to indemnify the college. This is sometimes called a Type 2 indemnity clause.

The third type of provision is one in which the indemnitor is to indemnify the indemnitee for the action or inaction of the indemnitee only. In this set of facts, the high school would have to indemnify the college only for liability directly attributed to and to the extent caused by the high school. This is sometimes called a Type 3 indemnity clause.

Even though the examples set forth above deal in the context of a high school and college for a local track meet, the concepts are analogous to any construction project. Both personal injury and property damage can occur at any time in any construction related situation. Even after a contractor completes the construction project, some passerby could injure himself or herself and, as a result of that injury, **could** look to the property owner for recovery. In turn the property owner can look to the general contractor for indemnification who in turn can look to the subcontractor for indemnification. As you can see, a number of parties can be involved in any given set of facts and everyone is essentially going to be looking to someone else to indemnify them. To the extent that your contracts contain indemnification clauses, it is imperative that the language set forth in those contracts have enough teeth in them to be able to provide to you the protection that you require.

The toughest indemnity clause, called a "Type I" indemnity, which has been upheld by the courts, does not indemnify one for his or her sole negligence or willful misconduct. However, it is tough on the indemnitor because it could require one who might only be ten percent negligent to indemnify the other who may be 90 percent negligent. It also does not distinguish between passive or active negligence. Therefore, a subcontractor may be required to indemnify a prime contractor, even though the prime contractor was actively negligent to a much greater degree than was the subcontractor. Further, if the clause is properly written, the indemnitor may be required to defend a claim, even though no negligence was shown during trial. The claim itself would trigger the indemnity provision.

E. Express Indeminity in Construction Cases

Express Indemnity is one that is created by contract. Typically, the contractual indemnity provision will be enforced unless it is otherwise illegal. As stated before, an illegality with respect to indemnity agreements are agreements to indemnify one against his or her sole negligence, or willful misconduct. An Appellate case that was decided a couple of years ago, highlighted the importance of a well drafted indemnity clause.

The prime contractor was responsible for construction of a commercial building. The subcontractor was the tile subcontractor on the project. The subcontract between prime contractor and subcontractor had a very broad indemnity provision that read as follows:

> "B. General Indemnity -- All work covered by this Agreement done at site of construction or in preparing or delivering materials or equipment, or any or all of them, to the site shall be at the risk of Subcontractor exclusively. Subcontractor shall, with respect to all work which is covered by or incidental to this contract, indemnify and hold

> Contractor harmless from and against all of the following:....."
>
> "1. Any claim, liability, loss, damage, cost, expenses, including reasonable attorneys' fees, awards, fines or judgments arising by reason of the death or bodily injury to persons, injury to property, design defects (if design originated by Subcontractor), or other loss, damage or expense, including any if the same resulting from Contractor's alleged or actual negligent act or omission, regardless of whether such act or omission is active or passive.... However, Subcontractor shall not be obligated under this Agreement [***3] to indemnify Contractor with respect to the sole negligence or willful misconduct of Contractor, his agents or servants or subcontractors who are directly responsible to Contractor, excluding Subcontractor herein."

As you can see, this is a very broad indemnity agreement. It requires the sub to indemnify the prime contractor for almost anything so long as it is not the prime contractor's sole negligence or willful misconduct.

At the end of the project, the owner made a number of claims against the prime contractor for defective workmanship, including a claim that the tile work was defective. The prime contractor settled all of the claims made by the owner and then demanded indemnity from all of the subcontractors whose work was claimed to be defective. Except for the tile subcontractor, each of the subcontractors eventually provided indemnity. Because the tile subcontractor did not provide indemnity, the prime contractor filed a complaint against the subcontractor in the amount of $12,000.00 plus the attorneys fees. The trial jury found that neither the subcontractor nor the prime contractor had been negligent. However, the court entered judgment in favor of the prime contractor. The subcontractor then filed an Appeal.

The subcontractor's argument was that it was not required to indemnify the prime contractor if it was not shown that the subcontractor had been negligent. Because the jury found that the subcontractor was not negligent, the subcontractor believed that the judgment should have been entered in its favor. The subcontractor also argued that the judge made a mistake in the law. The subcontractor argued that the prime contractor had the burden to prove that prime contractor was not negligent. The judge decided that the Subcontractor would have the burden to prove that the owner's claim arose out of the prime contractor's sole negligence or willful misconduct.

The appellate court held that an indemnity agreement in such a case arises out of a contractual agreement. The judge or jury is required to determine the intent of the parties in entering into the agreement. The intention of the parties should be determined from the clear and explicit language of the contract. The court will first look to the words of the contract to determine the intended scope of the indemnity agreement.

The appellate court held that since the indemnity agreement was "with respect to all work which is covered by or incidental to this subcontract," the trial court would not have to find that the subcontractor was negligent. The court further held that based on the language that all work performed by subcontractor "shall be at the risk of **subcontractor** exclusively" clearly expresses the intent of the parties that subcontractor should be responsible for the claim.

Importantly, the indemnity agreement required the subcontractor to indemnify the prime contractor from claims. The requirement to indemnify is triggered by the claim that arises out of work covered or incidental to the contract.

F. Illegal Indemnity Provisions

A situation that arises somewhat frequently raises some interesting questions. What happens if the party seeking indemnity creates the injury or damage as a result of his/her willful misconduct or as a result of his/her sole negligence? Can a party contract away their willful misconduct and/or sole negligence? The answer is no. As a general rule, one cannot contract away his or her sole negligence or withhold conduct. That is against public policy.

California Civil Code 2782(a) makes it against public policy for any construction contract to have language in it wherein the promisee (this is the party seeking to be indemnified) attempts to contract away his or her liability and/or responsibility for his/her/its willful misconduct or sole negligence.

Although there are exceptions to many rules, Civil Code Section 2782(a) provides in part:

"...provisions, clauses, covenants, or agreements contained in, collateral to, or affecting any construction contract and which purport to indemnify the promisee against liability for damages for death or bodily injury to persons, injury to property, or any other loss, damage or expense arising from the **sole negligence or willful misconduct** of the promisee or the promisee's agents, servants, or independent contractors who are directly responsible for such promisee or from defects in design furnished by such persons are against public policy and are void and unenforceable..." (emphasis added).

Similar language applies to contracts dealing with public agencies. Civil Code, Section 2782(b) provides in part:

"... provisions, clauses, covenants, or agreements contained in, collateral to, or affecting any construction contract with a public agency which purport to impose on the contractor, or relieve the public agency from, liability for the act of negligence of the public agency shall be void and unenforceable."

G. Conclusion

You can see that the law provides for parties to be able to contractually enter into agreements that provide for their protection against the wrongdoing of others. Even in situations where the parties don't enter into a written contract to protect themselves, the law applies a standard that will allow for the party who may be legally responsible to another to protect herself or himself from loss by seeking indemnification against the actual wrong party. Applying the laws of equity (fairness), the courts usually want to be able to make sure that the person who should be held responsible will be held responsible for his or her own fault, and not others who may in fact have a legal responsibility by way of some contractual relationship though they did not do the acts causing damages to another. However, rather than relying upon the courts to fully decide and apportion damages, you should have a written agreement for indemnity or an indemnity clause that sets out exactly what you want it to do.

IX.
BONDING IN THE CONSTRUCTION INDUSTRY

The issue of bonding is widely misunderstood. Many people think of a bond as if it were liability insurance. As an example of the difference between bonding and liability insurance, if you have an automobile accident, and it is your fault, your liability insurance carrier will pay the damages to the other party; however, the insurance company will not sue you for your negligence or fault. This is not true with respect to a bond. If you have obtained a bond to complete performance and/or make payment, and the bonding company is required to make a payment on your behalf, the bonding company has the right to come after you for reimbursement. Bonding is much more like a line of credit than liability insurance. When you obtain a bond, you sign an "indemnity agreement." That agreement states that in the event the bonding company has to expend any money with respect to claims, you will reimburse the bonding company. This indemnity agreement usually also covers costs such as the cost of investigating the claim as well as attorneys fees, etc.

In the construction industry, there are a number of bonds and each is discussed separately below.

A. Bid Bonds

Bid bonds assure the person to whom you are bidding (usually a public entity) that if your bid is accepted and you are awarded the contract, you will enter into that contract. Bid bonds are almost never required on private works of improvement, but are almost always required on public works of improvement.

When bidding on a public works job, if there is a bid bond, the contractor will know that if he/she refuses or fails to enter into the contract with the public body, that his/her bid bond will be forfeited. One commentator states that this penalty insures that only serious contractors who intend to construct the project will bid on public works.

The face value of the public works bid bond normally is a percentage of the amount bid. A standard percentage is ten percent (10%) of that amount. If the successful bidder fails to execute a contract, the surety (bond) is forfeited to the public entity. This makes the surety liable to the public entity for the face value of the bond.

Bid bonds are subject to the same defenses as are the bids themselves, mostly when a mistake is made. As discussed in the Bidding section of this book, relief may be given to the bidder on a project where that bidder has made a mistake based on a clerical error, rather than in judgment.

The method for being relieved from your mistake in bidding differs, depending on whether or not the job is a public works or private works project.

In a public works project, the bidder must advise the public entity of its mistake within five days of the opening of bids. The notice must specify in detail how the mistake came about. This must be done in writing. In addition, the mistake must be a clerical error in filling out the bid, and not an error in judgment. Generally, to be relieved of a mistake, the contractor must show that the mistake was material, and if the bid were enforced, it would be unconscionable; that the mistake related to a material feature of the contract; that the mistake was not the result of a violation of a public duty or from the contractor's negligence; and, the owner must be put in the status quo (a place where the owner was before) so that the owner suffers no serious prejudice except for the loss of its bargain. In California, the case of *Drennan v. Star Paving* allows for damages against a contractor for a bid that the contractor refuses to perform upon unless the contractor can show that a mistake was made and that the acceptance of the bid by the prime contractor was unreasonable.

That is to say that the prime contractor has to <u>reasonably</u> rely on the offer. If the mistake is obvious, it would probably be held that the person to whom you are bidding could not have <u>reasonably</u> relied on your bid to his/her detriment. A bid that is conspicuously less than any other party's bid should not be reasonably relied on.

Relief from the bid is also available where the terms and conditions of the contract are changed <u>after</u> bid submission, or where there is an unreasonable delay by the owner beyond the time for acceptance stated in the invitation to bid.

B. Payment and Performance Bonds

In California, when one purchases a performance bond, a payment bond is usually issued simultaneously at no additional cost. The performance bond protects the owner, public entity, or bank, and assures that the project will be completed. The payment bond protects subcontractors and material suppliers, and assures a means for payment to them if they are not paid.

1. Performance Bonds

   A performance bond is issued to insure performance of the project. That is to say if the work is not completed, the bonding company will then step in to complete the performance. As stated above, usually the performance and payment bonds are issued together, with the performance bond intended to protect the owner's interests, and the payment bond intended to protect the subcontractors' or material suppliers' interests.

2. Payment Bonds

   A payment bond is issued as a financial guarantee that if the bond principal (the person that obtains the bond, usually the general contractor) does not make payment on a certain project, and the claim for payment is valid, then the bonding company will step in and make payment. Clearly there are some conditions to that payment. As an example, you will have to give a notice to the bonding company of your claim.

C. Notice Requirements

Bond, stop notice, and mechanics' lien rights are bundled together, and the manner in which to perfect the right to make a claim against the bond is similar to those of stop notices and mechanics' liens. Ordinarily, to proceed on a claim against a payment bond, or to make a claim on a mechanics' lien or stop notice, persons not under a direct contract with the owner or entity must provide a preliminary notice to secure those rights. While non-compliance with those provisions bars any recovery on mechanics' liens or stop notices for the applicable period prior to complying with those rules, recent legislation provides that a claim may be made upon a bond even though some of the preliminary notice requirements were not met. Despite that legislation, it is always important to protect all mechanics' lien and stop notice rights by properly serving the preliminary notice.

A preliminary notice which satisfies the requirements of Civil Code section 3098 (for public works) or Civil Code section 3097 (for private works) must be served upon the owner and general contractor. In private works, the construction lender must also be served. The purpose of the preliminary notice, whether under a public works or private works project, is to put the owner of the project on notice that a person with whom the owner does not have a contract is doing work on the project. This is more fully discussed in the chapter dealing with liens and stop notices. The surety on the bond does not have to be notified on the 20 Day Preliminary Notice. However, it is a good idea to do so. The notice to the bonding company is discussed below.

The failure to give a preliminary notice within 20 days of when work first begins, if that notice is necessary, will bar any mechanics' lien or stop notice claim for the work done earlier than the 20 day period prior to serving the preliminary notice.

Further, on private works and public works projects, if a person serves the preliminary notice late, many times this does not mean that the person may not sue for stop notice or mechanics' liens for his/her work on the project, but it does mean that the person may not collect on a stop notice or mechanics' lien for the work done more than 20 days prior to the serving of the preliminary notice. As an example, if work commenced on April 1, 1997, and on April 20, 1997 a preliminary notice is served, the subcontractor or claimant may make a valid claim on a stop notice, mechanics' lien, and against any bond for all work performed. However, if work commenced on April 1, 1997, and a preliminary notice was not served until June 20, 1997, the subcontractor would only be able to recover on a mechanics' lien or stop notice for the work performed from June 1, 1997 and thereafter and cannot collect for any work done between April 1, 1997 and June 1, 1997 on a mechanics' lien or stop notice.

However, as indicated above, on contracts entered into after January 1, 1995, a bond claim may be made even if the preliminary notice was not served on the bonding company. On either private or public works bonds, the failure to comply with the preliminary notice requirements will be excused if a bond notice is served upon the bonding company within 15 days of the recording of a Notice of Completion with the County Recorder, or if no Notice of Completion is recorded, within 75 days after the completion of the work of improvement.

D. Contents of Bond Notice

As stated above, in order to make a claim against the bond, you must put the bonding company <u>on notice</u> of your claim. The California <u>Civil Code</u> provides for the method of delivery and contents of the written notice to the bonding company. The bond notice requirements are the same for both private and public works bonds, though on federal public works projects, the procedure is different and is discussed in the next section.

The notice itself is not required to be in any specific format. The notice can merely be a letter or other document but must state the kind of labor, services, equipment, or materials furnished or agreed to be furnished by the claiming party; the name of the person for whom the labor, services, equipment or services were furnished; and, the amount in value, as near as may be determined, of any labor, services, equipment, or materials already furnished or to be furnished. It must put the bonding company on notice that you are looking to it for payment.

In simpler terms, you may write a letter to the bonding company stating who you are supposed to do the work for, what work or services you are to provide and the amount in value of what you supplied that you contend has not been paid. In stating the amount that is unpaid, the best method is to state how much work you did in total, how much you have been paid for that work, and then the amount that is owing. In the notice, you should demand payment from the bonding company.

Once you have written your notice, you must then serve it on the bonding company. That notice may be given by personal delivery or by certified mail. As to the address to be mailed, if the surety is not a corporation, it would go to the surety's residence or place of business, if known. If that address is unknown, service may be made to the Clerk of the County in which the bond has been recorded.

As to a corporate surety, it may be filed with the agent designated by the surety on the bond itself, or it can be served on the agent for process as provided by that surety in the method and manner that service would be made in a civil action. Service may also be made at the office, or in the care, of any officer of the surety in this state, or it can be made to the bond principal at their last known address.

E. Federal Public Works

There are some slight differences for federal public works than what is stated above for state private or public works projects. The Miller Act governs federal works projects. Under the Miller Act, notice must be given to the general contractor within ninety (90) days after the last labor or material has been provided by you. There are some federal cases that hold that notice was invalid if it was not received by the general contractor prior to the expiration of ninety (90) days. However, there are other cases that have stated that it is effective upon mailing.

The bond notice on federal works must be served by registered mail. However, at least one federal court upheld a claim when the ninety (90) day notice was given by first class mail.

All that is essential, like the state notice requirements, is that the notice state that the claimant has furnished labor and/or materials to the job; is unpaid; has performed those services for a specified party; and is looking to the prime contractor for recovery. It is essential that the claimant state he or she is looking to the prime contractor for recovery in that the federal bonds are written with the intent to govern nonpayment by the general contractor. As cheap insurance, we suggest that you also serve the bonding company.

F. Premium On The Bonds

The premium on the bond will run somewhere between one and five percent depending on your financial wherewithal. That is to say that the better financial risk you are, the less it is likely to cost you to obtain the bond. It is also easier to obtain the bond if you are financially well off. The reason is, as we stated earlier, the bond is a financial guarantee that guarantees your performance. If the bonding company has to pay for your performance, then the bonding company has the right to come after you for its losses.

G. Limitation of Liability

The amount the bond can pay out in claims is limited to what is called the "penal sum" of the bond, which is the face amount of the bond itself. However, the limitation of liability can be waived by the bonding company.

Typically what happens in a construction project that goes sour is that the bonding company comes in to determine if, first of all, it can help the bond principal complete the project and pay the debts. That is clearly better than having the bond principal default (depending on how much the default would be). If it determines that the bond principal cannot adequately complete the project within some financial restraints, then the bonding company must decide what are the damages going to be to the various bond claimants including the owner, subcontractors and material suppliers.

If the bonding company determines that the payouts to claimants will be significantly less than or somewhat less than the amount of the bond, then the bonding company might wish to undertake completing the project and pay all of the debts. However, if the bonding company determines that the claims are going to exceed the penal sum of the bond, then the bonding company will probably elect to tender the bond amount. That is to say the bonding companies will pay the penal (face) sum of the bond to those making claims, or it may deposit the bond amount into court allowing the court to distribute the funds to the claimants, and walk away from the project. In this manner, the bonding company will limit its liability to the bond amount. However, as soon as the bonding company undertakes to complete the project, there is no further limitation of liability.

H. Bonding Company's Obligations

For the most part, the bonding company's obligations are identical with those of the bond principal (bonded contractor).

However, this is not always the case. As an example, if the bonded principal goes bankrupt, he/she no longer has any liability yet the bonding company is still on the hook to complete the project.

I. Release Bonds

There are different types of Release Bonds to release various disputed claims. As an example, if a Mechanics' Lien is recorded on a piece of property, and the claim is disputed, then the Mechanics' Lien can be released by recording a "Mechanics' Lien Release Bond." This is a bond in the sum of one and one-half times the amount of the Mechanics' Lien. The bond is substituted for the property as security for the claim.

A Release Bond can also be used to release Stop Notices.

J. License Bonds

The Business & Professions Code requires a bond as a condition to obtaining or renewing a contractor's license. The bond required for all contractors is in the amount of $10,000.

Like all other bonds, a license bond is not an insurance policy. However, many persons suing a contractor erroneously believe that the license bond is a performance bond or an insurance policy, or something that they can get if the contractor has no money. In order to proceed against and collect upon a license bond, the claimant must fall within one of the following categories:

1. A homeowner contracting for a home improvement on his/her personal residence who has been damaged as a result of a violation of the Contractors' License Law by the licensee;
2. Any person damaged as a result of a willful and deliberate violation of the Contractors' License Law by the licensee, or by the fraud of the licensee in the execution or performance of the construction contract;
3. Any employee of the licensee damaged by the licensee's failure to pay wages; or
4. A trust fund damaged as a result of the licensee's failure to pay fringe benefits to eligible employees represented by the union under a collective-bargaining agreement.

Only those persons falling within the above four categories can prosecute a claim against the bond. Further, unlike an insurance policy, a bond has a statutory face value limit for all claims total - not just all claims occurring from the same occurrence.

As an example, if a person has a claim against the license bond for work done on a job on Main Street, and another person has a claim against the license bond for work done on First Street, all claims will be limited to a maximum payment of the surety of the face value of the license bond. Thus, if a $10,000 license bond was issued, and $5,500 is paid out to the Main Street claimant, there only remains $4,500 to be paid out to any other claimant.

K. Disciplinary Bonds

There are some circumstances where a contractor who has been previously disciplined by the Contractors' State License Board may be required to have, in addition to a normal license bond, a disciplinary bond. This bond is in the amount of a penal sum not less than $15,000, but could be required to be as much as $75,000. Business & Professions Code section 7071.8(b) states that "sum shall not be less than $15,000 nor more than ten times that amount required by section 7071.6."

L. Contractor Judgment Bonds

A judgment bond is another form of a bond for a licensee who has had a construction related judgment entered against it. This bond is required to be filed in the amount equal to the unsatisfied judgment and must be filed within ninety (90) days from the date of notification by the Board to file the bond, or the contractor's license will be suspended. This bond is to serve as security to guarantee payment of the judgment should the contractor not pay that amount to the person who prevailed against it in a court or arbitration.

As with payment or performance bonds, all license bonds, judgment bonds, or disciplinary bonds carry an indemnification agreement, which makes the contractor liable to the surety should the surety be forced to pay out the penal amount under those bonds.

X.
INSURANCE

This chapter deals with the issue of insurance and specifically how insurance related matters are applied to construction related disputes. It merely highlights the issue to give you a general understanding. This chapter is written by construction attorneys and not insurance attorneys to highlight the issues. You should seek the aid and advice of competent professionals in your decisions to purchase a policy or when a claim is made.

At the outset, anyone in the construction industry knows that there is an insurance crisis in California. The major problem is that insurance companies have a hard time determining the risk that they are taking. Given that, they are either afraid to come into the market in California, or come into the market requiring such high premiums, that it is virtually impossible to obtain liability insurance for contractors. In addition, many insurance carriers are now excluding certain types of construction, such as condominium construction or mold. This makes it virtually impossible to obtain that kind of insurance unless the premium is very, very large.

This is the insurance crisis. However, this chapter is intended to give you some understanding of insurance itself.

The most often issued type of insurance policy dealing with construction is called a "CGL Insurance Policy." Although the definition of CGL Insurance Policy is "Commercial General Liability" policy, it has also been known and called a "Comprehensive General Liability" policy. For purposes of this chapter, the terms "Commercial General Liability" and "Comprehensive General Liability" will be used interchangeably. We will refer to the policy as a "CGL Policy."

For our purposes, the CGL policy is intended to protect individuals and businesses against general liability including the type of liability incurred while operating a construction business. The protection is intended to protect against potential liability caused to another party. Liability can arise in many ways. An owner and operator of a business could have potential liability from manufacturing a product, selling a service, or selling the product, either directly or indirectly.

Unlike the concept of indemnification, insurance is something that must be bought. As discussed elsewhere in this book, indemnification is based on an agreement, whether it is expressed in the contract or implied by the nature of the relationship between the parties. Insurance is never implied. You either have insurance or you don't. Insurance is something that you purchase by way of paying a premium. Indemnification is a right that you gain as a result of a relationship rather than by payment of premium.

However, there is a similarity between the concept of indemnification and the concept of insurance. The insurance policy is an agreement between an insured and an insurance company to indemnify and defend the insured in accordance with the policy provisions. If a situation arises where the insured is put in a position of having to answer for an injury or other damage to another person, aka third party, then the insured will look to his/her/its insurance company and ask the insurance company to defend and indemnify him/her/it for any potential loss. Essentially, the insured is asking for the insurance company to do two things: (1) to defend the insured against potential losses that might arise as a result of the insured's actions, and (2) if the insured is found responsible for the injuries or damages sustained by the party, then the insured is asking that those damages be paid by the insurance company.

The latter part dealing with payment to the third party is called indemnification. The investigation, negotiation and defense that takes place prior to the indemnification is called a defense portion of the relationship. Because of these two aspects of insurance, we come up with the concept of "defend and indemnify."

A. Contents of the Insurance Policy

All insurance polices are made up of different parts. Each part has its own purpose and importance. The policy is the insuring agreement between the insured and the insurance company. It defines the rights and liabilities of the parties just as any other contract. Although many insurance policies are written in legalese and they clearly are often hard and difficult to follow and understand, it is important to make sure that you are receiving the coverage that you believe you are purchasing.

Typically, the various parts of an insurance policy include such items as: declaration pages, definitions, conditions, insuring clause, exclusions, endorsements and binders. There is an additional item called a Certificate of Insurance which will be discussed separately.

We will review each of these below.

1. Binders

   A binder is a document that provides immediate insurance coverage even though all of the underwriting requirements may have not yet been completed. For example, a binder is necessary if you are involved in a situation where you need to immediately prove that you have insurance. Anytime that you apply for insurance you must complete an application form and go through an underwriting process which determines whether or not you in fact qualify for insurance. Underwriting will also determine the amount of premium to be charged. Often times initial information can be taken, money can be paid and you will be given a binder which gives you the insurance protection you are looking for during the underwriting process. However, you should be careful as it's very possible that once the underwriting process is completed, a determination can be made that you do not qualify for the insurance and therefore the binder will be canceled.

2. Declaration Page

   A declaration page is part of your insurance policy. It is usually one of the first pages in the policy and typically contains typewritten information that is specifically tailored to the type of insurance you are purchasing. The declaration page will include such personal information as: the name, address and telephone number of the insured, the policy period, the policy limits, any deductible that might be applicable, and a list of any and all endorsements. The declaration page may be the single most important page of any insurance policy and will usually define and set forth the type of coverage that you have.

3. Definitions, Conditions, Insuring Clauses, Exclusions and Endorsements

The balance of the clauses are generally pre-printed portions of the policy. The fact that they are pre-printed in boilerplate language does not limit their importance. Each one of these documents and clauses should be reviewed as well as any other clauses contained in the insurance contract so that you know exactly what you are purchasing. Special attention should be given to the exclusion portion of a policy. This area is going to describe what is <u>not</u> covered by your insurance policy. Often times people buy insurance with the understanding that they have a certain amount of coverage for a certain type of loss when in reality it is excluded from the policy. The most common exclusion that is relevant to contractors is a "work product" exclusion. This is discussed in detail later in this section. Pay particular attention to the exclusion portion of your policy.

B. Coverage

One of the most confusing and misunderstood portions of any insurance deals with the concept of coverage and specifically what is covered under your insurance policy. Insurance is expensive and particularly expensive in the area of construction. It is extremely important that as a contractor you know exactly what you are buying and what your coverage provides to you.

As a general rule, the standard CGL policy that a contractor will purchase will protect the contractor for both personal injury and property damage that is caused as a result of his or her conduct. The damage that is being referred to in these policies is the "consequential" damage. Consequential damage is defined as that damage that results as a consequence of your construction action. Your actual work product is not usually covered, unless specifically insured.

As an example of what is covered and what is not, the following example is helpful:

A roofing contractor is under contract to install a new roof on a commercial or residential property. The roofing contractor performs his or her work, but does so in a negligent manner. During a rain storm, the roof leaks, allowing water to get into the interior portion of the structure, causing damage to the interior of the structure. The owner of the property seeks to be compensated, not only for the damage caused to the interior of the property, but also for the cost involved in repairing the roof.

Under most CGL policies, the question becomes what is a covered item. Under the theory of consequential damages, the damage caused to the interior of the structure as a result of the rain coming into the structure is clearly covered as consequential damages. That is, as a consequence of the poor construction of the roof, damage occurred to the interior of the structure. That damage was consequential and triggers coverage. Is the repair of the roof covered? The answer is usually no. The construction of the roof was the "work product" of the roofing contractor and therefore is not usually covered under the policy because this is not a consequential damage of the construction. The roof itself is in the care, custody, and control of the contractor.

Knowledge of work product exclusions is very important, since often contractors believe that if they construct poor work their insurance is going to protect them for that work. This is not true. In almost all instances, the actual work product under a standard CGL policy will not be covered. A few carriers sell optional "work product" coverage, however, this is rare and expensive.

Personal injury is also covered under a policy as a consequential damage. Taking our roofing example a little bit further, suppose in addition to the roof leaking, the roof falls apart and shingles fall off the roof and hit someone, causing a personal injury. As stated above, the cost of repairing the roof is not a covered item; however, as a consequence of the poor construction, a personal injury was incurred by a passerby. The CGL policy will protect the insured for the injuries suffered by that individual.

In examining consequential damages, it is important to make sure that the consequential damages that one seeks to have covered by his/her insurance policy be damages arising as a direct result of the work performed by the contractor. In other words consequential damages are covered only if they flow directly from the work performed by the contractor. Lastly, the damage claimed must not be excluded somewhere else in the policy.

C. Types of Insurance Policies -- The Trigger of Coverage

Once a loss has occurred and a claim is being made for damages, it is necessary to be able to determine <u>when</u> that loss actually occurred. The time when a loss occurred is not as simple as you might think, particularly in the world of construction. The concept of when the damage occurred will have a direct effect on insurance coverage. For example, let us suppose a plumbing contractor in the course of his work installed pipes as part of his contract. Sometime after the installation and construction of the plumbing work, a pipe burst right in the area where one pipe was joined to another. Examination of the damage reveals that the work done at the joint (the area where the two pipes are joined) was performed improperly. Under this example, we have two different points in time. The first point in time is the time when the work was actually performed, i.e. the time when the plumbing contractor physically joined one pipe to the other. The second time that we are talking about is when the actual problem occurred (when the pipe actually burst and came apart). These two time periods can and often are months or years apart.

Because of the time concerns, it is extremely important to determine under which policy period coverage applies. Over a period of years there could be several different policies that any contractor might have and in some instances these policies could be issued by different insurance companies. Contractors are forever changing their policy coverage and most will look for the best price for coverage, and therefore could purchase insurance from different insurance companies over a period of years.

What needs to be determined in any loss or claim is what policy or policies will cover the insured for the loss being asserted. The common phrase used in the insurance industry is the term "trigger of coverage." In other words, what act or action triggers (determines) coverage?

An additional issue that is involved is that many times it is hard to determine when something actually did occur. Take for example, a contractor doing site work that over a period of years ends up sliding. One court case has held that all insurance policies that covered the work during the time of the slide were on the hook for coverage. That is to say that the trigger for the insurance coverage was a "multiple trigger," something that went on over years, and all policies in force from the time of the actual work until the claims are liable to indemnify and defend.

To further analyze the issue of the trigger of coverage more closely, we now need to look at the concept of "occurrence" versus "claims made."

1. "Occurrence" Policies

Under an "occurrence" policy, the question of coverage will turn on when the <u>occurrence</u> took place, as opposed to a "claims made" policy where the question will turn on when the <u>claim</u> was made.

Under an occurrence policy, the coverage period of such policy is said to be triggered once the occurrence occurs. That is, the policy in force at the time of the <u>trigger</u> (which is typically when the work is done) is liable. However, as stated above, the occurrence can often times be difficult to determine. Some claims will arise out of circumstances in which the occurrence is over a relatively short period of time, thus the occurrence would be clearly within a single policy period. Since most policies are sold for a one year period of time, if your occurrence occurred at anytime during that one year period of time, the question of coverage is relatively easy and uncontested since the trigger of coverage would occur during that one year policy period.

The question of coverage becomes a lot more difficult in those situations where the occurrence might develop over a longer period of time, such as the example described above. Other examples that create problems for coverage in the construction industry would be a situation that might deal with subsurface soils. For example, let's suppose that a contractor is involved in the construction of an entire building. After completion of the building and over a period of years the subsurface soil and compaction starts to fail. In turn, this causes damage to the concrete foundation, causing the building to crack and separate, which eventually causes major damage to the entire building. These facts are definitely going to raise an issue with regards to the period in which the "occurrence" occurred, thus raising the issue as to which insurance period will be applicable. There are several different time frames that anyone can look at for purposes of occurrence. We can look at the time of the construction, the time when the soil first started to deteriorate, the time when the foundation started to crack, or the time in which the resulting damage started to occur to the structure.

From the standpoint of the insured, it is a relatively easy situation if the insured has had continuous insurance with the same company throughout the entire time line set forth above. The insured's requirement is to submit the claim to his or her insurance company or companies. If the insured had more than one insurance company representing it during this period of time, **he or she must make sure to submit the claim to each one of those insurance companies**. The insurance companies will then be put in the position of having to make a determination as to who is responsible for coverage. The additional question will be which company or companies will cover you. A greater concern comes about for those people who have insurance for certain periods of time, but did not have insurance for other periods in the time line. That becomes a greater concern to the insured as a result of the fact that the occurrence might be deemed to have arisen during the period of time when the contractor had no insurance. **Most important is that the claim is submitted to all insurance companies possibly covering the risk**.

The occurrence situation discussed above is primarily directed to those situations where there is property damage. To the extent that there is bodily injury, the occurrence is generally very easy to determine. If someone is physically injured as a result of poor work, the date of that particular injury is usually easily determined and therefore it is usually easy to determine which insurance company's policy is on the hook. However, there are some injuries where the occurrence of the injury will be more difficult to determine, such as a bodily injury that is caused as a result of continuous exposure to a condition, such as a caustic or toxic chemicals.

2. "Claims Made" Policies

A "claims made" policy is very different than an "occurrence" policy. In a "claims made" policy, the trigger of coverage occurs when the claim is made as opposed to when the occurrence occurred. Usually, the damage occurs on a certain date, but the claim is not made until sometime thereafter. In this type of policy, the date when the claim is made is the date when the coverage is triggered. Thus, there can be an instance where the event occurs during one policy period but the claim is made in a different policy period. **Except where there are exclusions for prior acts**, as discussed below, the policy that is in effect at the time the claim is made is the policy that will cover you for the claim. An example of a "claims made" policy's effect the following example may be helpful: A loss occurs during the time that a person is insured by insurance company "ABC." The insured buys a new policy where the insurance company is "XYZ." Although the injury occurred during the policy period of ABC, the claim was made during the time in which the XYZ policy was in force. XYZ will be held responsible to defend the insured under a "claims made" policy.

One of the reasons why insurance companies write "claims made" policies is that they are then not generally liable for claims made when the occurrence for which liability is claimed occurred prior to the date that the policy was written. This means that the period covered is the policy period and not for sometime before or after. This would not be true where a policy had continually been renewed with the same company, and also is not true in the very limited circumstances where a person has purchased prior acts coverage.

The following additional example may be helpful:

A contractor buys "claims made" coverage on January 1, 1992. He/she performs work in March of 1992. He/she finishes that work in 1992 and goes on his/her way. In March, 1993, he/she is informed that there are problems with the job, and subsequently a lawsuit is filed also in 1993. However, in 1993, that contractor changed insurers and bought a new policy effective January 1, 1993. That new policy is also a "claims made" policy, but with a different carrier.

As stated before, on a "claims made" policy, the trigger for coverage is when the claim is made. The claim being made in 1993 would be tendered to the second insurance carrier. However, many "claims made" policies exclude coverage for prior acts. In this case the act occurred in 1992. Under most circumstances, the new insurance carrier will refuse to cover for the claim made, as it is a "prior act." Under the hypothetical stated above, if the claim had been made before the end of 1992, it is obvious that no problem would be had in tendering the claim to the first insurance carrier. The problem here is that the claim was tendered when it was known about, in 1993.

As briefly discussed above, there is another form of rider or coverage that can be bought along with a "claims made" policy. That is "prior acts" coverage. That is to say that under our prior example, when the contractor purchased a new policy from that second carrier in 1993, he/she could also have purchased from that carrier "prior acts" coverage which would cover him/her for acts that occurred prior to the effective date of that policy.

That form of coverage is more expensive, and is not always offered. However, if available, it covers the prior act. This is important to keep in mind when purchasing "claims made" coverage. That is, you are not necessarily receiving coverage that is worth anything. The best way for "claims made" coverage to be worth while having, is if you continue to have coverage with that carrier for an extended period of time.

3. Modified Occurrence Policies

A new type of policy that has reared its ugly head in California is a "modified occurrence" policy. This policy is a hybrid or mix of an occurrence policy as well as a "claims made" policy. This policy is really nothing more than a claims made policy that covers the prior acts so long as coverage continues with the same carrier.

This new kind of insurance policy in many cases will not cover claims made during the rather lengthy period under which someone may bring a lawsuit.

As discussed above, there are generally two classes of insurance. Most people are aware of an "occurrence" type policy, which covers a person for any "occurrence" during the policy period. An "occurrence" would be an accident, act, omission, or other thing done by the insured or his/her employees or agents that causes another damages. An "occurrence" with respect to a contractor could be the installation of a roof, the rewire of a kitchen, or the dropping of a hammer on a bystander's head. It could be any incident that causes someone an injury, whether physical or simply financial.

To be remembered is that not all "occurrences" are covered by insurance. As an example, most contractor's policies exclude "work-product." That means that if you install a bad roof, insurance will not pay for a new roof but will pay for damage caused by rain to contents in the house. The "occurrence" policy that may be liable for a claim is the policy in effect when the "occurrence" or act was done. As an example, if during 1994 you are covered by an "occurrence" type policy and the work you did in 1994 resulted in damages, and if you were sued in 1997 while insured by any carrier, the policy you had in 1994 would more than likely defend and indemnify you for any claims made (unless excluded for some other reason).

The other type of policy is a "claims made" policy. That type of policy covers a person for any lawsuit or claim made against them during the policy period. In the previous example, even though the work was done in 1994, the policy that would be liable would be the one in force when the claim is made. In our example, 1997, however, there may be policy exclusions, such as for work done prior to your buying insurance. This is called a "prior acts" exclusion. In essence, one instance looks to the policy in effect when the act occurred, while the other looks at the policy in effect when the claim was made.

Under a new type of policy, called a "modified occurrence policy," a claim must be made on a policy within 60 days of the incident that caused the damage, but no more than one year after the expiration of the policy. That one year is extended if you keep renewing the policy. What is particularly scary about this coverage is that it is very **inexpensive** in relation to other liability policies, so persons are buying it to save money not realizing that they may be getting something less than they expect.

The following example highlights the problem. In 1995, a subcontractor performs concrete work on a house. In 1997, that contractor is sued for problems caused by that concrete work performed in 1995. The contractor had a "modified risk policy" that was in force when the work was performed in 1995, but expired at the end of 1995. Under the provisions of that policy, a claim against the policy for the concrete work had to have been made either within 60 days of the performance of that work, or one year from the expiration of the policy. Under this policy it does not matter whether or not you know of the claim. Thus a claim against that policy, if not renewed, had to have been made before the end of 1996.

In this case, having not been sued until 1997, the contractor knew of no claim and could not make any claim against the insurance policy. The insurer denied coverage.

This form of insurance may be cheaper, and may be something you would want to look into, but only if you intend to continually renew coverage with that <u>same</u> carrier. If you are one of those persons who changes carriers every year or two, either to shop around and save money, or simply because your agent suggests something different, this type of policy may not be for you.

D. Duty to Defend/Reservation of Rights

As stated previously, the basic reason that insurance is purchased is to protect us against losses that occur as a result of our work. Although not necessarily looked at initially, the other reason that we all purchase insurance is to be able to have someone defend us against a loss that is being made. The duty to defend is as equally important as the duty to indemnify, and in many cases legal defenses are more costly than the alleged damages of the claimant. If all an insured was getting when it purchased insurance was protection against loss, and not a duty to defend, it could very well spend a large sum of money in defending itself even though the actual loss would be paid by the insured's insurance company, or if the insured was successful in its defense, would leave the insurance company paying nothing. This is especially true in condominium defect cases where defense costs are astronomical while liability may be minimal. The concept of duty to defend is therefore a very important concept.

As a general rule of law, the duty to defend is much greater than the duty to indemnify. Typically any type of claim that has a possibility of triggering coverage will raise the obligation of the insurance company to defend you. It doesn't necessarily raise the obligation of the insurance company to indemnify you.

In a legal setting, if a lawsuit is filed against you alleging damages as a result of work that you performed on a construction project, it is very possible that a complaint may have allegations that trigger insurance coverage even though there may also be allegations that are not covered by insurance. This type of complaint can be called a blended form of allegation. It is blended in the sense that there are allegations that are covered by insurance and allegations that are not covered by insurance.

The standard insurance policy and the laws as interpreting those insurance policies have determined that an insurance company's obligation is to defend <u>all claims</u> being brought against you by way of a civil lawsuit <u>if any</u> of the claims trigger insurance. Essentially, because the insurance company's duty to defend you is greater than its duty to indemnify you, the responsibility of the insurance company to defend you is triggered to defend you against all of those claims. Your insurance company will be required to retain an attorney for you and to pay that attorney to defend you.

In a situation where there is a duty to defend but there is a question as to whether or not the complaint filed provides full insurance protection, you will likely see what is called a "reservation of rights." A reservation of rights is a position taken by the insurance company to reserve all of its rights under the policy for a future determination as to whether or not coverage does in fact exist.

Insurance companies will generally protect themselves by way of a reservation of rights by sending to their insured a letter which sets forth their position regarding the claims being brought about and the fact that they are reserving their rights. They will state they are defending you even though they allege or claim not to be liable to indemnify you under the policy. This reservation of rights letter is generally a long letter containing boilerplate language from the policy and detailing the insurance company's position as to why it feels that it is not responsible for certain aspects of the claim being brought against you and what its rights are under the reservation of rights.

One of the remedies that are reserved by the insurance company is the remedy to cease further representation and defense of your claim. In other words, should the insurance company during the course of litigation make a determination that there is no coverage for the claims being brought, the insurance company would have the legal authority to advise you of this fact and to cease any further representation of your interests. Another form of reservation would be the insurance company's right to reserve any form of indemnification. For example, if an insurance company defends you throughout the course of your litigation and a determination is made at the end of the litigation that the damages are not covered damages, the insurance company would have the right to raise their non-responsibility to pay those damages since the damages are not covered under your policy.

A recent California case has ruled that after a case is over, an insurance company that reserved its rights can argue that attorneys fees were paid for non-covered items and can seek reimbursement of those attorneys fees from their insured.

A reservation of rights letter is more the rule than the exception particularly when dealing in the construction industry. Remember insurance generally will not cover you for your work product. **You should discuss this issue with your insurance company.**

E. Certificate of Insurance

Many times a contractor who enters into a contract, or for that matter a subcontractor who enters into a contract, is required to show proof of insurance. The certificate of insurance will accomplish this request. The certificate of insurance will provide such information as the name, address and telephone number of the insurance company, the insurance broker, the type of coverage you have, the limits of coverage you have, the policy number, the effective date of the policy, the expiration date of the policy, and any special type of representations.

The Certificate of Insurance should also state that the insurance will not be canceled without thirty (30) days written notice to the one holding the certificate.

Please keep in mind that the certificate of insurance is not an insurance contract. A certificate of insurance is only a document that represents that an insurance contract is in existence.

F. Conclusion

This discussion on insurance is really the tip of the iceberg when it comes to the review of insurance issues. The California court system as well as other courts throughout the United States have reviewed and analyzed insurance policies and insurance issues. There is a large body of law addressing a variety of issues in any given type of insurance policy. The analysis of insurance policies is a technical area of law and requires a clear and concise understanding. An attorney specializing in coverage issues should be consulted.

It is of the utmost importance that as the purchaser of insurance you know exactly what you are buying and exactly what coverage that you are obtaining.

XI.
DISPUTES

No matter how good a contractor you are, sooner or later you are going to be involved in a dispute. The difference between a good contractor and a poor one is that after a dispute arises a good contractor has already enhanced his or her likelihood of success.

At the outset you should know that there is no good lawsuit. You will never really recover all of your hard expenses nor any of your soft expenses, such as time lost from work and the emotional and business disruption that a major lawsuit can create. You should do everything you can to avoid the dispute.

A. How to Avoid a Dispute

There are a number of ways you can avoid a dispute. Probably the most important way is through communication. However, the more formalized methods will be discussed below:

1. Use A Written Contract

It is extremely important that a contract of any significance whatsoever be in writing. This is true because things that are in writing are easier to prove and much less likely to be forgotten. Further, if there is a dispute the judge or arbitrator is required to find the true intention of the parties. It is much easier to find the true intention of the parties if that intention is spelled out in writing. There is less for an arbitrator or a judge to determine if it is spelled out. It should also be remembered that swimming pool and home improvement contracts are required by law to be in writing.

2. Changes and Extras

As with having a contract in writing, it is best to document in writing changes or extras immediately. Lost time and additional monies resulting from extras are major sources of disputes. First of all, in order to determine if something is an extra, you must determine what is within the scope of the contract. A well written contract will do that because it spells out everything exactly. Secondly, you will never be in a better negotiating position than when your customer asks you to do something that is outside, or different from the scope of your present agreement. Therefore, you should negotiate all of the impact of that extra immediately. Remember, you presently have an agreement which requires you to do certain things and requires your customer to do certain things. Now your customer is asking for something different. You do not have to do that something different. That something different must be negotiated. Therefore, negotiate the entire impact such as cost, delay etc. Get it in writing immediately.

It is foolish to fear telling your customer the impact. In this way your customer can have a clear cut choice. The customer can either choose to make the change, and pay you the price by way of dollars and time, or the customer may choose to stay with the original written agreement. However, whichever way the customer decides, you will be better off if it has been documented in writing.

Recent legislation affecting home improvement contracts now mandates that change orders are not enforceable against the home owner or the person contracting for the home improvement work if they are not in a writing that describes the scope of the work and the price of the work to be performed. That means that the contractor may not be able to collect for the work performed. The Legislature however, has allowed for a basis of recovery on those oral change orders under a quantum meruit theory. This theory allows for recovery of the value of the work. While this is better than nothing, this is not necessarily the contract price, and may not include all contract profits that a contractor may make on the job. Therefore, it is best to have everything in writing.

3. Keeping a Journal

As attorneys, we are heavily involved in construction disputes. Because of that, we have found that it is very important that our clients keep a journal and a "Conversation Confirmer" during the construction process. In this way, you may be able to better remember and prove what happened, when, and in what sequence. Even if you are not able to remember all the facts of any particular instance, the journal itself may be good evidence of what happened.

Anytime that you are asked to do something different than what is called for in the original scope of the contract, immediately send or hand write a "Conversation Confirmer." This way, there will never be any confusion as to what you are directed to do. If you are asked to move a door, immediately write "Confirming your direction, we will move the door in the _____ room from ____________ to __________." At the same time, indicate if there will be any other impacts to this change such as delay or cost. After that, write a change order.

At the same time, while you are running the job, you should keep a journal of what transpired at all times. As an example, the number of workers on the job, whether there were any particular problems, whether it rained, whether another contractor interfered with your work, should be things that are documented in your journal.

4. Punch Lists

As stated previously, communication with your customer is a must. Therefore, frequent walk-throughs and written punch lists are a good idea. A punch list at the end of the job is most important. That way you will have documented what is left to be done so that that will not keep changing. (How many times has a customer given you punch list after punch list?)

Attempt to obtain the customer's signature to the final punch list(s) so that it will be documented that the two of you agreed upon the stage of completion at a particular time.

5. Frequent Invoicing

Again, in keeping with the theory of frequent communication, you should bill your customers frequently. It is axiomatic that this will help in your cash flow. Of equal importance is that it will keep your customer informed of what is going on by way of progress, changes, costs, etc. It will keep your customers informed and keep them from getting into debt without knowing about it and possibly raising that issue should a dispute occur.

B. Litigation

Even if you are the most careful contractor in the world, sooner or later you are going to be involved in litigation. What are your options? One of your options, the Mechanics' Lien will be treated in more detail elsewhere in this book. Therefore, we will discuss everything other than the Mechanics' Lien in this section.

You should keep in mind that litigation is costly and time consuming. It is very disruptive to your business. Therefore, you should attempt to settle the lawsuit before litigation. Attempt to look at the matter objectively, without emotion. It is strictly a matter of dollars and cents: what will it cost you to litigate the matter, and what is the likelihood of your success. In determining the cost of your litigation, make sure you add in the cost of business disruption on you and your employees. Think in terms of economics, not emotion.

1. Small Claims Court

Although you can't foreclose on a Mechanics' Lien in Small Claims Court, and the courts can only give a monetary judgment up to $5,000.00, we would suggest that you utilize the Small Claims Court if the amount sought does not greatly exceed $5,000.00.

The Small Claims Court is fast and economical. You can usually be heard within one month and the total cost is approximately $50.00. You should remember that you as a contractor do not make money while you are tied up in court. Therefore, the speed and economy of the Small Claims Court is something that you should seriously consider. Please note that there are some limitations on the use of these courts, such as the number of times you may use them.

Also be aware that if the defendant loses in Small Claims Court, there is an automatic right of appeal. However, even if that appeal is made, that appeal can usually be heard within two months. Those judgments are as binding as the judgment of any court.

2. Arbitration

Another means of settling disputes is through arbitration. Arbitration has a number of pluses and minuses. First of all, you will usually have someone deciding your dispute who presumably has some expertise in construction. It could be a contractor, an architect, or an attorney with some familiarity in construction law.

Secondly, arbitration is less formal than court action. You may not be allowed discovery, and therefore, it is typically less expensive than going to court. In fact, in arbitration you may wish to represent yourself (which a corporation cannot do in the court systems other than Small Claims Court). However, we do not believe that it is a good idea for you to represent yourself in any case of any magnitude at all. Whether or not you use an attorney, arbitration is usually quicker, less expensive, and is as binding as going to court. One of the drawbacks to arbitration is that it is virtually non-appealable. Due to its more informal nature, some of the protections that you have in the court system are not present in arbitration. One of these protections is a lack of control over what may be presented. When this lack of control is considered along with it's non-appealability, arbitration becomes risky. Arbitrators tend to allow much more evidence to be presented than in a formal court setting and if a judge were to make a mistake, that mistake may be appealable. This is not true in arbitration.

Third, you have no absolute right to "discovery" in arbitration. In the court system, you are entitled to "discover" what the other side contends that you did or didn't do in order to prepare for trial. This is not always the case in arbitration. There may be surprises in arbitration that would not be present in court.

3. Using the Court System

You may always use the court system for Mechanics' Lien and Stop Notice purposes. However, assuming that you have not protected those rights, or you wish to use the court system for other types of litigation as well as your Mechanics' Lien and Stop Notice rights, you should be aware that a contractor, like any other business person, is entitled to enforce his or her agreement. Typically, the means of enforcing those agreements is through the court system. You may file suit in Municipal Court for any amount up to $25,000.00. Anything over that amount is filed in Superior Court. If your customer does not pay when money is due, or in any other way breaches your agreement, you can have that suit resolved in the court system. The use of the courts is a technical matter that should be discussed with your attorney.

XII. MECHANICS' LIENS, STOP NOTICES AND BONDS

A. Introduction

In order for you to understand the procedures for enforcing Mechanics' Liens and Stop Notices, you should become familiar with the two concepts.

Unlike other business people, those who improve property have a preferred status. If you do everything properly, you are entitled to a lien on the property that you improve. A Mechanics' Lien is a lien on real estate as security for your being paid. A Stop Notice, in essence, is a lien on funds being held for construction, as security for you being paid.

Due to the nature of a Mechanics' Lien and Stop Notice, an owner may be forced to pay twice for the same work. **At the present time, a bill is before the Legislature, which would, on certain small residential projects, decide that the owner does not have to pay twice if the owner paid the contractor in good faith and the contractor did not pay its subcontractors and material suppliers. Various trade associations are vigorously fighting this legislation arguing that it is a violation of Contractors' Constitutional *Mechanics' Lien* rights.** Because of this you are required to follow the procedure rather carefully in order to protect your rights.

At the outset you should remember that a Mechanics' Lien is only one device for collection. There are other ways to collect. You may go to arbitration, file suit in Superior Court, or even in the Small Claims Court. However, only the Mechanics' Lien and Stop Notice will secure payment to one who does not have a direct contract with the owner through the owner's property.

Secondly, prime contractors should understand that Mechanics' Liens and Stop Notices are of greater benefit to other improvers of property. A person with a direct contract with the owner can sue the owner directly. Further, that person may be able to attach any of the owner's property (including the property that has been improved) without Mechanics' Lien rights. However, those people who are not in direct contract with the owner (subcontractors, material suppliers, laborers, etc.) cannot secure their rights through a remedy of attachment on any of the owner's property. Except for Mechanics' Lien and Stop Notice actions their only rights are against the person or entity that contracted with them.

B. What is a Mechanics' Lien

An owner has the right to expect that a project be completed in accordance with the contract. This means in accordance with the plans and specifications as well as other things in the contract such as schedule etc. The contractor or subcontractor is entitled to expect that payment is to be made when due. Unless the contractor agrees, the contractor is not "financing" the project. If the owner fails to meet the contractual commitments, the contractor will be put in a cash bind that could jeopardize this particular project as well as others. If the general contractor fails to pay his subcontractors or suppliers after being paid by the owner, the owner may be forced to pay twice. Because of the harshness of this remedy, people are required to strictly adhere to the Mechanics' Lien statutes.

C. Mechanics' Lien in Constitution

In 1879 the drafters of our State Constitution determined that certain people should be given protected status for the payment of monies due to the improvement of properties. Since that time, various statutes and court decisions have re-defined or fine-tuned the legal process used to enforce those Mechanics' Liens. However, it is important to note that Mechanics' Liens are in the State's Constitution and it would take a Constitutional Amendment rather than mere legislation to do away with Mechanics' Liens.

Mechanics' Lien statutes give lien claimants rights and special status that other people normally do not have. Because these laws could create severe problems for an owner who in good faith may have paid his general contractor and would be required to again pay a subcontractor, one must comply strictly with the Mechanics' Lien statutes. Built into the Mechanics' Lien statutes are certain rights for the protection of the owner. Those rights include the Preliminary 20 Day Notice, which will acquaint the owner with some of the persons who have lien rights to the property. Also with swimming pool and home improvement contracts, the owner is entitled to a document entitled "Notice to Owner" which explains the lien laws.

The owner may also require a performance and payment bond which when filed with the contract, limits the liability of the owner. The owner may also reduce his liability by requiring the use of a joint control company to monitor progress and disbursements.

D. The Nuts and Bolts of Mechanics' Liens

1. Prior to Entering Into a Contract

Get as much information as you can. At the time that you are negotiating a contract, there is a honeymoon between you and your client. At this time it is rather easy to obtain the information that you might require should you get involved in a dispute. This is the time to get it. Although you can get this information at any time, it may be much more costly after a dispute arises. Therefore, at contract negotiation time, I would suggest that you get the name of anyone who has any interest in the project, such as the owner (is it a corporation, a partnership, a husband and wife?). Get the name of any lender that has an interest in the property. Is there a construction lender? Is there a performance and payment bond? Get the address and legal description of the property. Obtain the home and business address of the owner as well as your customer. A good contract will have space for you to fill in all of that information.

2. Determine Your Status

Although this may seem to be rather elementary, your status will determine what is required to perfect your Mechanics' Lien. The law is somewhat confusing in this regard in using the term "original contractor". What you should determine is whether you are a prime contractor (one who has a direct contract with the owner) or a subcontractor (one who does not have a direct contract with the owner but a direct contract with another contractor be it prime contractor or subcontractor). Do not confuse the fact that you may be a specialty contractor (plumber, electrician, air conditioning, etc.) with whether you are a prime contractor. That is to say that if the owner is contracting for the plumbing directly with the plumbing contractor, that plumbing contractor is a prime contractor.

There has been some question as to whether a specialty contractor dealing with an owner-builder must give a Preliminary Notice. We feel that you should give the notice.

3. Who Can Record A Mechanics' Lien

The list of people who may claim liens is provided by the Constitution as well as the California Civil Code. The following people can record Mechanics' Liens: Mechanics, material men, contractors, subcontractors, lessors of equipment, artisans, architects, registered engineers, licensed land surveyors, machinists, builders, teamsters and dray men, and all persons and laborers performing labor or bestowing skill or other necessary services, or furnishing materials, or leasing the equipment to be used or consumed in, or furnishing appliances, teams, or power contributing to a work of improvement. Remember that these people do not have to have a direct contract with the owner. However, they must have a contract or have agreed to provide labor, materials for a person who has a contract with either the original contractor or a subcontractor below that general contractor. In addition, claimants can also be persons who have agreed to provide materials for someone who is an agent of the owner, such as the architect or construction manager. Therefore, anyone who has a contract with any of those people, has a right to a Mechanics' Lien. That is to say that a material supplier of a subcontractor has Mechanics' Lien rights. However, a supplier to a material supplier has no such Mechanics' Lien rights since the material supplier is not an agent of the owner.

Since the passage of the federal Employment and Retirement Income Securities Act ("ERISA"), there is a legal question as to whether express trust funds are entitled to Mechanics' Lien rights. The Legislature in 1999 modified the term "laborer" as defined in the Civil Code, and the preliminary notice statutes, in an attempt to allow express trust funds to assert Mechanics' Lien and bond rights for unpaid fringe benefits which are part of the laborer's overall compensation. While it is unknown at this time if that change will be held to be constitutional, there are changes to the preliminary notice statutes intended to give unpaid express trust funds Mechanics' Lien and bond rights. Whether that conflicts with federal law is unknown at this time.

Even if you fall within the above categories, your work and/or materials must be incorporated into the structure. A material supplier who does no more than drop lumber, has no Mechanics' Lien rights if the lumber is not installed. The material supplier has only contractual rights. Therefore, a material supplier must prove that the materials were actually installed in the work of improvement in order to be protected by lien rights.

Due to the fact that this book is written for the benefit of contractors and subcontractors, there will be no further discussion of laborers and/or material suppliers.

4. Stop Notices

As stated in the introduction, a Mechanics' Lien is a lien on property to secure payment for improvements made. A Stop Notice is a lien on funds to secure payment for the same work. The two remedies are not exclusive.

It should be remembered that in some instances a Stop Notice is the favored remedy. For example on public works, governmental entities will not allow you to file a lien on their property and sell it. They allow only Stop Notice rights. Therefore, that remedy is exclusive. For Federal projects Miller Act Bonds are your protection.

Additionally, if the property is over encumbered (there is more owed on the property including construction loans than the property is worth) a Stop Notice may be the preferred remedy. That may be the only way that you may satisfy your judgment.

E. Preliminary Notice

A Preliminary Notice is intended to notify an owner, lender and contractor that someone has a right to enforce a Mechanics' Lien or Stop Notice. It is intended to allow the owner to protect himself or herself from the harsh Mechanics' Lien remedy.

1. When Must a Preliminary Notice be Given

The law states that a Preliminary Notice must be given within twenty (20) days from first furnishing labor or materials. It is our suggestion that if you are required to give a Preliminary Notice, that you give the Preliminary Notice as soon as you enter into an agreement. This way there is less chance of your failing to give that notice. It should be remembered that there is no penalty for giving the notice early. As soon as you are under contract, you should give that notice.

If in fact you fail to give the notice within twenty (20) days from the time that you first begin work or furnish material, and you are still working on the job, you should still give that twenty (20) day notice. However, your lien rights are limited and will not extend to work or materials furnished anytime prior to the twenty (20) days prior to the service of the notice. If you are making more than one delivery under a single contract, only one Preliminary Notice is required. However, if there is more than one contract with more than one contractor, then you must give a Preliminary Notice as to each such subcontract.

2. Who Must Give the Preliminary Notice

It should be remembered that the theory behind the Preliminary Notice is to put the owner or lender on notice that certain people have Mechanics' Lien or Stop Notice rights with respect to the particular project. Therefore, the prime contractor need not give the Preliminary Notice. However, all others furnishing labor, services, equipment or materials for which a lien otherwise could be claimed, or Stop Notice given, must serve a Preliminary Notice on the owner. Therefore, the subcontractors and material suppliers or equipment suppliers must give the Preliminary Notice in order to enforce their Stop Notice or Mechanics' Lien rights. Specialty contractors doing business with an owner-builder should also give the Preliminary Notice (on California public works of improvement, the first tier subcontractor need not give a Preliminary Notice).

A major exception to this theory is that the people performing actual labor for wages, as well as express trust funds as described in the statutes (to the extent that they have lien rights - see explanation in chapter XII D 3), need not give the Preliminary Notice.

3. To Whom is the Preliminary Notice Given

The law requires you to give the Preliminary Notice to the owner, or reputed owner, the original contractor (that is the prime contractor), or reputed contractor, and the construction lender or reputed construction lender. However, if you believe or even suspect that someone has an interest in that property, we would suggest that you send the Preliminary Notice to that person. This is cheap insurance so that they do not later come back and state that they did not have notice of your entitlement. If there is a payment bond on the job, you should also send a copy of the notice to the bonding company.

4. How the Preliminary Notice Must Be Served

The Preliminary Notice may be served by delivering the notice personally or by leaving it at the address of residence or place of business with some person in charge. Or you may use first class registered or certified mail (return receipt requested), postage prepaid, addressed to the person to whom notice is to be given at the place of business or residence or at the address shown by the building permit.

If the person to be served resides outside the state, you may use any of the above methods. Recent legislation now allows those people required to give the Preliminary Notice to file the notice with the County Recorder. The Recorder will then notify those people filing the notice when a Notice of Completion or a Notice of Cessation of labor is recorded. Either of these notices serve to reduce the time within which you are able to record your lien (for that time period, please see below).

You may prove that you served the Preliminary Notice by an affidavit accompanied either by return receipt of certified or registered mail, or by a photocopy of a record of delivery and receipt maintained by the post office. This would show the date of delivery and to whom delivered. In the event of non-delivery, such as the person to whom it was sent refusing the delivery, you may prove service of the Preliminary Notice by the returned envelope itself.

After serving the Preliminary Notice you must prepare an affidavit of the person making that service showing the time, place and manner of service and the facts showing that the service was made in accordance with the service requirements indicated above.

5. Contents of the Preliminary Notice

The Preliminary Notice must have a general description of the items purchased (labor, services, equipment, or materials) and an estimate of the total price of the work or items furnished. In addition, your name and address should appear, the name of the person who contracted with you, a description of the job site sufficient for identification and a lengthy "Notice To Property Owner." The "Notice To Property Owner" should not be confused with the "Notice To Owner." The "Notice To Property Owner" is set out in full in the statute and must be complied with meticulously. If the person giving the Notice is required to pay into an express trust fund, then the Notice must give the name and address of the trust fund.

Based upon changes to the Preliminary Notice statute, as of January 1, 2000, at the time a subcontractor serves a Preliminary Notice, if there are unpaid wages due a laborer, including express trust funds, in accordance with the latest amendment of the law, the subcontractor must identify in the Preliminary Notice the identity and address of any laborer and express trust fund to whom employer payments are due.

Further, the contractor or subcontractor who owes unpaid wages to a laborer or owes fringe benefit or other payments to an express trust fund is required to give, not later than the date the wages became delinquent, a written notice to the laborers, their bargaining representatives, if any, and to the construction lender (or reputed construction lender), if any, that contains the name of the owner and contractor, a description of the jobsite sufficient for identification, the identity and address of any express trust fund to which employer payments are due, the total number of straight time and overtime hours on each job, and the amount then past due and owing.

Many construction trade associations or other construction printers have a form California Preliminary Notice, that may be utilized.

6. Summary

In essence, if you have any question as to whether you should or should not give the Preliminary Notice, we suggest that you do it. We suggest that this be done as a matter of course in every contract that you enter into at the time that you enter into the contract. This way there is less likelihood that you will forget to give the Preliminary Notice. Further, if there is any question as to whom you should send the Preliminary Notice to, give it to everyone as it is cheap insurance to make sure that you protect your lien and Stop Notice rights.

F. The Mechanics' Lien Itself

As we stated in the introduction, the Mechanics' Lien is a right given to those people who improve property and is granted by the Constitution of California. Therefore, mere legislation is not enough to do away with Mechanics' Lien rights. Further, if you have done all of the things necessary to perfect your lien (such as obtaining all the names of the owners, serving your Preliminary Notices etc.) you will be able to protect your payment and secure it, by means of the lien.

1. Who is Entitled To A Mechanics' Lien

Anyone who performs labor, skill or services, or furnishes material, equipment etc. to be used in a work of improvement, is entitled to claim a lien. The persons that are specifically named in the Constitution as well as the Civil Code are:

Mechanics, material men, contractors, sub-contractors, lessors of equipment, artisans, architects, registered engineers, licensed land surveyors, machinists, builders, teamsters and dray men, and all persons and laborers performing labor or bestowing skill or other necessary services, or furnishing materials or leasing equipment to be used, or consumed in/or furnishing appliances, teams, or power and contributing to a work of improvement.

Of course, anyone with a direct contract with the owner has a right to a Mechanics' Lien. However, the people mentioned above do not necessarily have to have a direct contract with the owner. They might have a contract with the agent of the owner and every contractor, subcontractor, architect, builder, or other person having charge of a work of improvement is held to be the agent of the owner. Since material suppliers are not those who may have "charge of a work of improvement," the supplier of a material supplier has no Mechanics' Lien rights. However, the material supplier of a subcontractor does have Mechanics' Lien rights.

Since the passage of the Employment and Retirement Income Securities Act there is a legal question as to whether trust funds are entitled to Mechanics' Lien rights.

It is also important to note that the work performed, materials, etc. supplied must have actually been used or consumed in the work of improvement. This means that a supplier who merely supplies items which are not incorporated into the structure, has no lien rights. However, the supplier may have contractual rights against the contractor for whom he furnished the material.

2. Where Must the Mechanics' Lien be Recorded

Since Mechanics' Liens deal with real property, a Mechanics' Lien must be recorded in the county where the construction occurs. It must be taken for recordation to the County Recorder's office in the county where construction (work of improvement) took place.

3. When Must the Mechanics' Lien be Recorded

Remember that a Mechanics' Lien is recorded with the County Recorder of the county where the property is located. When the Mechanics' Lien is to be recorded depends on a number of factors. One of the factors is the concept of "completion." This concept will be discussed further on.

Another factor deals with whether you are an original contractor or a subcontractor. Remember that the original contractor is one with a direct contract with the owner. A subcontractor is one who does not have a direct contract with the owner, but is dealing through an original contractor, or another subcontractor. The Mechanics' Lien laws make no distinction between a specialty or general contractor, only between prime and subcontractors.

a. Original Contractor

If you are an original contractor (prime contractor) you must record the Mechanics' Lien within ninety (90) days after completion of the work of improvement.

If the owner records a valid Notice of Completion, or a valid Notice of Cessation of Labor, then the original contractor has only 60 days after that recordation within which to record the Mechanics' Lien.

b. Other Mechanics' Lien Claimants

If you are not the original contractor, you must record your Mechanics' Lien within ninety (90) days after completion of the work of improvement, unless a Notice of Completion or a Notice of Cessation has been recorded. At this juncture it is important for you to understand that the time starts to run from the completion of the "work of improvement" and not from the completion of your work. You can record a Mechanics' Lien anytime you determine that you are entitled to be paid for your work but no later than the statutory time period. And that time period does not start to run until the entire work of improvement is completed. Therefore, one who does preliminary work on the site, such as a grading subcontractor, may have a substantial period of time within which to record a Mechanics' Lien whereas a finish carpenter or painter may have much less time since the work of improvement will not be completed until the finish work is completed.

If the owner records a valid Notice of Completion or Notice of Cessation, then the Mechanics' Lien must be recorded within thirty (30) days if you are not the original contractor.

c. What is Completion

The law states that completion means when the work is actually completed. This doesn't give much help. However, the law further states that occupation or use by the owner or his agent accompanied by a cessation of labor is equivalent to completion. Also, the acceptance of the owner or his agent, or cessation of labor for a continuous period of sixty (60) days would be the equivalent of completion. With respect to public works, the acceptance by the public entity is deemed completion. This is important for stop notice rights which will be discussed later.

Determination of the date of completion is a matter of fact and will be decided on a case by case basis. Typically actual completion consists of full performance of the contract. However, subsequent minor changes, or correction of defective work or repairs may be considered warranty work and not part of the original scope.

As you can see, it is not easy to define completion. It is also hard to distinguish between warranty work and completion work under the original contract. If you do any work of any substance that is not warranty work, chances are that it will be deemed work to complete the original agreement.

d. Notice of Completion

The owner can shorten the time within which a Mechanics' Lien can be recorded by recording a Notice of Completion. The Notice of Completion shortens the time limit for filing Mechanics' Liens and Stop Notices to sixty (60) days for the prime contractor and thirty (30) days for all the others. The Notice of Completion is a document that is signed and verified by the owner or his agent. The notice must contain the date of completion, the name and address of the owner, the nature of the owner's interest, and a description of the job site sufficient for identification. It should also contain the name of the original contractor and the kind of work done or material furnished. It must be recorded in the office of the County Recorder in the county where the site is located. It must be recorded within ten (10) days after completion. If it is recorded more than ten (10) days after completion, then the Notice of Completion is defective.

e. Notice of Cessation of Labor

Like a Notice of Completion, a Notice of Cessation serves to shorten the time period within which one can record a Mechanics' Lien. The Notice of Cessation is signed and verified by the owner or his agent verifying that the work has ceased. It must contain the following: the date when labor ceased, a statement indicating that labor has not again begun, the name and address of the owner, the nature of the interest of the owner, and the description of the site. It must also be recorded in the office of the County Recorder in the county where the site is located. It must also contain the name of the original contractor and is only effective after labor has ceased for thirty (30) days.

4. Contents of The Mechanics' Lien

Remember that the Mechanics' Lien just puts people on notice that you have a claim to the piece of property that you have improved. The following are the items that must be included:

(a) The amount demanded (the amount that is owed to you after all credits, set-offs etc.). If the amount is a good faith demand, the exact accurateness will not invalidate the lien. However, an excessive lien, (one that is not filed in good faith), will invalidate the lien;

(b) The name of the owner or reputed owner. (If you have done your homework, you will know this from the time you initiated the contract. However, if you have not done your homework, you might check with a title insurance company);

(c) A general statement of the labor, services, equipment, etc. furnished;

(d) The name of the person who employed you or to whom you furnished the items above;

(e) A description of the property sufficient for identification. This is very important since it will not bind the property if it is not described specifically;

(f) A claim of lien must be signed and verified by the claimant.

G. What to do After Recording a Mechanics' Lien

Many contractors believe that once they have "liened" the property, they are fully protected. That is not true. The lien indicates to all concerned, that the contractor claims an interest in that property. However, the lien becomes totally ineffective at the end of ninety (90) days. That is, ninety-one (91) days after the lien is recorded it means nothing unless a lawsuit is filed to foreclose that Mechanics' Lien. Therefore, within ninety (90) days you must file suit to foreclose that lien and at the same time record a "Lis Pendens." The Lis Pendens is recorded on the property telling people that there is litigation pending over that property.

Although you may be able to handle your own arbitration, file or record your own Mechanics' Lien, send out your Preliminary Notice, we do not believe it is wise for you to handle your own litigation. Instead, we suggest that you contact an attorney knowledgeable in construction and Mechanics' Liens well in advance of the ninety (90) days, so that the lawsuit may be filed.

The lawsuit must name everyone who has an interest in the property. Therefore, the information that you obtained during the negotiating process is extremely important at this time. Further, due to the time limitations in filing suit, you should give your attorney sufficient time to draft a good complaint.

1. Extension of Credit

What if the owner and you agree that there is a specific sum of money due you, but the owner needs an additional loan or an additional source of financing for the project? In essence, there is no dispute. The owner just cannot pay on time. However, the law requires you to file suit within a specific time. In this instance, you may enter into an agreement called an Extension of Credit. You may extend credit up to one (1) year. You must record a document named a Notice of Extension of Credit. This will protect your Mechanics' Lien rights. We never suggest that you extend credit for the full period of time. We suggest that credit be extended for shorter periods of time. Remember, you can always extend credit again if need be. However, you can never extend credit for a period in excess of one (1) year in total.

2. Who Should Be Named as Defendants in the Mechanics' Lien Complaint

Remember that a Mechanics' Lien complaint seeks to sell the property so that you may be paid for your improvement of the property. Therefore, you should name everyone who has an interest in the property. If you don't name those people, you will not be able to have their interest in the property sold. Therefore, you should name all of the owners, lenders, and anyone else who has an interest.

H. Lien Rights

Many people, including attorneys and sometimes judges, confuse the difference between the mechanics' lien and the right to a mechanics' lien.

The California Constitution grants a contractor, material man, and even a laborer the right to place a lien on a person's property to assure payment for the materials or services provided to that property. This right is not exclusive to construction, or even real property. These same rights are granted to persons such as auto mechanics and television repairmen. There has been some question whether express trust funds are entitled to claim Mechanics' Lien rights. There have been some cases which have stated that the federal ERISA laws prohibits liens by express trust funds. However, the Legislature recently redefined the term laborer, and has amended the Preliminary Notice law in an effort to allow express trust funds to claim lien rights which some courts had previously held they did not have. The Legislature's intent is to protect the entire compensation of laborers on a work of improvement, regardless of the form in which the compensation is to be paid. It is unknown how the courts may deal with claims by express trust funds in the future.

These lien rights, as discussed in other sections of this book, may be lost if certain procedures (such as the serving of a preliminary notice) are not followed. They are also lost when they are waived. A waiver is the voluntary giving up of a known right. The mechanism for enforcing or waiving these rights is discussed in this chapter.

I. Lien Releases - Waiver of Lien Rights

The subject of lien releases is one that comes up in conversations all the time. Indeed, the statute that created those lien releases (Civil Code section 3262) has been the subject of much litigation. Recently the section was discussed in the case that we argued to the Supreme Court dealing with the "pay if paid" clause, as well as in a later case that dealt with the "pay when paid" clause in public works.

A substantial part of the litigation in an important case called Halbert's Lumber was the lien release issue. The Halbert's Lumber case which is discussed below established the latest nuance in the lien release forms. A little history may be in order.

The statutory forms for releases were established by the Legislature to protect contractor's lien rights from unknowing waivers. Many years ago, a gentleman by the name of Bentz, gave his customer an Unconditional Lien Release. However, Bentz was not paid. When Bentz's customer's promise of payment turned out to be nothing, Bentz filed suit to foreclose on a Mechanics Lien. The owner filed a motion which essentially stated that even if all the facts in your motion are correct, you can't collect as a matter of law. In that case, the owner was saying that even if Bentz were otherwise entitled to a Mechanics Lien, Bentz could not enforce his lien because he had given an Unconditional Lien Release.

On appeal, the court stated that the constitutionally protected right to a Mechanics Lien could not be waived that easily. Therefore, the court held that the Mechanics Lien Release was not proper so long as Bentz was not paid.

This resulted in havoc in the construction industry. This was because the Bentz decision effectively turned all lien releases into Conditional Lien Releases rather than Unconditional Lien Releases. The only way that one could be sure that the Lien Release was valid was to make sure of payment. Therefore, the construction industry started to write joint payee checks with a substantial number of joint payees on the check. The law with respect to joint payee checks (at least with respect to mechanic's liens), is that once someone endorses a check, the maker of the check can assume that each endorser receives 100% of the amount of the check, whether that person actually received the money or not. Therefore, the maker of the check could write a check in favor of the prime contractor, subcontractor, and material supplier, and assume that each of them received 100% of the amount of the check for purposes of mechanic's liens.

Because of this chaos, the construction industry got together with the Legislature and drafted a change to Civil Code section 3262. That section now sets out the only way that one can release mechanic's lien rights. It sets out four different lien releases. Two are Conditional Lien Releases (on final and on progress payment) and two are Unconditional Lien Releases (on progress and on final payment). What that contemplated is that the owner would pay the prime contractor who would then hand over Conditional Lien Releases upon progress payment from his subcontractors. A condition is something that must happen before something else becomes legally effective. In this case, the condition is payment. Unless payment is made to the person giving the conditional release, the release is not effective. The Conditional Lien Release in effect states that upon payment of the sum shown in that lien release, the lien release would become unconditional. The only condition to the effectiveness of the lien releases contemplated by Civil Code section 3262 is payment. Therefore the Lien Release essentially says that before you rely on this release, make sure that I have been paid the amount shown in the lien release. In essence, on the first draw, the owner gets a Conditional Lien Release from the subcontractor for an amount. After payment of the first draw, it was contemplated that the owner would then get an Unconditional Lien Release for the first draw and a Conditional Lien Release for the second draw. This would go on until final payment. The only condition would be the payment.

There is another very important concept that people should keep in mind when dealing with lien releases. This is the problem with timing and dates on the Releases. The Conditional Lien Release has a date through which it is effective. That is to say that the Conditional Lien Release says "I release my lien conditionally through (a particular date)." What if there is a conflict between the date and the amount?

This was just the case in Halbert's Lumber, where Halbert had some glue-lam beams drop-shipped to the owner. At the time that

Halbert's prepared the Conditional Release upon Progress Payment, Halbert's was not aware of the glue-lam beams and therefore the amount was not included in the lien release. However, the lien release released Halbert's lien rights through and beyond the date of the drop shipment. This created a conflict between the amount (which did not include the glue-lam beams) and the period of time in which Halbert's was releasing its lien (which included the time of the drop shipment of the glue-lam beams). The court held that if there is a conflict, the time was the determinative factor. Here, Halbert's Lumber was determined to have released its lien rights to the glue-lam beams.

Therefore, if you are issuing Lien Releases through a particular date, make sure that all of your accounting information is recorded so that if the owner writes a joint check, or makes a payment in accordance with your lien release, all of the items to which you may have lien rights have been included in the sum that you are requesting.

You do not have to worry about retention or change orders that have not yet been documented. Those are specifically excluded in lien release forms contemplated by the statute. However, any items that are not change orders or retention will be included and released if you are paid the sum that is shown on your lien release.

A detailed look at the lien release process follows:

There are two categories of waivers of these lien rights that are specified by state law. The differences between these categories depend upon whether a contractor or other person entitled to the lien is waiving the lien right **before or after** a mechanics' lien has been recorded.

1. Release Of Lien Rights Prior To Recording A Mechanics' Lien

   Prior to recording a mechanics' lien, the details of which are discussed in greater detail in chapter XI of this book, the usual reason that a release of lien rights will be given to a property owner is that payment has been made.

   Prior to the recording of a mechanics' lien, there are four types of Releases of Lien Rights specified by law. Two are conditional releases, two are unconditional releases. Conditional means that the release is conditioned upon something else happening, usually the endorsement of a check and payment into the contractor's bank account. The four types, with their purpose are:

a. Conditional Waiver and Release Upon Progress Payment

This document only releases or waives the lien rights of a contractor or material man through the stated date on the document. **<u>The contractor must be careful that all materials and labor are included in the amounts charged, as the law enforces this waiver strictly, even for claims that are not known to the contractor</u>**. If you suspect such a problem you should state so in the release. This release is subject to the payment being endorsed and clearing the contractor's (or material man's) bank account. The release allows the contractor to retain all rights to any agreed upon retention, and for extras installed prior to the release date which are unpaid.

The contractor also retains certain legal rights that he has under the law, including the right to defend against the contract, or to seek to have it legally canceled.

b. Unconditional Waiver and Release Upon Progress Payment

This document also only releases or waives the lien rights of a contractor or material man through the stated date on the document. **<u>The contractor must be careful that all materials and labor are included in the amounts charged, as the law enforces this waiver strictly, even for claims that are not known to the contractor</u>**. If you suspect such a problem you should state that in the release. This release is **<u>not</u>** subject to the payment being endorsed and clearing the contractor's (or material man's) bank account. The release allows the contractor to retain all rights to any agreed upon retention, and for extras installed prior to the release date which are unpaid.

The contractor also retains certain legal rights that he has under the law, including the right to defend against the contract, or to seek to have it legally canceled.

c. Conditional Waiver and Release Upon Final Payment

This document is used for the final payment to be received by the contractor or material man, and releases or waives all lien rights on the property, **except** for claims specifically stated to exist due to a dispute over additional work. This release **is still** subject to the payment being endorsed and clearing the contractor's (or material man's) bank account. This release does not contain the language retaining legal contract rights to the contractor because it asserts that final payment has been received.

d. Unconditional Waiver and Release Upon Final Payment

This document is used for the final payment to be received by the contractor or material man, and releases or waives all lien rights on the property, **except** for claims specifically stated to exist due to a dispute over additional work. This release is **not** subject to the payment being endorsed and clearing the contractor's (or material man's) bank account. This release does not contain the language retaining legal contract rights to the contractor because it asserts that final payment has been received.

Obviously, if final payment is received without any dispute over payments for extras or other work, our discussion ends here. No mechanics' lien will be filed, and the contractor will go on to his or her next project. However, as stated in chapter XI of this book, in the event the contractor is not paid for all or part of its work, the contractor may record a mechanics' lien in the county where the work is being done, to enforce its mechanics' lien rights. **Remember a mechanics' lien is worthless in ninety days if a lawsuit to foreclose upon it is not filed.**

2. Release Of Mechanics' Lien That Has Been Recorded

As stated in the introduction to this chapter, the mechanics' lien is a simple mechanism for enforcing mechanics' lien rights. What gets confusing to some is that the lien itself may be lost, even if the right to the lien still exists. The difference is that the contractor is still entitled to be paid, but cannot rely upon the lien for enforcement against the property.

The distinction between the mechanics' lien as a tool and the mechanics' lien as a right was demonstrated in a recent court case. A mechanics' lien was recorded on the property, but not foreclosed upon, making it stale. Before the project was completed, another mechanics' lien was filed on the project. The first lien was released by the contractor voluntarily because it was stale. The contractor then sued to foreclose upon the second lien. This is permissible. The release of the mechanics' lien already recorded was not a waiver of the contractor's lien rights. So long as the second lien was properly and timely recorded (and in this case it was), the contractor did not waive any lien rights. One important difference on the lien release that was provided in this case was that the release only declared that the Mechanics' Lien that was previously recorded was "released". It did not say that the lien had been "fully satisfied" or that the claim had been "paid in full." The result may have been different if such language had been in the original lien release.

3. Priority Of A Mechanics' Lien

Usually, liens are a cloud on title to a property. All valid mechanics' liens have priority based on <u>when</u> work first started on the project. That means, first in time is first in right. Real estate loans have come to be called "first," "second," or "third" trust deeds, based on when a trust deed is recorded. Mechanics' liens are somewhat different.

As stated above, a mechanics' lien relates back to the date the first work commenced. For example: homeowner hires contractor to remodel the kitchen. Contractor begins work on January 3, 1995. On March 5, 1995, homeowner obtains a loan on the property from a lender. In June, contractor being unpaid, records a mechanics' lien. The lien is effective on the date work started, i.e., January 3, 1995, and has priority over the mortgage rights of the lender that were established March 5, 1995.

4. Stale Liens

Once a mechanics' lien has been properly recorded with the County Recorder in the county in which the property is situated, it becomes a cloud on the property's title. It continues to burden the property even if it the property is sold to a third party. If not removed, it could cause the loss of a potential sale, and prevent the owner from obtaining a mortgage on the property.

As stated throughout this book, if a lawsuit is not filed to foreclose upon the lien, it becomes unenforceable. Likewise, if a mechanics' lien is for an overstated value, or if a preliminary notice (when required) was not served, the lien is unenforceable. Despite its unenforceability, the stale lien may remain a cloud on the title of the property. There are methods for removing a stale lien, including making a motion to a court for an Order to have the lien removed. Such motions are uniformly granted.

Also, even though stale liens appear on title, many title companies will not raise a fuss over a lien that is more than one year old but which has not been foreclosed upon.

5. Mechanics' Liens May Be Bonded Around

In the event that a mechanics' lien is clouding title, a bond called a "Mechanics' Lien Release Bond" may be purchased in an amount that is one and one half times the lien amount. These bonds are expensive, as they must be collateralized (this usually means that the contractor or homeowner has to secure the bond with collateral such as other cash or property.) It is sometimes difficult for the smaller contractor to obtain these bonds due to the collateral requirements of most bonding companies. The lien claimant then must sue on the bond, and not the lien. The property is no longer at issue in the case.

6. Voluntary Release Of Mechanics' Lien

A contractor may release a mechanics' lien in a manner similar to the way it is recorded - by filing a document with the County Recorder. Procedurally, the principal differences between the two are that a mechanics' lien is "verified" under penalty of perjury, declaring that the amount is due and owing for labor or materials furnished to the property. The mechanics' lien does not need to be notarized. However, a Release of Mechanics' Lien contains no "verification" but it must be notarized. Such notarization is done by a notary public, and these can be found easily, including at many banks and escrow companies.

J. The Stop Notice

1. Introduction

As stated earlier, a Mechanics' Lien is a lien on property. A Stop Notice is a lien on funds. In some instances only the Stop Notice can be used. In public works projects, the public entity will not allow you to sell its property. You are only entitled to have it withhold funds. In essence the Stop Notice tells the person who is holding construction funds not to pay those funds to the person who might otherwise be entitled, due to the fact that you are owed money.

In private works projects, you may record a Mechanics' Lien and also pursue Stop Notice remedies. Most of the discussion dealing with Mechanics' Liens will apply equally to Stop Notices. That is to say Preliminary Notices etc. are required. However, in public works projects, a subcontractor to an original contractor is not required to give a Preliminary Notice. All other subcontractors or material suppliers must provide the notice to preserve their Stop Notice right.

2. Who is Entitled to Enforce a Stop Notice

Anyone other than the original contractor who has Mechanics' Lien rights has the right to serve a Stop Notice. An original contractor can also serve Stop Notices on a lender but not an owner.

3. Time Limitation

A Stop Notice must be served before the expiration of thirty (30) days after the recording of the Notice of Completion or Notice of Acceptance by the public entity, or Notice of Cessation. If no such notice is recorded, then service must be within ninety (90) days after completion. Note these time limits are identical to the Mechanics' Lien time limits. A Notice of Acceptance on public works projects may be issued later than actual completion. This is one difference between public works and private works procedures. The manner of service of a Stop Notice is identical to Mechanics' Lien service both in private works and public works. It may be served by personal service, or by registered or certified mail, return receipt requested. If you are not paid after serving the Stop Notice, you must file suit within ninety (90) days after the end of the time when Mechanics' Liens can be recorded. After filing suit, you must give notice within five (5) days to the public entity that you have done so.

4. Persons to Serve

You should serve your Stop Notice on anyone who is holding construction funds. That could be the owner, a lender, or anyone else holding the funds. If the person holding the funds is a construction lender, a Stop Notice bond must accompany the Stop Notice in order for the Stop Notice to be effective. This is a bond in the sum of 1 1/4 times the amount of the claim. The bond is intended to reimburse anyone who is injured due to a defective Stop Notice.

K. Release Bonds

The discussion above indicated how you could secure payment for your work of improvement on a specific construction project. You may secure payment through real property by way of the Mechanics' Lien procedure. You may secure your payment through cash by way of the Stop Notice rights. Both of these methods should be utilized when they can. However, what happens if there is a good faith dispute between you and either the contractor or the owner regarding the lien or the amount of the lien? The person disputing your Stop Notice or Mechanics' Lien can substitute a bond as your security. This is commonly called "bonding around a Stop Notice" or "bonding around a Mechanics' Lien." What happens, is the person disputing your claim goes to a bonding company and obtains a bond. That bond is a financial guarantee that will, in the event you are successful, pay you the amount of your claim through the bond. In essence, this frees the property that you have tied up (the real property or the construction funds) and substitutes a financial guarantee for that. In this way, construction can proceed or the property can be sold, but you will still be secured.

L. Bond Rights

If there is a Payment Bond on the project, subcontractors and material suppliers can sue on that bond as well. The method is explained in the Bonding chapter and the Public Works Procedure in this chapter.

M. Conclusion

Remember that Mechanics' Lien, Stop Notice and Bond rights are very technical. You should follow the enforcement procedure very carefully. If you have any questions whatsoever, seek the aid and advice of an attorney who is knowledgeable in the area.

Further, you should keep in mind that these procedures are not exclusive. You can sue for other claims, such as contractual damages, etc. You can also sue asking to foreclose on both a Mechanics' Lien and Stop Notice as well as any bond available.

Most of the forms that are discussed in this booklet are available through construction printers, or construction trade associations.

N. Public Works Procedure

The manner in which you can protect yourself for payment for work performed on public property in California is not very different from that of private works. Federal procedure is substantially different however.

Public works is defined as work that is contracted for by a public entity. However, as you can imagine, the State of California will not allow you to sell its property to foreclose on a Mechanics' Lien. Therefore, Mechanics' Lien remedies are not allowed in public works.

In this section we will discuss the procedure for enforcing other remedies on public projects. The first step is to separate them by type of project (State or Federal) since there is a difference between the two.

1. Federal Public Works Remedy

   a. Introduction

   Unlike state public works or a private work of improvement, federal public works are not subject to either Stop Notice or Mechanics' Lien rights. However, there is a payment bond that is intended for the protection of those who supply labor and material to the job. Recent legislation has increased the required amount of the bond to the full contract amount between the government and the general contractor, unless the contracting agency sets forth reasons why it is impractical to require such a large bond. This is the only non-contractual remedy for unpaid claimants (other than the prime contractor) on federal public works. It is known as the Miller Act Bond.

b. Public Work Defined - Federal

Public Work includes any work in which the United States is interested and which is done for the public, and for which the United States is authorized to expend funds. A federal public work includes work on property owned by the United States and works paid for by the United States for public use.

c. Comparison with Mechanics' Lien

The Miller Act only requires that labor and material be furnished and supplied and does not require that it be incorporated in the structure as is required under Mechanics' Lien Law. If the labor and material is furnished in good faith and under the reasonable belief that it is to be used in the work, then the Miller Act comes into effect.

d. Persons covered

The Miller Act protects those people with a direct contractual relationship with the contractor and/or a direct contractual relationship with a subcontractor. A material supplier who supplies material to a material man is not covered. An employee of a sub-subcontractor is not covered.

e. Notice Requirement

The code requires that anyone who is not in a direct contractual relationship with the prime contractor give a written notice to the contractor. That is to say that immediate first-tier subcontractors need not give notice, but their subcontractors or material suppliers must give notice. The form of notice is not spelled out. The statute only seeks to protect the contractor by making it possible for him to withhold monies due to the subcontractor in order to satisfy claims asserted by third persons. A letter informing the prime contractor that the supplier was looking to him for payment is probably sufficient.

f. Time and Service of the Notice

The notice must be served within ninety (90) days after the date you last furnished labor and materials under the contract. It must be served by personal service, or registered mail, addressed to the contractor at any place he or she maintains an office or conducts his or her business, or his or her residence.

g. Filing Suit

Every action on the Miller Act Bond must be brought after ninety (90) days and before one (1) year after the day on which you last performed labor or you supplied material. Attorney fees may be awarded against the surety only if the contract awards attorneys' fees if suit is required.

2. State Public Works

In addition to your contract rights against your customer, under the state public works procedure, you are entitled to both a Stop Notice as well as an action on the bond. However, there is no right to a Mechanics' Lien.

3. Public Work Defined - California

Public works is one contracted for by a public entity.

4. Stop Notice

a. Who is Entitled to Stop Notice Rights

Anyone other than the original contractor who has furnished material or services used in, upon, for or about the performance of the public work is entitled to Stop Notice rights (however, remember that a material supplier's material supplier has no such Stop Notice rights). In order to protect your Stop Notice rights you must give a Preliminary Notice if you are not a first tier subcontractor.

b. Failure to Give Preliminary Notice

As of January 1, 1995, the failure to give the notice on time will not preclude you from asserting Stop Notice rights for the period prior to twenty (20) days prior to your service of the Preliminary Notice.

Make sure to send a copy to the payment bond company as well.

c. Time for Service of Stop Notice

You must file your Stop Notice within thirty (30) days after a Notice of Cessation, or a Notice of Completion, or Notice of Acceptance has been recorded. If no such notice is recorded, then you have ninety (90) days after completion or cessation of labor in which to serve your Stop Notice.

d. Contents of the Stop Notice

The Stop Notice must be addressed to the directing body of the public entity and include your name, address, and capacity, what it was that you furnished, to whom you furnished your labor and materials, the value of that which you furnished, and the value of what you agreed to furnish. You should identify the location of the public work, and your work, also indicate how much you wish withheld. This must be verified (signed under penalty of perjury).

e. Notice of Notice of Completion

Unlike private works, if you pay the governmental entity $2.00 at the time you file your Stop Notice, the governmental entity will have to tell you when a Notice of Completion or Notice of Cessation was recorded.

f. When to File Suit

If you are not paid after serving the Stop Notice, you must file suit within ninety (90) days after the end of the time when Mechanics' Liens can be recorded. After filing suit, you must give notice to the public entity that you have done so within five (5) days.

5. Release of Stop Notice

If the stop notice is disputed the prime contractor can have the stop notice released by the use of a release bond or summary procedure.

A contractor can file with the public entity a corporate surety bond in an amount equal to 125% of the claim of the Stop Notice. If a release bond is filed, the public entity is relieved of any liability resulting from a subcontractor's Stop Notice. This substitutes the surety for the funds withheld. An action by a subcontractor on a Stop Notice release bond must be filed within three years of the day the contractor files the release bond.

If the original contractor disputes the claimant's Stop Notice to have the public entity withhold money from the general contractor, he/she may institute summary proceedings as follows:

a. Serve the public entity with an affidavit stating the reasons why the Stop Notice should be ineffective and demand payment of the funds being withheld.

b. The public entity must then serve the claimant with the affidavit and demand for the release together with a written statement stating that the public entity will release the funds, unless the claimant files a counter-demand not less than ten days and no more than twenty days after service upon the claimant.

c. The claimant can file a counter-affidavit stating his reasons why he is contesting. If the counter affidavit is not served on the public entity within the time allotted, the public entity can release the withheld funds to the original contractor.

d. If the counter affidavit is filed with the proof of service, the claimant or the original contractor may file an action with the superior court. A hearing must be granted by the court within 15 days after the motion is made. This is much quicker than a normal court action. The party who files the action must notify the public entity of the hearing date at least five (5) days before the hearing.

6. Payment Bonds

Many state projects require a payment bond. If a payment bond is required, in order to protect your right to collect on the bond you must serve the original (prime) contractor, and the bonding company, a Bond Notice unless you performed labor for wages or contracted directly with the prime contractor. You do that either by personal delivery, certified or registered mail. The

Notice must be served on the original contractor and bonding company within fifteen (15) days after recordation of a Notice of Completion. If no Notice of Completion is recorded, this time is extended to seventy-five (75) days. If you had timely served the bonding company with the twenty (20) day Preliminary Notice, you do not have to serve this bond notice.

7. Filing Suit on the Payment Bond

You must then file your lawsuit before the expiration of six (6) months after the period in which Stop Notices must be filed. If you will recall, Stop Notices must be filed within thirty (30) days after the recording of a Notice of Completion, Notice of Acceptance, or a Notice of Cessation, or ninety (90) days after the completion of the work of improvement if no notices were recorded.

XIII.
PROMPT PAYMENT LAWS

As a result of the advocacy of subcontractor trade associations with help from prime contractors, California now has a substantial body of law dealing with prompt payment. The statutes deal with retention and progress payments, as well as payments from the owner to the prime and the prime to the subcontractor.

Suppliers of material and services to state or local agencies are also protected by numerous provisions of both the Public Contracts Code as well as the Government Code. Unfortunately, unlike the private works provisions, the provisions dealing with public works are poorly organized and do not accurately demonstrate all of the contractor's rights. In the interests of putting only the information most needed by contractors in this book, the prompt-pay penalties that are listed in the following section are those that affect contractors in California most. In addition to these, the law may provide for other interest payments to the provider of public works goods and services. For example, the supplier or contractor may also be entitled to a penalty of .25% (.0025) percent per day for each day that the payment is late if the contractor is deemed a "small business." A "small business" is one whose annual gross revenues are less than $3,000,000.

A. Prime Contractor

1. Private Works of Improvement

   a. Progress Payments to Prime

   (1) With respect to private works of improvement, the owner must make progress payments to the prime contractor within 30 days after receipt of the request for payment unless this is modified in writing. If the owner does not, the owner is subjected to paying a penalty of 2% per month in lieu of interest. In addition, the prevailing party in litigation will be entitled to attorney's fees. If there is a dispute over the amount of the payment, the owner may withhold up to 150%

of the amount in dispute, so long as the amount is withheld in good faith.

b. Retention Payments to Prime

(1) With respect to retention, the retention must be paid by the owner to the prime contractor within 45 days after a certificate of occupancy or 45 days after a notice of completion depending on when the contract was entered into. Again, if the owner fails to pay, there is a 2% penalty per month. In addition, the prevailing party in litigation will be entitled to attorney's fees. If there is a dispute over the amount of the payment, the owner may withhold up to 150% of the amount in dispute, so long as the amount is withheld in good faith. With respect to retention, unlike progress payments, it is against public policy to waive this portion of the prompt pay statute. Therefore a waiver will probably not be upheld.

c. Progress Payments by Prime

(1) With respect to progress payments, they must be made within 10 days of receipt of the funds by the contractor. Again, this can be modified by a written agreement. There is a 2% per month penalty for failure to comply. The payor can withhold up to 150% of the disputed amount, if the dispute is in good faith. There is a provision allowing attorney's fees to the prevailing party.

d. Retention Payments by Prime

(1) Retention must also be paid within 10 days after receipt from the owner. Again, there is a 2% per month penalty in lieu of interest and the contractor can withhold no more than 150% of the disputed amount, if the dispute is in good faith. There is a provision allowing attorney's fees to the prevailing party. In this situation it is against public policy to waive the retention payments. Therefore, a contract that would waive that law would probably not be upheld.

2. State and Local Agency Public Works of Improvement (Other Than Utilities)

a. Progress Payments to Prime

(1) State (except California State University)

Progress payments must be made by the agency within 30 days of submission of an undisputed pay request. Interest in this case is 10% per year on the unpaid amount.

(2) California State University

Progress payments must be made by CSU within 39 days of submission of an undisputed pay request. Interest in this case is 10% per year on the unpaid amount.

b. Retention Payments to Prime

(1) Retention to the prime contractor must be paid within 60 days after completion, acceptance, recordation of a notice of completion, or, cessation of labor for 100 days due to factors beyond the contractor's control. Again, the owner can withhold only 150% of the disputed amount. On public works projects, the disputed amount need not be "in good faith," as required under private works projects. There need only be a "dispute." It is unknown whether a court would require the dispute to be a "good faith dispute." There is a provision allowing attorney's fees to the prevailing party. If the owner does not pay a valid progress payment request, there is a 2% per month penalty.

c. Progress Payments by Prime

(1) Progress payments must be paid within 10 days after receipt of the progress payment from the owner. In this case there is a 2% per month penalty. The prevailing party is entitled to attorney's fees.

d. Retention Payments by Prime

(1) Retention must be paid within 7 days after receipt and there is a 2% per month penalty. There is a provision allowing attorney's fees to the prevailing party.

B. Subcontractor

1. Private Works of Improvement

   a. Progress Payments to Subcontractor

   (1) With respect to progress payments, they must be made within 10 days of receipt of the funds by the contractor. Again, this can be modified by a written agreement. There is a 2% per month penalty for failure to comply with the section payable to the subcontractor. The payor can withhold up to 150% of the disputed amount. There is a provision allowing attorney's fees to the prevailing party.

   b. Retention Payments to Subcontractor

   (1) Retention must also be paid within 10 days after receipt from the owner. Again, there is a 2% per month penalty payable to the subcontractor. The contractor can withhold no more than 150% of the disputed amount. There is a provision allowing attorney's fees to the prevailing party. In this situation it is against public policy to waive the retention payments. Therefore, a contract that would waive that law would probably not be upheld.

2. State and Local Agency Public Works of Improvement (Other Than Utilities)

   a. Progress Payments to Subcontractor

   (1) Progress payments must be paid within 10 days after receipt of the progress payment from the owner. In this case there is a 2% per month penalty. There is a provision for attorney's fees to the prevailing party.

   b. Retention Payments to Subcontractors

   (1) Retention must be paid within 7 days after receipt and there is a 2% per month penalty. There is a provision allowing attorney's fees to the prevailing party. If there is a dispute, the payor may withhold only 150% of the disputed amount.

3. Payments by Subcontractors

   Progress payments by subcontractors to lower tier subcontractors must be paid within ten (10) days of receipt of funds by the payor. If there is a dispute, the payor can withhold no more than 150% of the disputed amount. A violation of this law subjects the contractor to 2% per month penalty payable to the subcontractor, and attorney's fees. This applies to both public and private works of improvement. On public works the ten (10) day payment period may not be modified by contract, while on private works the parties may agree to different payment terms for progress payments.

XIV.
CONTRACTORS' BOARD'S DISCIPLINE AND DISCIPLINARY STATUTES

A. Changes Since 1998

The most significant change in the laws affecting contractors, with respect to the disciplinary statutes, was the amendment to the Minor Works Exemption which increased and substantially changed what an unlicensed contractor can and cannot do in California.

As amended, the Minor Works Exemption now allows an unlicensed contractor to do work on a contract up to $500.00 in value. However, that same contractor must first give a contract form to the owner which informs that owner that the Contractors' License Board does not have jurisdiction over the unlicensed contractor on a job under $500.00. That same warning or notice also informs the owner that they could be liable to the contractor or his or her employees if they are injured on the job.

B. Introduction

Although the severity of the action will determine how the CSLB will proceed, all too often the method or punishment will be dictated by the staff handling the complaint.

C. Criminal

Under various sections of the license law, the Contractors' State License Board can proceed against a licensed contractor or an unlicensed contractor through the criminal courts. As an example, Business and Professions Code section 7028 makes it a crime to contract without a license and Business and Professions Code section 7108 states that using money received for a particular operation or project for another operation or project is a cause for discipline. Moreover, Penal Code section 484(b) makes such action a criminal offense and Penal Code section 484(c) makes the submission of false vouchers to obtain construction loan funds criminal embezzlement. Therefore, the Contractors' Board can proceed through the Attorney

General's office by way of disciplinary matters as indicated below, or go to the City Attorney or District Attorney and ask for a criminal complaint to be filed. This is not a usual procedure for the Contractors' Board and is used mainly when a person is a repeat offender or there is substantial injury.

D. Civil

Like the criminal procedure, the Contractors' State License Board can go into a civil court and get an injunction or a "Cease and Desist" order to prohibit a contractor from doing something that is illegal. In this case, it would be represented by the Attorney General's office. Again, this is something that is not usually done.

E. Accusation

Until the passage of the citation procedure, the most common means of discipline used by the Contractors' State License Board, was the accusation. An accusation is a pleading that tells the contractor what he or she has done that violates the law. The contractor can then deny the accusation and go to an Administrative Hearing. The hearing is held by the Administrative Law Judge who sits on behalf of the Registrar. That is to say that the decision of the Administrative Law Judge is not binding on the Registrar. The Registrar can adopt or refuse to adopt the decision of the Administrative Law Judge. The hearing before the Administrative Law Judge is formal. However, it is less formal than the rules of the civil or criminal courts and some of the rules, such as the hearsay rule are relaxed. Hearsay is a technical rule of evidence that essentially refers to a statement made by a third party outside of the courtroom.

There is no discovery (disclosure of facts, records, etc.) in the Administrative Procedures Act other than the discovery listed in the Government Code. That discovery is basically limited to the names and addresses of all witnesses, and any statements that were taken. The burden is on the Registrar to show that the licensee has violated the law.

F. Citation

The citation procedures implemented by the CSLB are an alternative to the more formal procedures that the Board had used in the past. Previously, the CSLB would have filed an accusation to revoke or suspend a license when they found that a contractor had violated the law. This meant that the contractor had to hire an attorney and proceed to an Administrative Hearing in order to defend him/herself. That procedure was costly, and in many cases, wasteful.

The citation procedure allows the Contractors' State License Board to issue a citation, requiring the contractor to do various things. It may require the contractor to correct a deficiency in his construction project, it may require the contractor to pay a penalty up to $5,000, or the citation may require the contractor to do both. Although the citation could require the contractor to do various things to correct any deficiencies in its work, more often the citation is issued after the owner is disenchanted with the contractor, or after repairs have already been made. In that case, the corrective order will be the amount that either the owner or the Contractors' Board's industry expert has stated is the amount of injury to the owner. Many times that determination is one-sided and hugely excessive compared to the actual loss to the owner. In no event can a citation for a single construction project have a fine in excess of $5,000. However, a penalty of $15,000 may be assessed for one who has a history of the same or similar violations, if the violation is grave, or if the cited person exhibits bad faith. This $15,000 assessment only applies to aiding and abetting an unlicensed contractor to evade the law or contracting with an unlicensed contractor. Issuing citations is a much simpler process than the more formal accusation process.

As any enforcement tool, the citation is both helpful and subject to abuse. The prior ultimate enforcement tool utilized by the CSLB, the accusation, which required going to a formal hearing, was costly to the contractor. Further, in many instances, the CSLB would use the fact that the contractor had violated technical portions of the law, for example: failure to put his or her license number on the contract, or the date of completion, to coerce the contractor into doing certain corrective work that it could not otherwise have the contractor do. In order to defend him/herself the contractor would have to hire an attorney and proceed to a formal hearing. The citation procedure allows the CSLB to issue a civil penalty in nominal sums thereby enforcing the law and not requiring the contractor to expend large sums of money in defense.

However, like any other enforcement tool, the citation procedure can also be abused. Some CSLB Deputies indiscriminately write citations for nonsensical things that do nothing to promote consumer protection. All these citations do is generate activity. Sometimes, the amount of the penalty is excessive in light of the alleged violations. In many instances, the purpose of the license is totally lost and punishment becomes the goal.

The CSLB has attempted to insure against such arbitrary use of the procedure by having their citations issued only by district offices, rather than Junior Deputy Registrars. Further, the rules themselves have a built-in appeal procedure. However, the appeal may be costly. In too many instances, the Regional Deputy Registrar is as overzealous as the investigator.

If a contractor is issued a citation, the contractor has various alternatives. A contractor may choose to pay the civil penalty and correct any deficiencies that are alleged in the citation. In the alternative, a contractor may wish to appeal all or any portion of the citation. A contractor can do this by checking off boxes, in the form that is provided along with the citation (see Appendix). **If you get one of these forms, you should contact an attorney immediately.**

A contractor may appeal the fact that he or she has not violated the Business and Professions Code section that is cited. A contractor may appeal the amount of the Civil Penalty, the Order of Correction, or both. This appeal must be made in writing and within fifteen (15) days. If a contractor wishes to appeal, he or she will still have the opportunity to be heard before an Administrative Law Judge. A contractor may represent him or herself, or have an attorney represent him or her.

The various forms that are used by the CSLB are enclosed as an Appendix to this booklet. You should look them over so you are familiar with what is being used. As stated previously, if you receive one of these forms, you should contact an attorney immediately.

Since the passage of the original citation procedure, the Contractors' State License Board has also been given the authority to cite unlicensed contractors. However, none of that information is included herein.

G. Disciplinary Guidelines

The Contractors Board through regulation has created a set of disciplinary guidelines for each type of violation. Unfortunately, the "recommended" minimum in practice becomes an actual minimum rather than a recommended minimum. Those disciplinary guidelines and their code sections can be found in Appendix G.

1. Short Title of Business and Professions Code Sections Affected by Citation Procedure:

Business & Professions Code Section

7018.5	Lengthy notice of Mechanics' Lien Laws.
7027.1	Contractors must have the proper license to do work for which it advertises.
7028	Contracting without a license is a misdemeanor.
7028.1	It is a misdemeanor to perform asbestos related work without an asbestos certification.
7028.5	Officers, Directors and RMO's cannot individually contract without their own license.
7029	Two or more individual licensees must have a joint venture license to work together.
7029.1	Joint venture license required.
7029.5	Identification requirements for plumbers, electrical sign contractors, and well-drilling trucks or rigs.
7030	Contract must contain notice of Contractors' License Law. Also sets out another Notice required prior to entering into a contract.
7030.1	Sets forth requirements regarding disclosure of disciplinary actions.

7030.5	Contractor's identification requirements.
7034	Contracts may not contain any indemnity against certain negligence or willful misconduct, or waiver of lien rights.
7048	Requires unlicensed contractor to give notice to owner of unlicensed status.
7068.1	Requirements and responsibilities of a qualifying individual.
7068.2	Notice and replacement required regarding loss of RMO or RME.
7071.11	Claims against license bond or deposit.
7071.13	Contractors cannot refer to their license bond in selling jobs.
7075	Failure to display license and renewal.
7076	Continuing to do business after cancellation of license.
7083	A contractor must report changes in name, address, of managing personnel.
7083.1	Address correction of licensees that have expired, been canceled, or become inactive.
7090	Citation and discipline process including failure to pull permits.
7099.10	Advertising without proper license.
7099.11	Advertising for asbestos related work.
7107	Abandonment of a project.
7108	Diversion of funds.
7108.5	Prime contractor must pay subs within 10 days of receipt from owner.
7108.6	Payment of transportation charges.
7109	A contractor cannot willfully disregard the plans and specifications or do work in an unworkmanlike manner.
7109.5	Violation of safety provisions of Labor Code.
7110	Violation of State, City or County Building and Safety, Health and Safety, Civil, or Water Codes.

7110.1	A contractor cannot require a release of claims on wages unless full payment is made.
7111	A contractor must keep records of all transactions on a job and maintain them for three years afterwards.
7111.1	Failure to cooperate in investigation.
7112	Misrepresentation in a contractor's license application.
7113	Failure to complete the contract for the price stated.
7113.5	Avoiding obligations or settling for less than the amount owed.
7114	Aiding and abetting an unlicensed contractor.
7114.1	Making false statements on a certificate of experience.
7116	Willful or fraudulent acts.
7117	Contractor must act in the name of the licensee.
7117.5	Acting under an inactive or suspended license.
7117.6	Working out of classification.
7118	Contracting with an unlicensed contractor.
7118.4	Asbestos related inspection.
7118.5	Contracting with uncertified contractor.
7119	Failure to diligently complete a project.
7120	Failure to pay money when due.
7123	Criminal convictions.
7125	Reporting Worker's Compensation Carrier.
7125.1	Certificate of Worker's Compensation Insurance.
7154	Employing an unregistered home improvement salesman.
7157	No kickbacks or compensation to customers.
7158	False certificate of completion.
7159	Requirements of Home Improvement or Swimming Pool Contracts.
7161	Misrepresentation and false advertising.

7162 Representation with respect to trademark or brand name or quality.

7164 Contract and changes to be in writing - notice regarding bonds.

2. Business and Professions Code Sections and Recommended Civil Penalties

The following are shorthand explanations of portions of the Business and Professions Code, and the penalties available for their violation. It is not an exhaustive explanation. You should seek the aid and advice of a knowledgeable construction attorney for more detail.

7018.5 **$50.00 - $150.00**

The Legislature has prepared a lengthy form entitled "Notice to Owner" which clearly describes in common laymen's language the pertinent provisions of the California mechanics' lien laws and the rights and responsibilities of a property owner and a contractor under these laws. This also includes the possibility of filing a contract with the county recorder, and the recording of a contractor's payment bond for private work in the county recorder's office. Each licensed contractor must give a copy of this "Notice to Owner" to the owner, his agent, or the payer, before entering in a contract with an owner for work which is described as "home improvement" or swimming pool construction.

7027.1 **$50.00 - $150.00**

It is a misdemeanor and a violation of the license law to advertise for construction or work of improvement unless the person advertising holds a valid license in the classification advertised.

7028. **$200.00 - $2,000.00**

Contracting without a license is cause for discipline unless he or she is exempt from the provisions of the contractors law.

7028.5 **$50.00 - $500.00**

A person who is or has been a member, officer, director or responsible managing officer of a licensed contractor, cannot individually engage in the business, or individually act in the capacity of a contractor without having a valid contractor's license.

7029.

A joint venture license may be acquired by a combination of individuals, corporations, or others, who each hold a valid active license. Such a joint venture license is required in order for two or more individually licensed contractors to jointly submit a bid or otherwise act as joint venturers. This does not appear to be subject to citation.

7029.1 **$200.00 - $2,000.00**

Two or more licensees may not act in a joint capacity unless they receive a joint venture license.

7029.5 **$50.00 - $150.00**

Every plumbing contractor, electrical sign contractor, and well drilling contractor must have displayed on each side of the motor vehicle used in his/her business his/her name, permanent business address and contractor's license number in letters and numerals not less than one and one half inches (11/2") high. This includes any drill rig used for drilling of water wells.

7030. **$50.00 - $100.00**

Contractors must include the following statement in at least 10-point type on all written contracts where he or she is a prime contractor ***(not subcontractor).***

"Contractors are required by law to be licensed and regulated by the Contractors' State License Board which has jurisdiction to investigate complaints against contractors if a complaint regarding a patent act or omission is filed within four years of the date of the alleged violation. A complaint regarding a latent act or omission pertaining to structural defects must be filed within 10 years of the date of the alleged violation. Any questions concerning a contractor may be referred to the Registrar, Contractors' State License Board, P.O. Box 26000, Sacramento, California 95826."

This statement must be reprinted "word for word."

In addition to the above, any contractor, ***at the time of making a bid or prior to entering into a contract*** to perform work on residential property with four (4) or fewer units, whichever occurs first, must provide the following notice in writing:

"STATE LAW REQUIRES ANYONE WHO CONTRACTS TO DO CONSTRUCTION WORK TO BE LICENSED BY THE CONTRACTORS' STATE LICENSE BOARD IN THE LICENSE CATEGORY IN WHICH THE CONTRACTOR IS GOING TO BE WORKING--IF THE TOTAL PRICE OF THE JOB IS $500 OR MORE (INCLUDING LABOR AND MATERIALS).

LICENSED CONTRACTORS ARE REGULATED BY LAWS DESIGNED TO PROTECT THE PUBLIC. IF YOU CONTRACT WITH SOMEONE WHO DOES NOT HAVE A LICENSE, THE CONTRACTORS' STATE LICENSE BOARD MAY BE UNABLE TO ASSIST YOU WITH A COMPLAINT. YOUR ONLY REMEDY AGAINST AN UNLICENSED CONTRACTOR MAY BE IN CIVIL COURT, AND YOU MAY BE LIABLE FOR DAMAGES ARISING OUT OF ANY INJURIES TO THE CONTRACTOR OR HIS OR HER EMPLOYEES.

YOU MAY CONTACT THE CONTRACTORS' STATE LICENSE BOARD TO FIND OUT IF THIS CONTRACTOR HAS A VALID LICENSE. THE BOARD HAS COMPLETE INFORMATION ON THE HISTORY OF LICENSED CONTRACTORS, INCLUDING ANY POSSIBLE SUSPENSIONS, REVOCATIONS, JUDGMENTS, AND CITATIONS. THE BOARD HAS OFFICES THROUGHOUT CALIFORNIA. PLEASE CHECK THE GOVERNMENT PAGES OF THE WHITE PAGES FOR THE OFFICE NEAREST YOU OR CALL 1-800-321-CSLB FOR MORE INFORMATION."

This notice must be in either capital letters in 10-point roman boldface type or in contrasting red print in at least 8-point roman boldface type.

7030.1 **$1,000.00 - $5,000.00**

Prior to entering into a contract to perform work on residential property of four (4) or fewer units, a contractor who has his or her license suspended or revoked *two or more times* within an eight year period, must disclose any disciplinary, license suspension, or revocation during the last eight years as a result of a violation of the Contractors' License Law, in either 10-point roman boldface type, or in contrasting red print of at least 8-point roman boldface type.

7030.5 **$50.00 - $100.00**

Licensed contractors must include their license number in: (a) all construction contracts; (b) subcontracts and calls for bid; and (c) all forms of advertising.

7034. **$50.00 - $150.00**

(a) Licensed contractors cannot be a party to any contract which contains a provision, clause, covenant, or agreement, which indemnifies them against liability for any personal injury, death, or property damage, or any other loss, damage, or expense caused by their sole negligence, willful misconduct, or defect in design furnished by them, or their agent, servant or subcontractor.

(b) Licensed contractors cannot require any subcontractors, employees, or suppliers to waive their lien rights unless they give their written permission as provided by Civil Code section 3262.

7048.

The Registrar of Contractors is empowered to issue citations containing orders of abatement and civil penalties against persons acting in the capacity of or engaging in the business of a contractor without having a license in good standing to do so. The Registrar may also issue a citation for the failure of an unlicensed contractor to provide the notice required in Section 7048.

7068.1 **$50.00 - $1,000.00**

The person qualifying on behalf of an individual or firm shall be responsible for exercising enough direct supervision and control of their employer's or principal's construction operations as is necessary to secure full compliance with State law, and the qualifier shall not act in the capacity of the qualifying person for an additional individual or firm unless one of the following conditions exists:

(a) There is a common ownership of at least 20 percent (20%) of the equity of each individual or firm for which the person acts in a qualifying capacity.

(b) The additional firm is a subsidiary or a joint venture of the first. "Subsidiary" means any firm at least 20 percent (20%) of the equity of which is owned by the other firm.

(c) With respect to a firm under Section 7068(b) or (c), the majority of the partners or officers are the same.

"Firm" means a co-partnership, a limited partnership, a corporation, or any other combination or organization described in Section 7068.

"Person" is limited to natural persons.

A "qualifier" may qualify only three licenses.

7068.2 **$50.00 - $150.00**

If a Responsible Managing Officer or Employee stops being employed or associated with the firm, a notice must be given to the Registrar by the licensed contractor or firm, or the Responsible Managing Officer or Employee, in writing within ninety (90) days from the disassociation. The licensee shall replace the qualifier, within ninety (90) days from the date of disassociation.

If the required notice is not received by the Registrar within ninety (90) days, the license is automatically suspended. The Registrar may accept a petition of a licensee who disputes the date of disassociation or who has failed to notify and replace the qualifier within the ninety days, for one additional ninety (90) day extension to replace the qualifier.

7071.11 **$50.00 - $500.00**

When a contractor's bonding company makes payment on any claim against a bond, whether through court action or otherwise, the bonding company will notify the Registrar within thirty (30) days of payment. Any judgment against the bond, or a good faith payment by the bonding company on the bond, is grounds for discipline unless the contractor notifies the bonding company in writing not to make the payment.

7071.13 **$50.00 - $100.00**

A contractor cannot refer to its license bond in any advertising, soliciting, or any other presentation to the public.

7075. **$50.00 - $100.00**

A license is not transferable.

7076. **$50.00 - $1,000.00**

An individual license is canceled upon the death of a person licensed as an individual. A partnership license is canceled upon the death of a partner. A partnership license is also canceled upon the disassociation of a partner or upon the dissolution of the partnership. A joint venture license is canceled upon a cancellation, revocation, or disassociation of any of its entities or the dissolution of the joint venture. In the above situations, the Registrar may allow the entity to continue for ninety (90) days to wrap up their affairs. Failure to give notice of any of the above events, is grounds for disciplinary action.

7083. **$50.00 - $100.00**

Contractors must report to the Registrar, all changes of personnel, name style, addresses or other license information within ninety (90) days after the changes are made.

7083.1 **$50.00 - $100.00**

If a contractors license has expired, been canceled, or became inactive, the contractor must notify the Registrar, in writing, of any change of address of record within ninety (90) days, and the contractor will maintain a current address of record during the three (3) year period following expiration, cancellation, or inactivation of the license.

7090. **See below**

This section talks about the disciplinary process as well as making it a violation of the law to violate state or local laws regarding the issuance of building permits with some exceptions. As of this writing, there is some question as to the amount of penalty, if any.

7099.10 **$50.00 - $1,000.00**

Advertising for construction or for work of improvement in an alphabetical or classified directory without being properly licensed is cause for discipline, unless an exemption applies.

7099.11 **$50.00 - $1,000.00**

A contractor cannot advertise for work for the removal of asbestos unless the contractor is certified to engage in asbestos related work. A contractor must also be registered in accordance with section 6501.5 of the Labor Code. A contractor must include his or her certification and registration numbers in all forms of advertising.

7107. **$100.00 - $1,000.00**

Abandonment of a construction project without legal excuse is a cause for discipline.

7108. **$100.00 - $1,000.00**

A contractor who diverts funds or property received for use on a specific construction project or operation, or for a specified purpose in the construction project or operation, or who fails to substantially account for the application or use of the funds or property on the construction project or operation is subject to disciplinary action.

7108.5 **$100.00 - $1,000.00**

Prime contractors must pay their subcontractors within ten (10) days of receipt of each progress payment for which the subcontractor has performed. However this can be waived in writing. If there is a good faith dispute over the amount to be paid, then the prime contractor can withhold 150% of the disputed amount. In addition to discipline, this section allows for a penalty of 2% per month to be paid to the subcontractor.

7108.6 **$100.00 - $1,000.00**

Contractors must pay transportation charges to dump truck carriers by the 20th day of the month after the transportation was performed. This can be waived in writing.

7109. **$50.00 - $1,500.00**

A willful departure in any material respect from accepted trade standards for good and workmanlike construction is grounds for disciplinary action, unless it was done in accordance with plans and specifications prepared under the direct supervision of an architect.

Willful departure or disregard of plans and specifications in a material respect, which is prejudicial to another, without the consent of the owner or the person entitled to have the particular construction project completed, is also grounds for disciplinary action.

7109.5 **$50.00 - $1,500.00**

A violation of any safety provision in the Labor Code is grounds for discipline.

7110. **$50.00 - $1,000.00**

Disregard of the Building Code, Health and Safety Code, the Notice of Recision provisions, Workers Compensation requirements, or Water Code is grounds for discipline.

7110.1 **$50.00 - $150.00**

Obtaining a labor release before the employee is paid is grounds for discipline.

7111. **$50.00 - $500.00**

Licensed contractors must keep records showing all contracts, documents, records, receipts and disbursements of all their transactions as a contractor, and make those available for the Registrar's inspection, for a period of not less than five (5) years after completion of any construction project or operation to which the records refer. A contractor cannot delay, obstruct or refuse to comply with the written request of the Registrar for information or for a request to make that information available.

7111.1 **$50.00 - $1,000.00**

A contractor cannot refuse to respond to a written request to cooperate in the investigation of a complaint.

7112.

Misrepresentation of a material fact in a contractors license application is cause for disciplinary action. The regulations have not yet been updated to show the amount of the civil penalty for violating this section.

7113. **$50.00 - $1,500.00**

A licensed contractor's failure to complete any construction project or operation for the price agreed upon is grounds for disciplinary action.

7113.5 **$50.00 - $500.00**

Licensed contractors' avoidance or settlement for less than the full amount of their lawful obligations *incurred as a contractor*, whether by (a) composition, arrangement or reorganization with creditors under *State law*, (b) composition, arrangement or reorganization with creditors under any agreement or understanding, (c) receivership, (d) assignment for the benefit of creditors, (e) trusteeship, or (f) dissolution, constitutes a cause for disciplinary action.

Licensed contractors will *not be subject to disciplinary action* for avoiding or settling their obligations in bankruptcy, or by composition, arrangement or reorganization with creditors *under Federal law.*

7114. **$200.00 - $15,000.00**

Aiding and abetting an unlicensed contractor is grounds for discipline.

7114.1 **$50.00 - $1,000.00**

Making false or misleading statements on a Certificate of Experience in support of someone else is grounds for discipline.

7116. **$50.00 - $1,500.00**

A licensed contractor who does any willful or fraudulent act which substantially injures another is subject to discipline.

7117. **$50.00 - $150.00**

Contractors must act in the name that is on their license and in accordance with the personnel of the license. (Those persons listed on the application form.)

7117.5 **$200.00 - $2,000.00**

A person who acts under an inactive or suspended license is subject to disciplinary action.

7117.6 **$200.00 - $2,000.00**

Doing work out of classification is grounds for discipline.

7118. **$200.00 - $15,000.00**

Entering into a contract with an unlicensed contractor is a cause for disciplinary action.

7118.4 **$50.00 - $1,000.00**

A contractor making an examination dealing with the presence of asbestos must disclose orally and in writing, if it is owned or has a common ownership or any financial interest in or any relationship whatsoever with an entity in the business of performing the corrective work.

7118.5 **$50.00 - $1,000.00**

Contractors are subject to discipline if they knowingly or negligently enter into a contract with another person, who is required to be, and is not, certified for asbestos related work.

7119. **$100.00 - $1,000.00**

Contractors who injure another due to their willful failure or unjustified refusal to carry out a construction project or operation with reasonable diligence are subject to disciplinary action.

7120. **$100.00 - $1,000.00**

Failure to pay money when due for any materials or services when a contractor is able to pay, or when the contractor was paid, is a cause for disciplinary action. Also, denying of the amount due made with the intent to secure any discount or with the intent to hinder, delay or defraud the person to whom the debt is due is a cause for disciplinary action.

7123. **$500.00 - $1,500.00**

A conviction of a crime substantially related to the qualifications, functions and duties of a contractor is cause for disciplinary action.

7125. **$50.00 - $150.00**

Licensed contractors must report in writing the name and address of their workers' compensation insurance carrier after any policy of insurance is issued to them.

The carrier must then report to the Registrar any cancellation or lapse of the policy within ten (10) days after the cancellation or lapse.

The filing of a false statement is grounds for disciplinary action.

7125.1 **$500.00 - $1,500.00**

A contractor is required to file with the Registrar of Contractors, a Certificate of Workers' Compensation Insurance unless the contractor is exempt from the requirement of having workers' compensation insurance. If a contractor is exempt, he or she must file an Exemption Certificate. The filing of a false statement is grounds for disciplinary action.

7154. **$50.00 - $500.00**

Home improvement contractors who employ an unregistered home improvement salesperson to sell home improvement contracts are subject to disciplinary action.

7157. **$50.00 - $500.00**

(a) A contractor cannot give compensation or reward of any kind to an owner for referral sales regarding home improvement contracts.

(b) A contractor, his agent or salesperson may give tangible items to prospective customers for advertising or sales promotion purposes where the gift is not conditioned upon obtaining a contract for home improvement work if the gift does not exceed a value of five dollars

($5.00) and only one such gift is given in connection with any transaction.

(c) Salespeople or contractor's agents cannot accept any compensation of any kind, for or on account of any work of improvement transaction, from any person other than the contractor whom they represent, nor shall they make any payment to any person other than their employer on account of sales.

"Owner" also means "tenant" under this rule.

(d) A contractor cannot make a payment or give other consideration to a contractor or salesperson unless he or she is licensed, except where the person who the contractor is paying is exempt from licensing or where the project is exempt.

7158. $50.00 - $1,500.00

It is unlawful for any person to accept, receive and use a false Certificate of Completion or other evidence of completion on a work of improvement with knowledge that the document is false. Use of any such false document in connection with the making or accepting of any assignment or negotiation of the right to receive any payment from the owner with regard to the contract, or to use such a false document in order to obtain or grant any credit or loan on the security of the right to receive any payment is subject to discipline.

7159. $50.00 - $1,000.00

This is a long list of contractual requirements in one or more Home Improvement and Swimming Pool contracts totaling more than $500.00. It says that these contracts must be in writing and signed by parties, and shall include all of the following:

(a) The name, address and license number of the contractor, and the name and registration number of any salesman who solicited or negotiated the contract.

(b) The approximate dates when the work will begin and be substantially completed.

(c) A plan and scale drawing showing the shape, size, dimensions and construction equipment specifications for a swimming pool and for other home improvements, a description of the work to be done and a description of the materials to be used or installed and the agreed consideration for the work.

(d) If there is a down payment, the down payment shall not exceed $200 or two percent (2%) of the contract for *swimming pools*, or $1000 or ten percent (10%) of the contract for home improvements, **whichever is less**.

(e) A schedule of payments showing the amount to be paid in dollars and cents (not just percentages). The schedule of payments shall be referenced to work performed and any material or equipment supplied. You can never receive proportionately more money than the work performed (except for the down payment). On swimming pool contracts, the final payment may be made at the completion of the final plastering phase, so long as any installation of equipment, decking or fencing required under the contract is also completed. If you fail to substantially commence work within 20 days of the date specified in the contract, the next payment due will be postponed for the same period.

(f) The contract shall also state that upon satisfactory payment being made for any portion of the work, the contractor, before receiving any further payment, shall give to the person contracting for the work, a full and unconditional release from any claim or mechanics' lien for that portion for which payment has been made.

(g) The down payment or payment schedule provisions of (d) and (e) do not apply when a contractor furnishes a payment and performance bond, lien and completion bond, or a joint control approved by the Registrar. A contractor must also place a notice in at least 10-point type, within three inches of the signature line, telling the tenant or owner that he has the right to require a performance and payment bond.

(h) No extra or change order work shall be required to be performed without the prior written agreement of the person contracting for the construction. Any change order forms shall be incorporated in and shall become a part of the contract.

No change order is enforceable against the person contracting for the home improvement work or swimming pool construction unless it clearly sets forth the scope of work encompassed by the change order, and the price to be charged for the changes. However, the contractor who fails to have a written change order may still be able to recover on a "quantum meruit" basis for the reasonable value of the work they performed.

(i) Any salespersons commission can only be paid in proportion to the schedule of payments.

(j) A contractor must give the notice required by Section 7018.5.

(k) A statement defining what constitutes substantial commencement.

(l) A notice that failure by the contractor without lawful excuse to substantially commence work within twenty (20) days from the approximate date specified in the contract when work will begin is a violation of the Contractors' License Law.

(m) If the contract provides for a contractor to furnish a joint control, the contractor shall not have any financial or other interest in such joint control.

A contractor must give a signed copy of the contract to the owner.

A violation of this section is also a misdemeanor, which can subject a person to imprisonment or criminal fines as well as civil penalties pursuant to a disciplinary proceeding. Such an action would have to be brought within four years from the signing of the contract against an unlicensed contractor, and within one year against a licensed contractor.

7161. $50.00 - $1,500.00

The following acts are misdemeanors, and any licensed contractor or applicant who commits one of these acts is subject to disciplinary actions:

(a) Using false, misleading or deceptive advertising to induce a person into any contract for a work of improvement.

(b) Making any substantial misrepresentation in obtaining a home improvement contract or other work of improvement, or making any false promise of a character likely to influence, persuade, or induce any person to enter into such a contract.

(c) Any fraud in the execution of, or in the material alteration of any contract, trust deed, mortgage, promissory note or other document relating to a home improvement or other transaction involving a work of improvement.

(d) Preparing or accepting any trust deed, mortgage or promissory note for any work of improvement transaction with knowledge that it is for more money than the real value of the improvement work.

(e) Publishing any advertisement which is in any way false, deceptive or misleading. Advertising any improvement work while intending not to accept contracts for that particular work or at the price which is advertised or offered to the public.

If a contractor violates sections b, c, d, or e above as part of a plan or scheme to defraud an owner of a residential or non-residential structure, including a mobile home or manufactured home, for damage caused by natural disaster, it is a violation of law.

7162. $50.00 - $1,000.00

A representation by a contractor with respect to a trademark or brand, name, quality or size of any goods or material in reference to bathroom fixtures, a sink, stove, refrigerator, lighting, carpeting or other floor surfaces, burglar and smoke alarms, paints, textured coatings, siding and other wall surfaces, installation, roofing, air conditioning and air heating systems, and appliances to be provided pursuant to a home improvement contract shall be set forth in writing in the contract or specifications and shall include a description of the goods and materials by brand name, model number, or similar designation. Failure to install specific goods or materials is grounds for disciplinary action.

7164. $50.00 - $1,000.00

Every contract between an owner and a contractor for the construction of a single family dwelling that is going to be retained by the owner for at least one year must be in writing and signed by both parties. The writing must contain (a) the name, address and license number of the contractor, (b) the approximate dates when the work will begin and will be substantially completed, (c) the legal description of the location where the work will be done, (d) the Notice to Owner prescribed in Section 7018.5 of the Code.

The writing must contain any other matters that the parties agree to and they must be legible and clearly describe any other documents incorporated into the contract. Before commencement of the work, the owner is to be furnished a copy of the agreement signed by the contractor. It should also contain, close to the signature line, in 10 point bold type or in all capital letters, a statement that the owner has the right to require the contractor to have a performance and payment bond and that the expense of the bond may be borne by the owner.

G. Warning letter

In many instances, if a contractor is not a repeat violator, and there is merely a technical violation, the Contractors' Board will send the contractor a warning letter. The warning letter may state something like, your contract does not contain your contractor's license number. Then it will warn the contractor that further violations will result in disciplinary action. Those warning letters are kept in the file as a "flag" on the licensee in the event of further violations of the licensee.

H. Appeal

The appeal of a decision of the Registrar, whether it be through a citation or through an accusation, is called a "Writ Proceeding" to the Superior Court in the County where the action took place. This is a rather technical issue that should be left to attorneys specializing in this type of matter. It really serves no purpose to discuss it here. You should know however, that you are entitled to appeal the Registrar's decision.

XV.
APPENDIX

A. **Private Works Mechanics' Lien, Stop Notice and Bond Checklist**

B. **Private Works Stop Notice, Mechanics' Lien and Bond Flow Charts**

C. **Prompt Pay Law Flow Chart - Private Works**

D. **Prompt Pay Law Flow Chart - Public Works**

E. **Index of Selected Cases**

F. **Sample Citation**

G. **Disciplinary Guidelines**

APPENDIX A.
PRIVATE WORKS MECHANICS' LIEN, STOP NOTICE AND BOND CHECKLIST

I. Preliminary To Starting:

These determinations will save you money in the long run.

- Obtain the legal description of the property. (Map book and page number, etc.)
- Determine the name of the owner and the extent of his interest in the property.
- Determine whether the owner is the one who is requesting the improvement. If not, what is the interest of the person requesting it, and, are there any others who claim an interest in the property (lenders, etc.)?
- Determine whether you are a prime contractor, subcontractor, laborer or material man.
- The name of the construction lender or holder of construction funds (if any).
- Consider the effect of a bond or joint control.

II. If You Are A Subcontractor, A Contractor Working For An Owner/Builder, Or Material Man:

A. Within twenty (20) days from first furnishing labor or materials:

1. Subcontractors and material suppliers shall send out a Preliminary 20-day Notice to the owner, original contractor, and construction lender or holder of construction funds (if any). Contractors working for an owner/builder shall send out a Preliminary 20-day Notice to the construction lender or holder of construction funds (if any) only. For purposes of collecting on a payment bond, all parties should serve the bonding company as well.

No matter how many deliveries you make, or the time span over which you furnish labor or materials, only one

Preliminary Notice is required. If you furnish materials or services under separate contracts or with more than one contractor or subcontractor, you must furnish a separate notice for each subcontractor.

The contractor or subcontractor who owes unpaid wages to a laborer or owes fringe benefit or other payments to an express trust fund is required to give, not later than the date the wages became delinquent, a written notice to the laborers, their bargaining representatives, if any, and to the construction lender (or reputed construction lender), if any, that contains the name of the owner and contractor, a description of the jobsite sufficient for identification, the identity and address of any express trust fund to which employer payments are due, the total number of straight time and overtime hours on each job, and the amount then past due and owing.

2. Service: The most common method is by first class certified or registered mail, return receipt requested, postage prepaid, addressed to the residence or place of business of the person being served, or at the address shown by the building permit, or at an address contained on a recorded mortgage or trust deed. Be sure to keep post office receipts for later use if you need to file a claim and prove it in court. A Preliminary Notice also may be served by personal delivery or by leaving it with "some person in charge" at the residence or place of business of the person you wish to serve (must be an adult).

3. County Recorder: You may file a copy of the Preliminary Notice with the County Recorder so that they will notify you if a Notice of Completion or Notice of Cessation is recorded.

B. After work is completed or work ceases, if you are a contractor working for an owner/builder go to Section III below dealing with prime contractors, otherwise follow the procedure below:

1. If the owner records a Notice of Completion after completion of the work of improvement (requires signature of owner or his agent) you should not do additional work under the contract. (While this Notice provision is designed

to primarily protect the owner, it might serve to increase the funds accessible to satisfy your claim, and indicate that you have performed your contractual obligations.)

2. If the owner records a Notice of Cessation of Labor or a Notice of Completion, then: (NOTE: Labor must have ceased for at least thirty (30) days before the owner is entitled to record the Notice of Cessation.)

a. Within thirty (30) days of recording of either of these, the subcontractor must record a Claim of Lien in the office of the County Recorder. Also at this time, serve Stop Notices (see below).

b. File Lien Foreclosure action within ninety (90) days of recording Claim of Lien, and record a Lis Pendens at the same time. You must also file an action on the Stop Notice at this time if applicable. If you want more than ninety (90) days in which to foreclose, then after recording lien, but before ninety (90) days elapses, give credit to the owner and record a notice of the fact and terms of credit. The code section that provides for the Notice of Extension of Credit might lead one to believe that the lien claimant (contractor, subcontractor, supplier, etc.) can unilaterally extend credit by recording a Notice of that. Most construction attorneys do not believe that that is the case and believe that you should get the owner's agreement to the extension of credit well. To the best of our knowledge, there are no cases that have decided this either way. We believe that you should get your signature and the owner's signature on the Notice notarized and then recorded. It seems prudent to either get the owner's notarized signature on the document, or file suit before ninety (90) days has elapsed.

Within ninety (90) days after your Notice of Extension of Credit expires, you must file suit to foreclose. You can keep granting extensions by the above procedure, but you must file suit to foreclose within one (1) year after work is completed.

This action should be brought to trial within two (2) years after commencement.

3. If no Notice of Completion or Cessation is recorded and:

a. The project is actually completed; or,

b. Labor ceases and owner or agent uses work of improvement; or,

c. Owner or agent accepts improvement; or,

d. Labor ceases for a continuous period of sixty (60) days; then:

(1) Within ninety (90) days of any of the above acts, record a Claim of Lien. Also at this time, serve Stop Notice. (See below)

(2) Within ninety (90) days of recording lien, file a Lien Foreclosure action and record a Lis Pendens at the same time.

If you want to extend the time in which to file a foreclosure action, after you record the claim of lien, but before ninety (90) days elapses, give credit to the owner and record a notice of the fact and terms of credit. The code section that provides for the Notice of Extension of Credit might lead one to believe that the lien claimant (contractor, subcontractor, supplier, etc.) can unilaterally extend credit by recording a Notice of that. Most construction attorneys do not believe that that is the case and believe that you should get the owner's agreement to the extension of credit well. To the best of our knowledge, there are no cases that have decided this either way. We believe that you should get your signature and the owner's signature on the Notice notarized and then recorded. It seems prudent to either get the owner's notarized signature on the document, or file suit before ninety (90) days has elapsed.

The extension will be for ninety (90) days after the credit expires, but even with extensions you must file suit to foreclose within one (1) year after the work is completed.

The action should be brought to trial within two (2) years after commencement.

4. Stop Notices

a. Serve Stop Notices on owner, bonded Stop Notice on construction lender, or anyone holding funds.

b. If no mechanics' lien has been recorded, and a surety on a payment bond has been recorded, then the Notice must be served on the surety.

c. File suit on the Stop Notice at the same time that you file a lien foreclosure action.

III. If You Are A Prime Contractor And Work Is Completed Or Ceased:

A. Within ten (10) days after completion, you may wish to have a Notice of Completion recorded. (While this Notice provision is designed to primarily protect the owner, it might serve to increase the funds accessible to satisfy your claim, and indicate that you have performed your contractual obligations.)

Do not do additional work under the contract. This notice requires the signature of the owner or his agent.

B. If the owner records a Notice of Cessation of Labor or a Notice of Completion, then: (NOTE: Labor must have ceased for at least thirty (30) days before the owner is entitled to record the Notice of Cessation.)

1. Within sixty (60) days of recording of a Notice of Cessation or a Notice of Completion, the contractor must record a Claim of Lien. You should also serve a bonded Stop Notice on the construction lender if applicable.

2. File a Lien Foreclosure action, within ninety (90) days of recording Claim of Lien and record a Lis Pendens at the same time, as part of the action, you should also file suit on the Stop Notice if applicable.

3. If you want more than ninety (90) days in which to foreclose, then after recording the Lien, but before the first ninety (90) days elapses, give credit to the owner and record a notice of the fact and terms of credit. The code section that provides for the Notice of Extension of Credit might lead one to believe that the lien claimant (contractor, subcontractor, supplier, etc.) can

unilaterally extend credit by recording a Notice of that. Most construction attorneys do not believe that that is the case and believe that you should get the owner's agreement to the extension of credit well. To the best of our knowledge, there are no cases that have decided this either way. We believe that you should get your signature and the owner's signature on the Notice notarized and then recorded. It seems prudent to either get the owner's notarized signature on the document, or file suit before ninety (90) days has elapsed.

Within ninety (90) days after your "extension of credit" expires, you must foreclose. You can keep granting extensions by the above procedure, but you must file suit to foreclose within one (1) year after work is completed.

The action should be brought to trial two (2) years after commencement.

C. If no Notice of Completion or Cessation is recorded, and:

1. The project is actually completed; or,

2. Labor ceases and owner or agent uses the work of improvement; or,

3. Owner or agent accepts improvement; or,

4. Labor ceases for a continuous period of sixty (60) days, then:

a. Within ninety (90) days of any of the above acts, record Claim of Lien and serve a bonded Stop Notice on the construction lender at the same time, if applicable.

b. File Lien Foreclosure action within ninety (90) days of recording Claim of Lien and record a *Lis Pendens* at the same time, you should also include an action to foreclose on the Stop Notice if applicable.

c. If you want more than ninety (90) days in which to foreclose, then after recording lien, but before the first ninety (90) days elapses, give credit to the owner and record a notice of the fact and terms of credit. The code section that provides for the Notice of Extension of Credit might lead one to believe that the lien claimant (contractor, subcontractor, supplier, etc.) can unilaterally extend credit by recording a

Notice of that. Most construction attorneys do not believe that that is the case and believe that you should get the owner's agreement to the extension of credit well. To the best of our knowledge, there are no cases that have decided this either way. We believe that you should get your signature and the owner's signature on the Notice notarized and then recorded. It seems prudent to either get the owner's notarized signature on the document, or file suit before ninety (90) days has elapsed.

Within ninety (90) days after your offer expires, you must foreclose. You can keep granting extensions by the above procedure, but you must file suit to foreclose within one (1) year after work is completed.

The action should be brought to trial within two (2) years after commencement.

IV. Filing Suit On Payment Bond If Applicable

This is only applicable to subcontractors and material suppliers. Prime contractors cannot file suit to recover on a payment or performance bond.

A. The Preliminary 20 Day Notice given to the bonding company as indicated in Section II A 1 will be sufficient notice to the bonding company.

B. If you didn't give the Preliminary 20 Day Notice indicated above, then you must serve the notice on the bonding company within fifteen (15) days after recordation of a Notice of Completion. If no Notice of Completion is recorded, this time is extended to seventy-five (75) days after completion.

C. You must then file your lawsuit before the expiration of six (6) months after the period in which Stop Notices must be filed. If you will recall, Stop Notices must be filed within thirty (30) days after the recording of a Notice of Completion, Notice of Acceptance, or Notice of Cessation, or ninety (90) days after the completion of the work of improvement if no notices were recorded.

As stated previously, you should become thoroughly familiar with procedures yourself and discuss them with a construction attorney prior to putting the checklist to work in your office.

APPENDIX B.

PRIVATE WORKS, STOP NOTICE, MECHANICS' LIEN AND BOND FLOW CHARTS

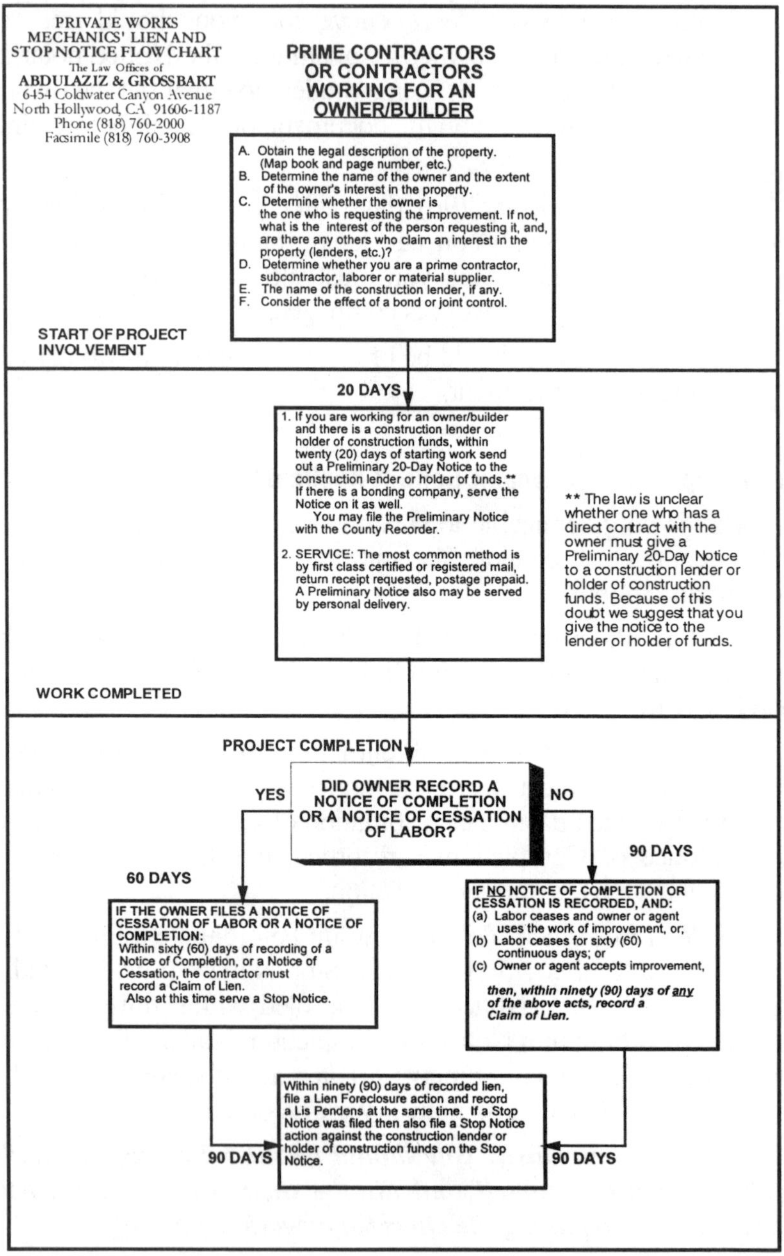

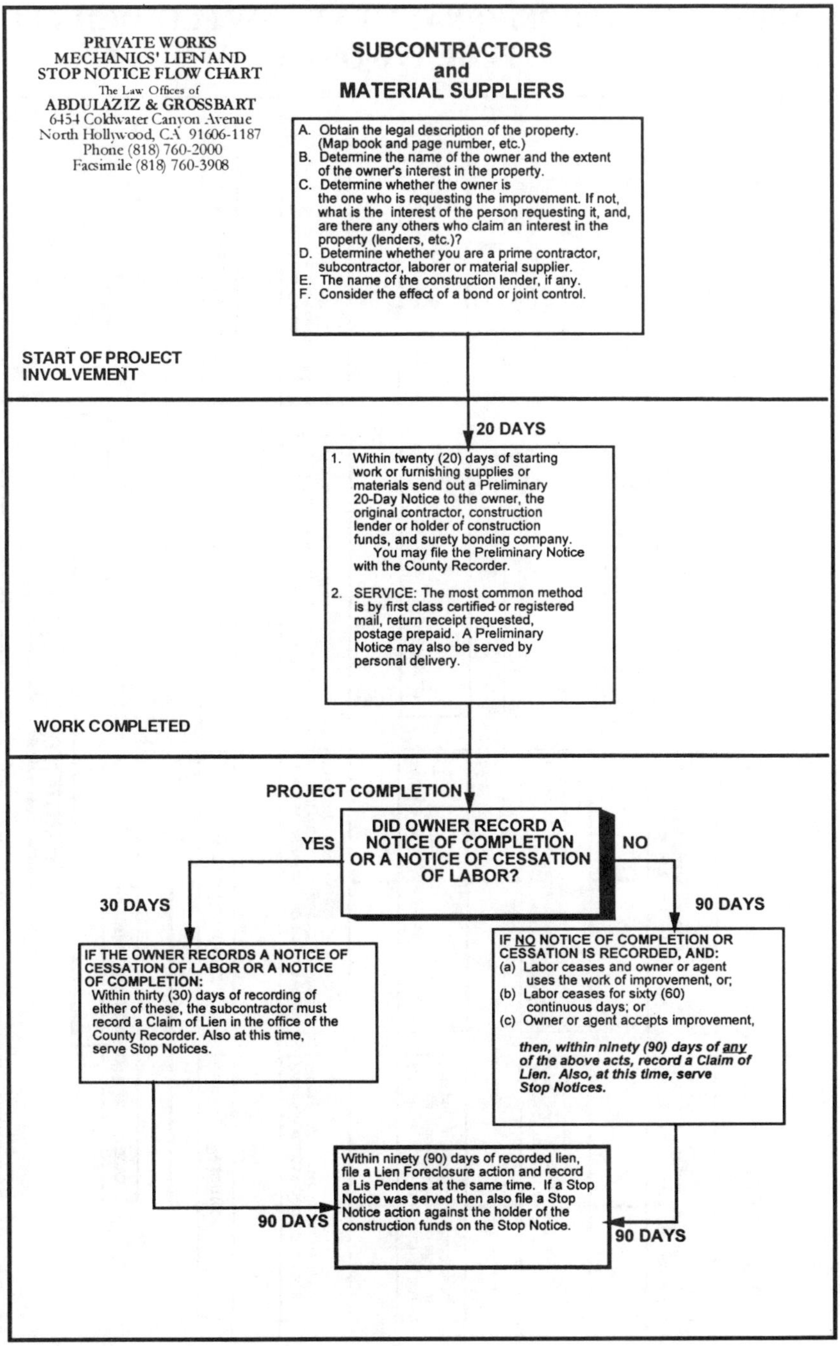
PRIVATE WORKS
MECHANICS' LIEN AND
STOP NOTICE FLOW CHART
The Law Offices of
ABDULAZIZ & GROSSBART
6454 Coldwater Canyon Avenue
North Hollywood, CA 91606-1187
Phone (818) 760-2000
Facsimile (818) 760-3908
SUBCONTRACTORS
and
MATERIAL SUPPLIERS
A. Obtain the legal description of the property. (Map book and page number, etc.)
B. Determine the name of the owner and the extent of the owner's interest in the property.
C. Determine whether the owner is the one who is requesting the improvement. If not, what is the interest of the person requesting it, and, are there any others who claim an interest in the property (lenders, etc.)?
D. Determine whether you are a prime contractor, subcontractor, laborer or material supplier.
E. The name of the construction lender, if any.
F. Consider the effect of a bond or joint control.
START OF PROJECT INVOLVEMENT
20 DAYS
1. Within twenty (20) days of starting work or furnishing supplies or materials send out a Preliminary 20-Day Notice to the owner, the original contractor, construction lender or holder of construction funds, and surety bonding company. You may file the Preliminary Notice with the County Recorder.
2. SERVICE: The most common method is by first class certified or registered mail, return receipt requested, postage prepaid. A Preliminary Notice may also be served by personal delivery.
WORK COMPLETED
PROJECT COMPLETION
DID OWNER RECORD A NOTICE OF COMPLETION OR A NOTICE OF CESSATION OF LABOR?
YES
NO
30 DAYS
90 DAYS
IF THE OWNER RECORDS A NOTICE OF CESSATION OF LABOR OR A NOTICE OF COMPLETION: Within thirty (30) days of recording of either of these, the subcontractor must record a Claim of Lien in the office of the County Recorder. Also at this time, serve Stop Notices.
IF NO NOTICE OF COMPLETION OR CESSATION IS RECORDED, AND:
(a) Labor ceases and owner or agent uses the work of improvement, or;
(b) Labor ceases for sixty (60) continuous days; or
(c) Owner or agent accepts improvement,
then, within ninety (90) days of any of the above acts, record a Claim of Lien. Also, at this time, serve Stop Notices.
Within ninety (90) days of recorded lien, file a Lien Foreclosure action and record a Lis Pendens at the same time. If a Stop Notice was served then also file a Stop Notice action against the holder of the construction funds on the Stop Notice.
90 DAYS
90 DAYS

APPENDIX C. PROMPT PAYMENT LAW FLOW CHART – PUBLIC WORKS

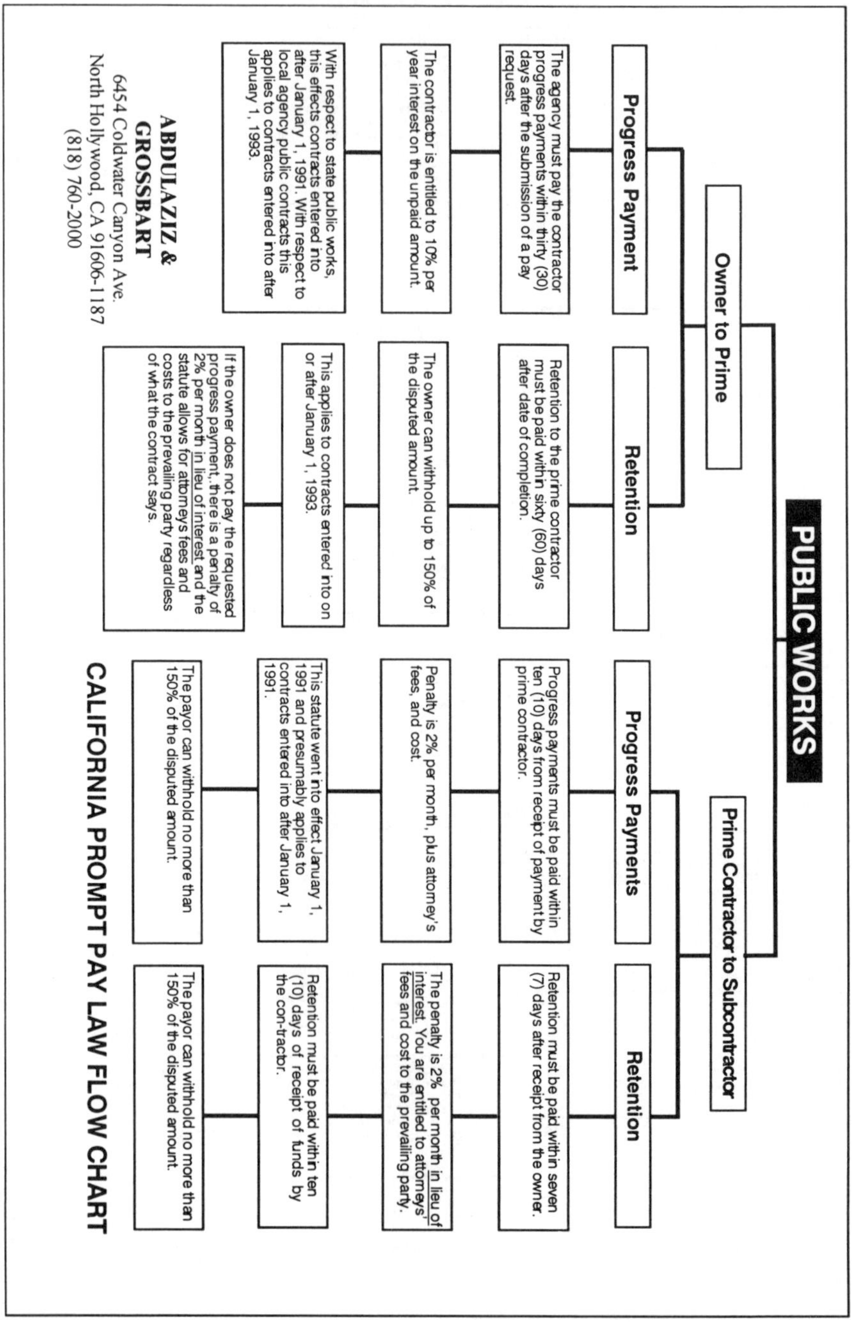

APPENDIX D. PROMPT PAYMENT LAW FLOW CHART – PRIVATE WORKS

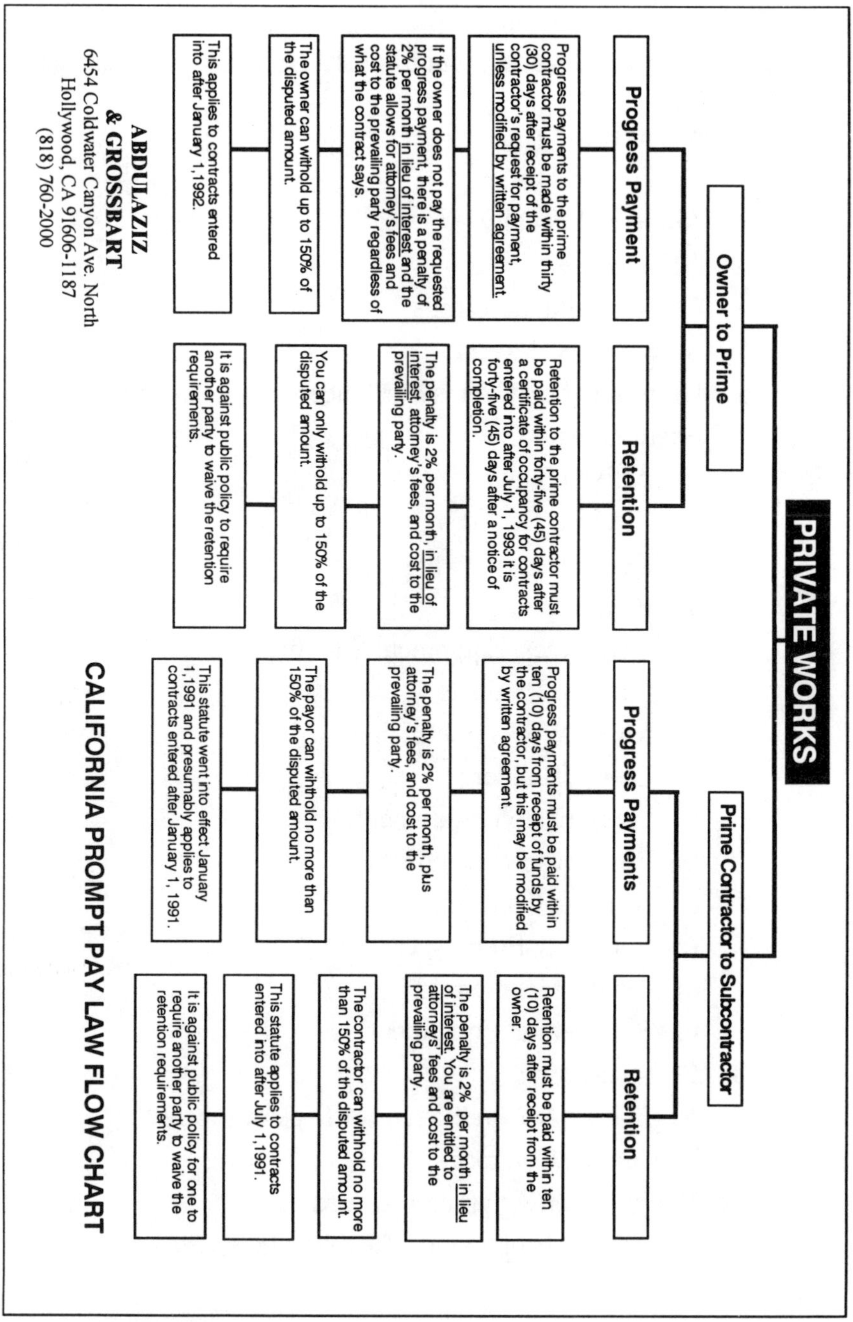

APPENDIX E.
INDEX OF SELECTED CASES

I. Selected Cases Covering contractors' License Law, License Necessity

A. License necessity

1. General
2. Additional Penalty
3. "B" License
4. California Public Works
5. Scope of "B" License
6. Discrimination Claims by Unlicensed Contractor
7. Exemptions
    a. Affixed Signs
    b. Cleaning Services
    c. Developer
    d. Employees
    e. Employees, Equipment Suppliers
    f. Finished Products
    g. Minor Works Exemption
    h. Owner/Builder
    i. Prefabricated Equipment
    j. Project Superintendents
    k. Separate Contracts
    l. Suppliers, Employees
    m. Small Operations
    n. Suppliers of Equipment
8. Floor Covering
9. Negligence Not an Excuse for Lack of License
10. To Enforce Contract
11. Review of an Arbitration Award
12. Licensing – Employing a Revoked Licensee

II. Substantial Compliance With License Law

A. Substantial Compliance

1. Individual
2. Separation of Tasks
3. Out of State Contractor
4. Qualifier for Two Entities
5. Failure to Obtain New Qualifier
6. New "Knowledge" Requirement

III. Selected Cases Covering Disciplinary Proceedings

A. Disciplinary Proceedings

1. Insurance Defense
2. Materiality
3. Relationship
4. Warranty
5. Settlement
6. Specificity of the Accusation
7. Violation Does Not Create Civil Remedies
8. Willfulness

IV. Selected Cases Covering Home Improvement Contracts

A. Home improvement Contracts

1. Right of Recovery on Mechanic's Lien where Section 7159 is Violated
2. "Sophisticated" Homeowner

V. Selected Cases Covering The Home Solicitation Act

A. The Home Solicitation Act

1. Failure to Comply
2. Quantum Meruit
3. Inability of Contractor to Recover

VI. Selected Cases Covering California 20-Day Preliminary Notices And Mechanic's Lien

A. Preliminary Notice

1. Strict Compliance with Statutory Requirement
    a. Exception
    b. Amount Stated

B. Mechanic's Liens/Bonds/Stop Notices

1. Priority of Liens
2. Stop Notices – Amounts in Construction Funds Subject to Lender's Interest Charges
3. Overstated Liens
4. Validity of Subsequent Liens
5. Stop Notice Release Bond
6. Substantial Compliance with Requirement of Bond Notice
7. "Pay if Paid" Clause
8. Tenant Improvements

VII. Corporations – Ability To Get At The Principal Where A Corporation Is Not Properly Identified

A. Corporations

1. Requirement to Avoid Personal Liability
2. Authority of Officers
3. Liability of Officers

VIII. Selected Cases Covering Construction Claims

A. **Emotional Distress Damages**
   1. Recovery

B. **Warranty**
   1. Implied Warranty of Quality and Fitness

C. **Indemnity**

D. **Selected Cases Covering Hirers for Employee of Others**

E. **Arbitration**

F. **Architect's Liability**

G. **Limitations of Claims**

IX. Selected Cases Covering Public Works

A. **Prehire (Project Labor) Agreements**

B. **Liability to Listed Subcontractors**

C. **Public Entity's Lack of Liability for Changes Under Abandonment Theory**

D. **Arbitration**

E. **Prevailing Wages**

F. **Debarment**

X. Selected Cases Covering Surety Liabilities

A. **Prompt Pay Laws**

B. **Damages**

C. **Attorneys Fees**

SELECTED CASES COVERING CONTRACTORS' LICENSE LAW LICENSE NECESSITY

SUBJECT MATTER: License Necessity - General

NAME OF CASE: *Contractors Labor Pool, Inc. v. Westway Contractors, Inc.* (1997)

HOLDING:

Contractor licensing requirements provide minimal assurance that all persons offering such services have the necessary skill and character to do the work and that they understand applicable local laws and codes, and know the basics of administering a construction business.

SUBJECT MATTER: License Necessity - Additional Penalty

NAME OF CASE: *Brown v. Solano County Business Development, Inc.* (1979)

HOLDING:

By enacting the statutes dealing with contractor licensing, the Legislature showed its determination that both criminal penalties and substantial civil penalties needed to be provided to make sure that a license is important. The Legislature decided that there needed to be a strong deterrent to prevent the conduct prohibited by the licensing statutes.

SUBJECT MATTER: License Necessity - "B" License

NAME OF CASE: *Hazard, Jr. Enterprises, Inc. v. Insurance Company of the West* (1997)

HOLDING:

Under the licensing law, a general building contractor can do work that is not solely the building of structures.

SUBJECT MATTER: License Necessity - "B" License

NAME OF CASE: *Denver D. Darling, Inc. v. Controlled Environments Construction, Inc.* (2001)

HOLDING:

This case arose from a transaction occurring prior to the modifications to the "B" contractor's statute by the Legislature following the *Home Depot* Decision by the Court of Appeal. The "B" contractor statute now expressly allows a "B" contractor to subcontract jobs involving less than two trades to a duly licensed contractor. In the *Denver D. Darling* case, the Court held that a "B" general building contractor could perform and collect for work it performed under a structural concrete subcontract for a cold storage facility construction project, even though the definition of a "B" contractor is a contractor whose principal contracting business is in connection with structures requiring the use of more than two unrelated building trades or crafts, where the subcontractor used a variety of properly licensed subcontractors to perform that work. Again, the law has changed to allow a "B" contractor to itself perform jobs involving two or more trades (excluding framing), or to take jobs for less than two trades where it subcontracts the work to properly licensed subcontractors.

SUBJECT MATTER: License Necessity - California Public Works

NAME OF CASE: *K&K Services, Inc. v. City of Irwindale* (1996)

HOLDING:

Contracts for state public works are not exempt from requirements of Contractors' State License Law. There is no legal requirement for a California Contractor's License for federal public works projects; however, the federal owner can require one.

SUBJECT MATTER: License Necessity - "B" License - Scope of

NAME OF CASE: *Home Depot, U.S.A., Inc. v. Contractors' State License Board* (1996)

HOLDING:

The statute that provides for a general building contractor defining his work as principal contracting business in connection with structures requiring use of more than two unrelated building trades or crafts did not keep the general building contractor from taking any prime contract that required less than three unrelated trades.

NOTE HOWEVER, THIS HAS BEEN CHANGED BY STATUTE. A GENERAL BUILDING CONTRACTOR MAY NOW TAKE A PRIME CONTRACT OR A SUBCONTRACT FOR FRAMING OR CARPENTRY. HOWEVER, THE GENERAL BUILDING CONTRACTOR ("B") MAY NOT TAKE A PRIME CONTRACT FOR ANY PROJECT INVOLVING TRADES OTHER THAN FRAMING OR CARPENTRY UNLESS THE PRIME CONTRACT REQUIRES AT LEAST TWO UNRELATED BUILDING TRADES OR CRAFTS OTHER THAN FRAMING OR CARPENTRY, OR UNLESS THE GENERAL CONTRACTOR HOLDS THE SPECIALTY LICENSE OR SUBCONTRACTS WITH AN APPROPRIATELY LICENSED SPECIALTY CONTRACTOR.

SUBJECT MATTER: License Necessity - Discrimination Claims By Unlicensed Contractor

NAME OF CASE: *Holland v. Morse Diesel International, Inc.* (2000)

HOLDING:

The Court of Appeal held that an unlicensed minority business that had participated in a construction project at a state university could not sue for contract claims because of its lack of a contractor's license, but that the lack of a contractor's license did not prevent that business from seeking damages it claimed stemmed from racial discrimination and retaliation.

SUBJECT MATTER: License Necessity - Exemptions - Affixed Signs

NAME OF CASE: *Johnson v. Mattox* (1968)

HOLDING:

Permanent signs affixed in the ground in concrete are not personal property and therefore, one must be a licensed contractor to recover for putting those in.

SUBJECT MATTER: License Necessity - Exemptions - Cleaning Services

NAME OF CASE: *Attorney General's Opinion* (1957)

HOLDING:

People who enter into contracts for window cleaning, or general cleaning and hauling, or cleaning fireplaces, or sanding of concrete porches, patios, etc. in excess of the minimum required for a contractors license, are not contractors within the meaning of the license law and therefore not required to hold a license.

SUBJECT MATTER: License Necessity - Exemption - Developer

NAME OF CASE: *Ranchwood Communities Ltd. Partnership v. Jim Beat Const. Co.* (1996)

HOLDING: Where unlicensed developer was suing for negligence against subcontractors, the court held this is outside the contractual claims and not barred by licensing requirements since the developer was not suing for compensation for work which required a license.

SUBJECT MATTER: License Necessity - Exemption - Employees

NAME OF CASE: *Fillmore v. Irvine* (1983)

HOLDING:

There is a presumption in the Labor Code that a worker performing services for which a license is required is an employee rather than an independent contractor unless that person has a contractor's license. However, this presumption is not applicable as to whether one can sue or not sue for compensation.

SUBJECT MATTER: License Necessity - Exemption - Employees, Equipment Suppliers

NAME OF CASE: *Dahl - Beck Electric Co. v. Rogge* (1969)

HOLDING:

Backhoe owner not licensed as a contractor, who furnished both backhoe and an operator, was deemed not an independent contractor when evidence showed that operation of backhoe was under the control and direction of the hiring contractor. Therefore, backhoe operator not barred from bringing action for compensation.

SUBJECT MATTER: License Necessity - Exemption - Finished Products

NAME OF CASE: *E.A. Davis & Co. v. Richards* (1953)

HOLDING:

The court held that the installation of a prefabricated kitchen unit, consisting of seven wall cabinets, six base cabinets, a dishwasher, and a sink, which required that fixture to be attached to the floor and walls, did not require a contractor's license under Business and Professions Code section 7045. The court found that the manufacturer's necessity to do minor plumbing, electrical, and linoleum work was incidental to the installation of the finished unit.

SUBJECT MATTER: License Necessity - Exemption - Finished Products

NAME OF CASE: *Walker v. Thornsberry* (1979)

HOLDING:

Where the contract between the manufacturer of metal prefabricated restrooms and the customer did not require the manufacturer to do any installation of concrete foundations, rough plumbing, or installation of plumbing fixtures, stalls, wood roofing, and painting upon which to place the prefabricated restrooms, and the employees of the manufacturer merely assembled the pieces and bolted the structure to the foundation, that activity is exempt as being within the definition of "finished products." Therefore no license was required and the manufacturer could sue for compensation if it was not paid.

SUBJECT MATTER: License Necessity - Exemption - Minor Works Exemption

NAME OF CASE: *People v. Vis* (1966)

HOLDING:

Although the amount of a particular contract was less than the amount stated in the Minor Works Exemption, the operation came within the requirements for licensing where the price for the performance of the entire contract, including furnishing the materials, exceeded the amount of the Minor Works Exemption.

SUBJECT MATTER: License Necessity - Exemption - Owner/Builder

NAME OF CASE: *Moon v. Goldstein* (1945)

HOLDING:

A landowner who constructs a building or other structure, not for his own occupancy, is a "contractor" within the license law. An exception is allowed and the owner will not have to comply with the license requirements if the structure is not intended for sale, and the work is being done by the owner him or herself or through his or her own employees with wages as their sole compensation. Otherwise, the owner of the property must utilize all licensed subcontractors.

SUBJECT MATTER: License Necessity - Exemption - Prefabricated Equipment

NAME OF CASE: *Costello v. Campbell* (1947)

HOLDING:

A contract for the installation of a cold storage plant on the owner's premises was divisible from the balance of the contract so that the contractor making the installation, who was unlicensed, was allowed to recover for the value of the equipment. This is especially true since the equipment was prefabricated and did not become a permanent fixture.

SUBJECT MATTER: License Necessity - Exemption - Project Superintendents

NAME OF CASE: *Dorsk v. Spivak* (1951)

HOLDING:

A construction manager under contract with the owner, acting as the owner's agent and superintendent of a construction project, is not required to be licensed as a contractor. The construction manager is not binding himself or herself to any construction agreement, but is merely acting as the agent for the owner.

SUBJECT MATTER: License Necessity - Exemption - Separate Contracts

NAME OF CASE: *Ranchwood Communities Ltd. Partnership v. Jim Beat Const. Co.* (1996)

HOLDING:

Where an unlicensed contractor is also a party to a separate contract for which no license is required, the unlicensed contractor can collect on a contract which does not require a license. Contractor's unlicensed status will not bar contractor from obtaining relief for breach of separate contract.

SUBJECT MATTER: License Necessity - Exemption - Suppliers, Employees

NAME OF CASE: *Cargill v. Achziger* (1958)

HOLDING:

Although one may furnish materials as a supplier and then install the materials as an employee of someone, that person does not require a contractor's license. This is because two exemptions apply. First exemption is the supplying of material only. The second exemption dealing with fabrication, is exempt as a result of the employee status.

SUBJECT MATTER: License Necessity - Exemption - Small Operations

NAME OF CASE: *E.A. Davis & Co. v. Richards* (1953)

HOLDING:

The evidence showed that a kitchen unit consisting of cabinets, dishwasher, and sink assembly with a garbage disposal unit did not become a permanent fixture. Therefore, even though the amount for that work was in excess of the Minor Works Exemption, the installer did not need a contractor's license. Also, if the work that did require a contractor's license was in excess of the Minor Works Exemption, then a license would be required. However, if the work done did become a fixed part of the structure and was in excess of the Minor Works Exemption, then the work would require a contractors license.

SUBJECT MATTER: License Necessity - Exemption - Suppliers of Equipment

NAME OF CASE: *Contractors Labor Pool, Inc. v. Westway Contractors, Inc.* (1997)

HOLDING:

A person or a company in the business of supplying equipment or hiring out laborers, is not required to have a contractor's license when the company only furnished laborers and did not supervise the workers. Even the furnishing of equipment is not enough if full supervision and control of the workers was the responsibility of a subcontractor which actually performed the construction services on work.

SUBJECT MATTER: License Necessity - Floor Covering

NAME OF CASE: *Attorney General's Opinion* (1951)

HOLDING:

Where linoleum or other flooring material is affixed to the subfloor or structure by means of liquid cement or mastic so that it could not be removed without damaging it so that it could not be reused, the material becomes a fixed part of the structure and would require the installer to have a contractors' license.

SUBJECT MATTER: License Necessity - Negligence Not an Excuse for Lack of License

NAME OF CASE: *Construction Financial, LLC v. Perlite Plastering Co.* (1997)

HOLDING:

The statute prohibiting an unlicensed contractor from suing on a contract as a result of failure to obtain a license based on his own negligence, does not excuse the contractor from having a contractor's license because the Legislature expressly reviewed and rejected a rule allowing exemptions for minor lapses from strict applications of the law.

SUBJECT MATTER: License Necessity - To Enforce Contract

NAME OF CASE: *Hydrotech Systems, Ltd. v. Oasis Waterpark* (1991). **This is the leading case at this time dealing with failure to have a contractors license.**

HOLDING:

Even if the unlicensed operator alleged and sued for fraud, if the work that was being done was work for which a license would be required, that person could not recover. The reasoning is that otherwise everyone would sue for fraud in that regard.

SUBJECT MATTER: License Necessity - To Enforce Contract

NAME OF CASE: *K&K Services, Inc. v. City of Irwindale* (1996)

HOLDING:

A statute providing that no person engaged in business or acting in the capacity of a contractor may bring an action in any court for collection of compensation for performance of any act or contract for which a license is required without alleging and proving that he is a duly licensed contractor, prevents the contractor from suing for breach of contract as well as the collection of any compensation such as the exclusive right to run a "fill" operation on the land under which it would collect dumping fees from third parties. This is because the act involved performance of duties of a "contractor."

SUBJECT MATTER: License Necessity - Review of an Arbitration Award

NAME OF CASE: *Lindenstadt v. Staff Builders* (1997)

HOLDING:

The Court of Appeal reviews de novo the trial court's order confirming an arbitration award where the status of the unlicensed contractor has been determined. This is because a contract with an unlicensed contractor is an illegal contract.

SUBJECT MATTER: Licensing – Employing a Revoked Licensee

NAME OF CASE: *Attorney General's Opinion - Holding*

HOLDING:

The Attorney General of the state of California rendered an opinion that a licensee could employ a revoked contractor so long as the revoked contractor is not an officer, director, associate, partner, or qualifying individual of the licensee and his/her employment does not include any right to control or discretion in the manner of the performance so as to determine the final results that were performed.

SUBSTANTIAL COMPLIANCE WITH THE LICENSE LAW

Business and Professions Code section 7031 requires that as a prerequisite to sue for money damages, that the contractor be duly licensed. That includes not only a mere license, but a proper license for the craft or work that was being performed. This rule means that an unlicensed contractor, which in some cases includes a person who was licensed but for some reason was unlicensed for any portion of the work, may not collect.

Due to the harshness of this rule, the courts began crafting an exception which became known as the Doctrine of Substantial Compliance. Under this exception, if the contractor "substantially complied" with the License Law, it would be allowed to collect even though it may not have been licensed during the entire period of time, or at the time the contract was executed, etc.

The following cases, in chronological order, detail the evolution of the Doctrine of Substantial Compliance, though by changes to the statutes itself, these cases may have been overruled.

SUBJECT MATTER: Substantial Compliance - Individual

NAME OF CASE: *Asdourian v. Araj* (1985)

HOLDING:

This case had two issues, one of which is discussed in the Home Improvement Act realm. The other issue was the fact that the contractor obtained a license under a fictitious name, but thereafter entered into a contract with an owner under his own name, rather than the fictitious name stated on his license.

The Supreme Court held that the competence and experience of the plaintiff formed the basis of the license, and that issuance of the license to the individual in his own name would not have provided the owner any greater assurances he was dealing with an experienced and competent contractor. Therefore, the Court held that the public was protected and allowed the contractor to recover.

SUBJECT MATTER: Substantial Compliance - Separation of Tasks

NAME OF CASE: *Johnson v. Mattox* (1968)

HOLDING:

In this case, a person who was not licensed as a contractor entered into a contract to provide materials to a job site and installed some of those materials. The court ruled that the items could be separated, allowing recovery for the items that did not require a contractor's license, while no recovery could be obtained for those items of work that did require a license.

SUBJECT MATTER: Substantial Compliance - Out of State Contractor

NAME OF CASE: *Hydrotech Systems, Limited v. Oasis Water Park* (1991)

HOLDING:

This was one of the first cases that came down during a period where the Legislature had completely barred the Doctrine of Substantial Compliance. Even if the doctrine had been enforced, on these facts, the contractor probably would not have been able to collect. In this case, the contractor induced Hydrotech, who was an out-of-state contractor, to come to California and perform work on a project it was constructing. The issue of licensure came up, and the allegations were that the Hydrotech was fraudulently induced to come to California to perform work under promises that it would be paid regardless of its licensure. The Supreme Court stated in Hydrotech that strict application of the law means that a contractor who is not licensed may not collect, regardless of any inducement to enter into that contract. While there was no issue as to the work performed, the court reiterated the policy behind the rule by stating that "the license requirements provide minimal assurance that all persons offering such services in California have the requisite skill and character, understand local laws and codes, and know the rudiments of administering a contracting business."

SUBJECT MATTER: Substantial Compliance - Qualifier for Two Entities

NAME OF CASE: *G.E. Hetrick & Associates, Inc. v. Summit Construction and Maintenance Co., Inc.* (1992)

HOLDING:

This case was very similar to the Asdourian and Knapp cases. G.E. Hetrick & Associates held a sole proprietorship license. G.E. Hetrick & Associates, Inc., a company qualified by the owner of the sole proprietorship, entered into a contract to perform construction work. Hetrick, Inc. was not licensed, but sued when it was not paid for the work it performed. This case ruled that the statutory changes to section 7031 were not to be applied retroactively to contracts that were executed prior to the change in this statue that had eliminated substantial compliance. Relying on Asdourian and Knapp, the court ruled that if Gary Hetrick was the responsible managing officer of Hetrick Inc. to a degree sufficient to establish substantial compliance, then Hetrick, Inc. substantially complied with the License Law.

SUBJECT MATTER: Substantial Compliance - Failure to Obtain new Qualifier

NAME OF CASE: *Construction Financial, LLC v. Perlite Plastering Co., Inc.* (1997)

HOLDING:

This was one of the first cases after the Doctrine of Substantial Compliance was reenacted by the Legislature. Under this new version, neglect by the contractor that was allowed under Latipac is not allowed. In Perlite, a plastering subcontractor was not properly licensed because its qualifier left the firm and was not replaced. Because Perlite didn't have a qualifier for that type of job, it was not properly licensed to enter in the contract to do that work. The plasterer argued that it substantially complied with the law. However, the Court of Appeal stated that where the failure to be licensed was due to ordinary negligence by the contractor, the Doctrine of Substantial Compliance would not allow the contractor to recover. This case also had a discussion as to retroactivity, in that the contract at issue was entered into at the time when the Doctrine of Substantial Compliance was not allowed to be used. Just like the doctrine could not be used to take away retroactively in Hetrick, it could not be given back retroactively under this case.

SUBJECT MATTER: Substantial Compliance With License Requirements – New "Knowledge" Requirement

NAME OF CASE: *Slatkin v. White* (2003)

HOLDING:

As long as a contractor fulfills subdivision (e) of the Business & Professions Code § 7031, he or she can recover on a mechanic's lien against the homeowner even if the contractor was not licensed throughout all of construction. The three requirements under this section are: 1) Duly licensed as a contractor in California prior to the performance of the act or the contract, 2) Acted reasonably and in good faith to maintain proper licensure; and 3) Did not know or reasonably should not have known that he or she was not duly licensed. With regards to these three requirements, the court will make a determination to see whether substantial compliance with the state contractor licensing requirements has been satisfied. If there is substantial compliance, then the contractor may recover on the mechanic's lien.

SELECTED CASES COVERING DISCIPLINARY PROCEEDINGS

SUBJECT MATTER: Disciplinary Proceedings - Insurance Defense

NAME OF CASE: *Certain Underwriters At Lloyd's, London v. Superior Court (Powerine Oil Company, Inc.)* (2001)

HOLDING:

In this holding, the California Supreme Court held that an insurer's obligation to pay damages or to defend their insured arises from an action brought in a court, and thus the insurer did not have a duty under the terms of their insurance policies at issue to defend their insured in an administrative proceeding brought by a governmental agency. Although this case dealt with environmental issues dealing with an oil refinery, the case would likely apply to disciplinary actions against a contractor, architect, engineer, etc.

SUBJECT MATTER: Disciplinary Proceedings - Materiality

NAME OF CASE: *Terminix Co. v. Contractors' State License Board* (1948)

HOLDING:

If the particular statute which a contractor is alleged to have breached states that there has to be a material injury or material prejudice, then if there is no harm, the contractor could not have violated that statute. This would be true even if the contractor offered to make things right and the owner did not allow the contractor to do that.

SUBJECT MATTER: Disciplinary Proceedings - Relationship

NAME OF CASE: *Linda Jones General Builder v. Contractors' State License Board* (1987)

HOLDING:

Some sections of the Contractors' License Law require a contractor/owner relationship. If one is doing work on his or her own residence, some of those disciplinary sections may not apply.

SUBJECT MATTER: Disciplinary Proceedings - Warranty

NAME OF CASE: *Viking Pools, Inc. v. Maloney* (1989)

HOLDING:

If the contractor breaches the express written warranty, this is an abandonment and failure to complete the construction project as contracted, and thus is a ground for discipline.

SUBJECT MATTER: Disciplinary Proceedings - Settlement

NAME OF CASE: *Terminix Co. v. Contractors' State License Board* (1948)

HOLDING:

Where the contractor performed unsatisfactory work for the customer, but prior to the initiation of disciplinary proceedings by the Contractors' Board the contractor offered to settle with the customer on terms that were more favorable than what the customer was entitled to, but the offer was refused, then there is no violation of the License Law.

SUBJECT MATTER: Disciplinary Proceedings - Specificity of The Accusation

NAME OF CASE: *Cooper v. Board of Medical Examiners* (1975)

HOLDING:

In this case, Cooper was a licensed psychologist. An accusation was served alleging violations of the laws governing such professionals. Cooper had alleged that he could not be disciplined because the accusation, which is the charging document, was not specific as to certain allegations against him. The Court ruled that if the pleading gives the licensee notice of the charges against him or her, and affords the basic elements of Due Process, variations between the pleadings will not be material. The issue revolves around whether or not the licensee was misled to his prejudice by the pleading. Generally, the License Board can amend the pleading, even orally, up to the time of the hearing. If there is any surprise, the Administrative Law Judge will grant a continuance.

SUBJECT MATTER: Disciplinary Proceedings- Violation Does Not Create Civil Remedies

NAME OF CASE: *Swickheimer v. King* (1971)

HOLDING:

In this case, The Court of Appeal ruled that violations of the License Law that would subject a licensee to discipline by the Contractors' State License Board does not create any right to civil damages in favor of individuals for whom the contractor or his or her employees were working.

SUBJECT MATTER: Disciplinary Proceedings - Willfulness

NAME OF CASE: *Bailey - Sperber, Inc. v. Yosemite Insurance Company* (1976)

HOLDING:

Some sections of the Disciplinary Statutes require willfulness in order for there to be a violation. However, when willfulness is not part of the statute, then a contractor may be disciplined even if the violation is inadvertent.

SUBJECT MATTER: Disciplinary Proceedings – Willfulness; Material Injury

NAME OF CASE: *Tellis v. Contractors' State License Board (2001)*

HOLDING:

This case touched on the "willfulness" and "material injury" issues in disciplinary cases. As to "willfulness," the Court of Appeal held that the evidence that the contractor knew his work was substandard as to seventeen items was sufficient to prove the departure from trade standards was "willful" under the charging statute.

As to material injury, the Court held that because Tellis was paid in full for such work, he could be disciplined despite his offer to repair the defective work. The contractor alleged that under *Terminix v. Contractors' State License Board*, he could not be disciplined because his offer to correct the work eliminated the "material injury" element of the charge. The Court of Appeal held that because Tellis had been paid in full, his offer to correct the work was not the same as the offer made in *Terminix,* where the rejected offer was made when a balance was allegedly due to the contractor. This was said to eliminate the "material injury."

SUBJECT MATTER: Disciplinary Proceedings – Willfulness

NAME OF CASE: *Mickelson Concrete v. Contractors' State License Board (1979)*

HOLDING:

A contractor who knowingly performs work in a manner that is contrary to trade standards, even with the written consent and agreement as of the owner as to that departure, has willfully departed from trade standards and is subject to discipline by the Contractors' State License Board.

SELECTED CASES COVERING HOME IMPROVEMENT CONTRACTS

SUBJECT MATTER: Home Improvement Contracts - Right of Recovery on Mechanics' Lien where Section 7159 is Violated

NAME OF CASE: *WM. R. Clarke v. Safeco Insurance Company of America* (1997)

HOLDING:

This case, which is also discussed elsewhere, ruled that the "pay-if-paid" clause is unenforceable and unconstitutional in California as an infringement of the contractor's mechanics' lien rights. In its discussion, the Supreme Court stated that no mechanics' lien may be recovered where there is no "contract price" as is required by Civil Code section 3140 for recovery on a mechanics' lien. While the case has not been cited for this proposition by another appellate court, it can be argued that where a home improvement contract is voidable or rescinded by operation of Business and Professions Code section 7159 this case's result is that the contractor is not entitled to foreclose upon any mechanics' lien on the property.

SUBJECT MATTER: Home Improvement Contracts - "Sophisticated" Homeowner

NAME OF CASE: *Davenport & Co. v. Spieker* (1988)

HOLDING:

This was a case that followed the Asdourian case (discussed above), where the Court of Appeal ruled that a home owner was "sophisticated" within the definition of Asdourian, allowing a contractor to recover for oral change orders which were in violation of Business and Professions Code section 7159. In this case the homeowner was a partner in a large commercial real estate and development concern.

SUBJECT MATTER: Home Improvement Contracts - "Sophisticated" Homeowner

NAME OF CASE: *Asdourian v. Araj* (1985)

HOLDING:

A Home Improvement Contract that does not comply with Business and Professions Code section 7159, which is intended to protect residential homeowners, may be deemed voidable at the discretion of the home owner. An exception to this rule is where the homeowner is "sophisticated." A "sophisticated" homeowner could be someone who relies on his or her own expertise to make decisions concerning the improvements to the residence. In Asdourian, the Supreme Court ruled homeowners to be deemed "sophisticated" also based upon a social relationship with the contractor which made it "understandable" that the parties' contract did not comply with section 7159. Note that the case did not discuss what the remedy is for a contractor if the contract is voidable, and application of quantum meruit (value of the work done) recovery for the homeowner could be argued in such circumstances.

SELECTED CASES COVERING THE HOME SOLICITATION ACT

SUBJECT MATTER: The Home Solicitation Act- Failure to Comply

NAME OF CASE: *Weatherall Aluminum Products Co. v. Scott* (1977)

HOLDING:

A home improvement contract which fails to comply with the provisions of Civil Code section 1689.5 (which requires a "Notice of Cancellation" and language in the contract discussing that right of cancellation) may be rescinded at any time before the contractor has complied with these 1689.5 provisions. The contractor may be required to remove the improvements and refund all money paid by the homeowner to the contractor or the contractor may be precluded from recovering payment. Where the homeowner cancels the contract and the contractor fails to pick up the merchandise installed within 20 days, the home owner may keep the products supplied with no obligation to pay for them. (This case has been partially modified by Beley v. Municipal Court, which is discussed below.)

SUBJECT MATTER: The Home Solicitation Act - Quantum Meruit

NAME OF CASE: *Beley v. Municipal Court* (1979)

HOLDING:

Although a home improvement contract may be rescinded where the contractor has failed to comply with the Home Solicitation Act, the contractor who has done substantial work that improves the value of a home owner's property may be entitled to recover the value of the work that was done even though the contract itself has been legally rescinded by operation of Civil Code section 1689.5 et seq. This case partially modified the Weatherall decision discussed above, but may have itself been modified in certain circumstances by the Louis Luskin & Sons case, discussed below.

SUBJECT MATTER: Home Solicitation Act - Inability of Contractor To Recover

NAME OF CASE: *Louis Luskin & Sons, Inc. v. Samovitz* (1985)

HOLDING:

Where a contractor has "spiked" the job by entering into a contract to do repairs to residential property without complying with Civil Code section 1689.5 et seq., and started work immediately without awaiting the three-day period in which the owner has time to cancel (doing work which would cause the owner to hesitate or fail to exercise his or her legal right to cancel), that contractor will not be entitled to recover for the work that was done, including the value of the work that was done. There is a question whether this case only applies to "spiking cases" such as what occurred here, or applies to all failures of a contractor to comply with the Home Solicitation Act. The Court stated that contractors can inexpensively protect themselves by including the right to cancel provision in their contract, and their failure to do so is at their own risk. Some would argue this language means the Court intended its rule to apply in all circumstances.

SELECTED CASES COVERING CALIFORNIA 20-DAY PRELIMINARY NOTICES AND MECHANICS' LIENS

SUBJECT MATTER: Preliminary Notice - Strict Compliance with Statutory Requirement

NAME OF CASE: *IGA Aluminum Products v. Manufacturers Bank* (1982)

HOLDING:

The California Civil Code requires any contractor and/or material supplier who is not in a direct contractual relationship with the owner of the property must, as a prerequisite to the recording of a Mechanics' Lien, timely serve a California 20-Day Preliminary Notice. The Civil Code also sets forth the method upon which the Preliminary Notice should be served. Service can be done in one of two methods. Either by personal service or by Certified or Registered Mail, return receipt requested. In this case, a material supplier who was not in a direct contractual relationship with the owner of the property served its Preliminary Notice but did so by regular First Class Mail. Thereafter, it recorded its Mechanics' Lien and sought to recover monies that were owed to it by foreclosing on the Mechanics' Lien. The construction lender asserted that the Mechanics' Lien was invalid because the service of the Preliminary Notice was invalid. The material supplier argued that even though the Preliminary Notice was sent by regular mail, this form of service represented "substantial compliance" with the notice requirement. The court held that in order to perfect a Mechanics' Lien, a Preliminary Notice must be given in strict compliance with the statutory requirements and where notice does not meet such requirements, a lien cannot attach to funds or property. In this instance, the material supplier was not allowed to pursue its claim for foreclosure of the Mechanics' Lien or a claim against the funds of the construction lender.

SUBJECT MATTER: Preliminary Notice - Strict Compliance with Statutory Requirement

NAME OF CASE: *Kim v. JF Enterprises* (1996)

HOLDING:

The *Kim* case ruling is similar to that of the *Truestone* ruling. The facts of this case are that Kim, the plaintiff, filed his original complaint for foreclosure on a Mechanics' Lien. Kim was not in a direct contractual relationship with the owner and therefore under all accounts would have been required to serve a Preliminary Notice. Kim did not serve a Preliminary Notice as required by the Civil Code. The defendants defended the foreclosure of Mechanics' Lien action on the basis that the plaintiff failed to serve a Preliminary Notice. Kim argued two theories in support of his argument that he was exempt from serving a Preliminary Notice. First, Kim argues that even though the agreement was between himself and a tenant, the owner had knowledge of the work being performed by the plaintiff and as a matter of law, that is the same as being under a direct contractual relationship. Second, the tenant with whom Kim entered into a contract, was the agent of the owner and therefore the owner is responsible as a principal of the agent. Using the theory of *Truestone*, that knowledge of construction being performed may be an exception to the service of a proper Preliminary Notice, Kim attempted to claim the same thing. However, in the *Kim* case, the court held that if the owner had any knowledge at all, it was constructive notice as opposed to actual notice and that constructive notice is not as sufficient as actual notice. Therefore, the court determined that the failure to serve a Preliminary Notice is a bar to the foreclosure of a Mechanics' Lien.

SUBJECT MATTER: Preliminary Notice - Strict Compliance with Statutory Requirements - Exception

NAME OF CASE: *Truestone, Inc. v. Simi West Industrial Park* (1985)

HOLDING:

A similar case to the *IGA Aluminum* but a different ruling. Here, Truestone, a material supplier, sought to foreclose on its Mechanics' Lien against Simi West, the owner of property in which it supplied materials for incorporation into the construction project. The owner of the project defended the Mechanics' Lien action on the basis that the Preliminary Notice served by Truestone violated the Civil Code in that it was not served by Certified Mail or by personal service. Truestone argued that it should be able to overcome the failure to serve by Certified Mail, since the owner admitted to Truestone that it had received the Preliminary 20-Day Notice and that Truestone made a separate promise to pay. Even though the *IGA Aluminum* case held that there must be strict compliance in the service of the Preliminary Notice, in this case, the court implied that there may be an exception to the strict compliance if the party to whom the Preliminary Notice was mailed had knowledge that materials were being supplied or work was being performed by others and made a separate promise to pay, even though it did not receive the Preliminary Notice in strict compliance with the statutory requirement of the Civil Code. The distinguishing factor between the *Truestone* case and the *IGA Aluminum* case was that in the *IGA Aluminum* case, the defendant did not acknowledge receipt of the Notice whereas in the *Truestone* case, the defendant did acknowledge receipt of the Notice, and agreed to pay.

SUBJECT MATTER: Preliminary Notice – Mechanic's Liens – Strict Compliance with Statutory Requirement – Amount Stated

NAME OF CASE: *Rental Equipment, Inc. v. McDaniel Builders, Inc.* (2001)

HOLDING:

In this very factually specific case, the Court of Appeal ruled that an equipment rental company could not foreclose upon a mechanic's lien where it did not make a good faith effort to estimate the value of its services on the required Preliminary 20-Day Notice. In the case, the evidence was that the rental company arbitrarily chose a number, which had no rhyme or reason with regard to the actual charges for the rented equipment.

SUBJECT MATTER: Mechanics' Lien - Priority of Liens

NAME OF CASE: *Schmitt v. Tri Counties Bank* (1999)

HOLDING:

A developer obtained a construction loan. The loan was secured by a construction deed of trust recorded on June 9, 1994. In July 1995, the developer contracted for site improvements including grading and paving of roadways. When the developer was unable to pay for the site improvements, the contractor who performed that work filed a lawsuit to foreclose on its mechanics' lien. The issue in the case was the priority of the mechanics' lien as opposed to the construction deed of trust which was recorded earlier. Although deeds of trust recorded before the commencement of a work of improvement generally have priority over mechanics' liens, there is a statutory exception to this preference for site improvements. However, there are exceptions to the exception, including when the owner of the land or the lender obtain a payment bond, or where the lender holds the construction funds pursuant to a contract with its borrower and uses those funds to pay all claimants for the work they performed. That is to say, the lender is required to put the money into a fund control or escrow and assure that all mechanics' lien claims were paid before it disburses the construction funds to the borrower, in this case the developer. The lender did not do that in this case. That is why the Court of Appeal affirmed a lower court's ruling holding that the site improver had priority over the construction deed of trust even though the construction deed of trust was recorded earlier.

SUBJECT MATTER: Mechanic's Liens - Stop Notices - Amounts In Construction Funds Subject To Lender's Interest Charges

NAME OF CASE: *Steiny and Company, Inc. v. Citicorp Real Estate, Inc.* (RULED NOT TO BE PUBLISHED BY SUPREME COURT)

HOLDING:

The importance of this case to the construction industry is that it is not the law of this state. However the logic and reasoning are important to understand. This case had departed from a previous case, *Familian Corp. v. Imperial Bank* (1989), however, the *Steiny* decision, based upon the action of the California Supreme Court only applies to Steiny. In *Familian*, the court had held that a construction lender must make available to Stop Notice claimants the amount that the lender had segregated and preallocated to a fund to pay loan costs, including interest on the construction loan.

Familian may be factually specific, as in that case, the construction lender had effectively "front-loaded" the construction fund by allocating from the initial loan proceeds all of the loan fees including future interest that would be charged over a period of time on the construction loan. In the *Steiny* case, the bank had charged interest to the construction fund on a monthly basis. The trial court had followed the holding in *Familian* and stated that all funds, including those that the bank had deducted for earned interest, must be made available to Stop Notice claimants.

The Court of Appeal in Steiny, reversed, holding that the construction lender was not required to make available to Stop Notice claimants the amount that the lender had earned and already disbursed to itself from the loan fund for interest on the loan. Due to the de-publication by the Supreme Court, the *Familian* decision should now remain the state of the law of California. However, in future cases, a distinction may be made between earned interest and preallocated interest.

SUBJECT MATTER: Mechanics' Liens - Overstated Lien Amount

NAME OF CASE: *Basic Modular Facilities, Inc. v. Ehsanipour* (1999)

HOLDING:

In this case, a licensed contractor entered into a contract for improvements to an owner's property. After change orders, the contract price was $154,884.00. The owner paid the contractor $137,092.00, leaving the balance of $17,792.00. On January 27, 1997, the contractor recorded a mechanics' lien for $18,192.00. Thereafter, the contractor continued work. On April 17, 1997, the contractor sent the owner a demand letter and billing statement seeking among other things the past due balance, extended overhead, additional work and delay damages, all totaling $245,299.00. The contractor recorded a second mechanics' lien in that amount.

The owner then filed a motion with the court to remove the lien on the grounds that it was overstated. It was contended that under Civil Code section 3123, the lien cannot include such items as extended overhead, and can only include reasonable value of labor, services, equipment, or materials furnished to the property. Although the contractor voluntarily agreed to reduce the amount of the second lien to $192,062.00, the court ordered that lien removed in its entirety. The owner argued that the claim could not be greater than the amount due in the contract. The Court of Appeal disagreed. The Court of Appeal held that the amount of a mechanics' lien can include the amount for the reasonable value of labor, services, equipment or materials furnished based on the owner's breach of contract, even if based on oral modifications to the contract.

SUBJECT MATTER: Mechanics' Liens - Validity of Subsequent Lien After Earlier Lien is Released

NAME OF CASE: *Solit v. Tokai Bank* (1999)

HOLDING:

This case reversed an earlier Court of Appeal holding on the effect of a petition to release a mechanics' lien. Generally, a mechanics' lien must be recorded within 90 days of the completion of the project, though that time can be shortened by the recording of a Notice of

Completion or a Notice of Cessation of Work. Earlier cases have held that if a mechanics' lien is recorded and then released, a subsequent mechanics' lien can be recorded on the same project by the same contractor so long as the recording of the second lien is timely. The exception to that is where a Release of Lien specifically states that the claim was satisfied or otherwise released and discharged.

In this latest case, a contractor filed an earlier lien which was released by the contractor after he was threatened with a petition to have that lien released (because it was more than 90 days old and a suit had not been filed). The contractor released that lien, but later recorded a new lien which was timely because the project had not yet been completed. The contractor filed a lawsuit to foreclose on the later lien, but inadvertently referred to the earlier lien's document number. When the contractor sought to amend his complaint to refer to the later recorded lien, the owner claimed that the release of that earlier lien barred any recovery on the subsequent lien. The Superior Court agreed, relying on an earlier case from the Court of Appeal which held that once a court ordered the mechanics' lien released pursuant to Section 3154, there was no longer a lien on the property.

However, the recent Court of Appeal decision distinguishes between the specific <u>lien</u> and the <u>right</u> to claim a lien. While the petition may release a specific lien, the right to the claim of lien is governed by the California Constitution and other statutes, and is not dependant on whether the earlier lien was no longer valid. So long as the subsequent lien was timely recorded, it is not effected by the release of an earlier lien, whether that release was voluntary or by court decree. The exception is in the circumstance where the Release of Lien used words to the effect that it discharged <u>all</u> lien rights that the claimant had on the property.

SUBJECT MATTER: Mechanic's Liens - Stop Notices - Stop Notice Release Bond

NAME OF CASE: *National Technical Systems v. Commercial Contractors, Inc.* (2001)

HOLDING:

On a public works project, after a contractor has filed a Stop Notice and the prime contractor obtained a Stop Notice Release Bond, requiring the public entity to release the funds to the contractor, the subcontractor must sue the surety issuing the Stop Notice Release Bond to enforce its rights against the Release Bond.

In this case, the court discussed the differences between a Release Bond issued after the filing of a lawsuit and one given prior to the commencement of litigation. During litigation, bonds are often obtained for a number of reasons to secure payment in one form or another. Following the litigation, the prevailing party may in some cases obtain a judgment against the bond surety through "summary proceedings." A motion can be made to recover on bonds issued during litigation, and in that circumstance a separate lawsuit against the surety is not necessary. It seems that in the present case, the Contractor obtained a Stop Notice Release Bond prior to the suit brought by its subcontractor. The subcontractor did not sue the surety who issued that bond in the case itself, but after getting a judgment against the contractor, the subcontractor sought to recover from the surety through summary proceedings.

The Court of Appeal held that one could not collect on a Stop Notice Release Bond that is given prior to the commencement of litigation through summary proceedings (as discussed above, through a motion procedure) after receiving a judgment in the construction dispute. For those bonds, the surety has the right to be added as a party to the court action pursuant to the Code of Civil Procedure. The Court reasoned that where a bond is given before an action is commenced, the surety might not have notice of the filing of the lawsuit. That prevented the surety from protecting its rights during the litigation.

It is important to note that if the Statute of Limitations has not run on the bond, the subcontractor could file a separate case against the bond surety, allowing the surety to then defend itself in the action. The issue in this particular case was the summary enforcement of a Stop Notice Bond where the surety was not joined in the action and therefore could not defend itself.

SUBJECT MATTER: Payment Bond Claims – Substantial Compliance with Requirement of a Bond Notice

NAME OF CASE: *American Buildings Company v. Bay Commercial Construction, Inc. (2002)*

HOLDING:

On a public works project, a material supplier provided a surety with a "Preliminary Notice on Payment Bond" more than 20 days after furnishing the materials. The payment bond surety claimed that it was not obligated to pay the supplier because the supplier did not timely comply with the preliminary notice rules. The supplier contended that its Preliminary Notice on Payment Bond complied with the provisions of Civil Code Sections 3227 and 3252, which allow for notice to a surety after the work has been performed so long as it is within 75 days of the completion of the project, or fifteen days following the notice of completion (or acceptance). The Court of Appeal ruled that the preliminary notice and bond notice sections are complimentary, and that notice under the bond statute may be given where the preliminary notice was faulty or insufficient, and the supplier may then enforce a claim on a payment bond for the full amount of the labor, material, and services. Therefore, the supplier's notice was not faulty as a Bond Notice even though it was faulty as a Preliminary Notice.

SUBJECT MATTER: 'Pay if Paid' Clause Ruled Unconstitutional by California Supreme Court

NAME OF CASE: *WM. R. Clarke v. Safeco Insurance Company of America* (1997)

HOLDING:

This case, which is also discussed elsewhere, ruled that the "pay-if-paid" clause is unenforceable and unconstitutional in California as an infringement of the contractor's mechanics' lien rights. In its discussion, the Supreme Court stated that no mechanics' lien may be recovered where there is no "contract price" as is required by Civil Code section 3140 for recovery on a mechanics' lien. While the case has not been cited for this proposition by another appellate court, it can be argued that where a home improvement contract is voidable or rescinded by operation of Business and Professions Code section 7159 this case's result is that the contractor is not entitled to foreclose upon any mechanics' lien on the property.

SUBJECT MATTER: Mechanic's Liens and Tenant Improvements

NAME OF CASE: *Howard S. Wright Const. Co. v. Superior Court* (2003)

HOLDING:

Contractors who do tenant improvement work essentially have two owners. One is the person who owns the land and the building (lessor), and the other is the lessee. The lessee has an interest in the property by way of the lease that was signed, called a leasehold interest. Mechanic's Lien rights run as to both owners. Usually, tenant improvement work is contracted for by the tenant, but it goes on the property that is owned by the owner of the real estate. The owner may shield itself by posting and recording a Notice of Non-Responsibility within ten days of when they first become aware of the work going on on their property. However, an owner that participates in the construction cannot shield its property interest from a mechanic's lien. The court in this case stated that if alterations to the real estate were required under the lease, then the owner of the property actively participated in, and retained control over the construction. Thus, the owner of the land would not be shielded from mechanic's liens.

CORPORATIONS - ABILITY TO GET AT THE PRINCIPAL WHERE A CORPORATION IS NOT PROPERLY IDENTIFIED

SUBJECT MATTER: Corporations - Requirement to Avoid Personal Liability

NAME OF CASE: *G. W. Anderson Construction Company v. Mars Sales* (1985)

HOLDING:

When a person enters into a contract that does not indicate a corporate status or corporate identity, the individual will be liable as well as the corporation because the person contracting for the services did not know he or she was looking solely to the corporation for any obligations under the contract. The Court held that the individual can protect him or herself from personal liability by clearly disclosing the fact that the corporation, not the individual is the party to the contract.

SUBJECT MATTER: Corporations - Authority of Officers

NAME OF CASE: *Snukal v. Flightways Manufacturing* (2000)

HOLDING:

In this case, the plaintiff leased a residence to a corporation. The residence was occupied by an individual who was the corporation's president, chief financial officer and secretary. That individual alone executed the lease agreement on behalf of the corporation and designated his title as President without indicating his other offices. The rental was not paid and the plaintiff sued to recover lost rents against the corporation. The corporation raised the defense that the particular officer was not authorized to enter into the agreement. The corporation was relying on Corporations Code section 313, which appears to require a signature from two corporate officers, one that is from the operational category (i.e., Chairman of the Board, President, or a Vice-President) and one from the "financial category" (i.e., Secretary, Assistant Secretary, Chief Financial Officer, or Assistant Treasurer). This case made it to the California Supreme Court, which held that one individual who holds a position from both categories of corporate officers, may bind a corporation to an agreement.

SUBJECT MATTER: Corporations - Liability of Officers

NAME OF CASE: *Michaelis v. Benavidez* (1998)

HOLDING:

This case is troubling to the small corporation. One of the main reasons for setting up a corporation is to shield the officers from liability. Typically, if everything is done correctly, officers or directors of the corporation are not responsible to third persons for simple negligence. However, this case held that directors or officers of a corporation may be personally liable for the torts of their corporation if they participate in wrong doing or authorize or direct that it be done. In this case, an individual, who is the president, director, and majority shareholder of a cement contracting firm which contracted with a general contractor to pour a patio and driveway for a residence, could be held personally liable for property damage resulting from negligence where that individual was the only person at the firm with the contractors' license, personally bid the job, personally made all construction decisions, and when the complaint alleged that the individual breached his duty to the owners as third parties, rather than that the corporation breached its duty to third parties. As a result of this case, it appears that corporate officers may be held responsible for acts that would otherwise be shielded from responsibility by incorporation.

SELECTED CASES COVERING CONSTRUCTION CLAIMS

SUBJECT MATTER: Emotional Distress Damages - Recovery

NAME OF CASE: *Fuentes v. Perez* (1977)

HOLDING:

In this case, a contractor who was re-roofing a residence failed to cover the roof properly. The owners frantically called several times during a heavy downpour for the contractor to come out and cover the roof but the contractor did not come. The owner subsequently called the fire department who came in the middle of the night and covered the roof. In the meantime, the house was heavily flooded, and significant damage to the property resulted. The owners complained that they also suffered severe emotional distress from the helplessness of the situation. The Court of Appeal ruled that in this type of case, where no actual physical injury occurred to the owner, the owner cannot collect damages for emotional distress. This court limited the type of case that would allow emotional distress damages to specific instances that are really not relevant to contractors, such as an insurer who commits bad faith, or a jeweler who loses a family heirloom while knowing its sentimental value to the owner.

SUBJECT MATTER: Emotional Distress Damages - Recovery

NAME OF CASE: *Cooper v. Superior Court* (1984)

HOLDING:

In this case, a runaway tractor crashed into the front of a home causing damage to the property. The homeowners sued for their damages and alleged emotional distress. While the owners were entitled to recover for their property damage, the court stated that absent a preexisting relationship or an intentional act by the contractor, emotional distress damages cannot be recovered.

SUBJECT MATTER: Emotional Distress Damages- Recovery

NAME OF CASE: *Erlich v. Menezes* (1999) **Supreme Court**

HOLDING:

The contractors in the state of California won a substantial victory by a recent California Supreme Court case, *Erlich v. Menezes*. Last year we reported that the case was on appeal. The Supreme Court decision holds that a homeowner could not recover for emotional distress based only on the contractor's breach of contract resulting in construction defects discovered in her home.

The Supreme Court's reversal of the Court of Appeal decision in this case is very important because this was the only case to allow emotional distress damages to the owners of residential real property where the damages did not relate to a physical injury caused to them. That is to say, we are not talking about the situation where a contractor drops a hammer on someone, or a ladder falls on a resident. The situation involved in this case was the alleged mental distress caused to an owner merely by the poor workmanship of a contractor.

No previously reported California case had allowed such damages for negligence or as a result of a breach of contract in a single family residential remodel. The Supreme Court decision now puts the law back where it was prior to the decision of the Court of Appeal, which was overruled.

In Erlich, the trial court found that Menezes had performed the home improvement contracted for by the Erlichs in a negligent manner. The jury found that as a result of the defective condition of the house, the Erlichs suffered emotional distress. The jury also found that Menezes breached his contract with the Erlichs by negligently constructing their home and awarded the Erlichs compensatory damages for repairs. This portion of the trial appellate court's decision was appropriate. If one does something that is not correct, the person who does something incorrectly should be held responsible.

A general contractor and a structural engineer found that there were defects in the roof, exterior stucco, windows and waterproofing, and serious errors in the structural components. None of the 20 shear or load bearing walls specified in the place were properly installed.

Turrets on the roof were inadequately connected to the roof beams and began to collapse. Three decks were in danger of "catastrophic collapse." In fact, the experts said it was easier to list what was right with the home, that what was not.

Prior to this case, no reported California case had allowed an award for emotional distress damages based upon a breach of contract to build a house or from any negligence in building or remodeling. The California Supreme Court held that since Menezes' negligence caused only economic and property damage, the Erlichs were not entitled to recover damages for the emotional distress.

The court upheld the long established policy in the state of California that emotional distress can only be recovered based on an independent duty <u>other</u> than the contract between the owner and the contractor, or where a <u>special</u> pre-existing relationship exists between the parties. In this case, Menezes was merely a contractor, and the Erlichs were merely the owners of the property. There was also no breach of an independent duty that did not arise out of the contract.

The previous decisions of the Supreme Court had always held that except in very rare circumstances, the courts should deny recovery of emotional distress damages for tort (negligence) because of the different objectives of the parties, in the absence of a physical injury to the claimant. In contract cases, the predictability of assuring commercial stability in contractual dealings is very important. The potential for changing every contract action into a tort, with an accompanying non-economic damages recovery, would be something that would not fulfill that purpose. The jury did not find any intentional acts on Menezes' part. Only that Menezes acted negligently in the construction of the house.

With this Supreme Court ruling, the law is now settled that a mere breach of contract, or negligence in carrying out the terms of a construction contract, will not lead to damages for emotional distress.

SUBJECT MATTER: Implied Warranty of Quality and Fitness

NAME OF CASE: *Pollard v. Saxe & Yolles Development Company* (1974)

HOLDING:

This case presented the issue of whether the doctrine of implied warranties of quality and fitness which is applicable to the sale of goods and is also applicable in some contract situations, should be applicable to the sale of newly constructed real property. In this case, a general contractor built five new apartment buildings in San Jose. More than three years after the owners took possession of the apartment buildings, the owners complained of construction defects to the general contractor. A lawsuit was filed in February 1967 which was more than three years but less than four years after both actual and constructive notice of the damage to their property. In spite of the fact that the trial court concluded that implied warranties of quality and fitness do not attach to the sale of real property, our California Supreme Court overruled that decision and found that the implied warranties of quality and fitness of purpose do attach to the sale of newly constructed real property. In these set of facts however, the Supreme Court agreed with the lower court that the owners of the newly constructed real property were barred from prosecuting their action for failure to give timely notice of the breach of warranty.

SUBJECT MATTER: Construction Disputes - Indemnity

NAME OF CASE: *Centex Golden Construction Company v. Dale Tile Company* (2000)

HOLDING:

In this case, a subcontractor had a contract with a general contractor that required the subcontractor to indemnify (defend) and hold the general contractor harmless for any claims made pertaining to allegedly defective tile work. Such a claim was made. The subcontractor argued that it had no obligation to indemnify the general contractor because the jury found that the subcontractor was not negligent. The Court of Appeal strictly interpreted the indemnity provision that was at issue and held that a subcontractor must defend and indemnify a general contractor under this type of indemnity clause even where it was not in any way negligent so long as the person or entity being indemnified was not solely responsible nor was the claim as a result of willful misconduct. The trigger for the duty to indemnify was the claim that alleged an event covered by the contract clause.

SUBJECT MATTER: Liability of the Hirer to the Employees of the Contractor

NAME OF CASE: *Hooker v. Department of Transportation (2002)*

HOLDING:

In two recent Supreme Court cases, the court evaluated the liability of the hirer to employees of a contractor, where the employee is injured or killed on a jobsite. In the first of two cases decided on the same day, the California Supreme Court held that the hirer of a licensed general contractor was not responsible for damages resulting from the death of the contractor's employee unless the hirer retains control over the independent contractor's work in a manner in which the hirer would be able to prevent or eliminate, through the exercise of reasonable care, a dangerous condition causing injury to the employee. Mere retention of the ability to control safety conditions is not enough. It must be direct control over the means or methods of the work as to be accomplished.

SUBJECT MATTER: Liability of the Hirer to the Employees of the Contractor

NAME OF CASE: *McKown v. Wal-Mart Stores, Inc.*

HOLDING:

In the second case from the Supreme Court on the issue of hirer liability, the hirer of the licensed contractor, Wal-Mart Stores, was held liable for the employee of its independent contractor, where the hirer (store) requested that the contractor use its forklift, which was defective and unsafe. In this case, the key difference was that the hirer's (store's) equipment, which the hirer wanted the contractor to use, contributed to the injury.

SUBJECT MATTER: Workers' Compensation – Homeowner's Liability for Unlicensed Contractor's Employees

NAME OF CASE: *Hernandez v. Lawson* (2003)

HOLDING:

Ordinarily, when a person hires someone who is required to have a license in order to perform work but does not in fact have a license, the employees of this unlicensed person become the "statutory employees" of the hirer. The hirer is then liable for injuries to these "statutory employees." However, tree trimming is a service connected with the maintenance of a house and the land connected with it. As such, tree trimming is considered a "household domestic service," and is not required to comply with OSHA requirements. Therefore, the hirer in this case was not liable for injuries sustained by employees of an unlicensed tree trimmer.

SUBJECT MATTER: Liability for Failing to Take Safety Precautions

NAME OF CASE: *Kinney v. CSB Construction Inc.* (2001)

HOLDING:

When a hirer, a general contractor, retains control over a jobsite and an employee of a subcontractor gets injured, there are two theories of liability against the general contractor. One is a negligent exercise of the general contractor's retained supervisory powers. The second is a failure to exercise its powers, thus affirmatively causing the hazard, which caused the injury. In this case, Kenny, an employee of the subcontractor, fell while working as an ironworker on a construction project. Kenny argued that the general contractor was completely responsible for the working conditions and for the safety of all persons and property on the site. In order to recover for his injuries, Kenny needed to show either one of the theories of liability, that the general contractor negligently exercised his retained supervisory powers, or that the general contractor's failure to require the subcontractor to take safety precautions affirmatively contributed to the creation or persistence of the hazard causing the plaintiff's injuries. Kenny was unable to show either.

SUBJECT MATTER: Construction Dispute - Arbitration

NAME OF CASE: *Villa Milano Homeowners Association v. Il Davorge* (2000)

HOLDING:

In this case, the Court of Appeal held that an arbitration provision that was contained within the recorded covenants, conditions and restrictions ("CC&R") was legally unconscionable, and could not be used to compel the arbitration of a dispute. Condominium owners and their homeowners association had filed a construction defect suit against a developer. The developer alleged the parties were required to arbitrate the dispute because there was an arbitration clause in the CC&R document that was recorded. Recording of a document is interpreted in many cases to convey knowledge of the document's contents on interested persons. Relying on the fact that an arbitration agreement must be freely agreed to by the parties, the Court of Appeal held that the plaintiffs were not required to arbitrate their dispute based upon the clause that they did not specifically individually agree to.

SUBJECT MATTER: Waiver of Mandatory Arbitration Provision

NAME OF CASE: *Vicki Simms et al., v. NPCK Enterprises, INC, et al.*

HOLDING:

There is a strong public policy favoring contractual arbitration. Thus, the party who claims a waiver to the arbitration clause has a heavy burden of showing that there will be some prejudice absent the waiver. Some of the things that the court will look at in deciding if there was a waiver of the arbitration clause are how far the litigation had gone, if the litigation machinery has been substantially invoked, whether and when anyone asked for arbitration, and whether a counter-claim was filed. Most importantly, the courts will examine whether there is a delay and whether the delay "affected, misled, or prejudiced" the opposing party.

SUBJECT MATTER: Arbitration - Contracts of Adhesion May Be Upheld

NAME OF CASE: *McManus v. CIBC World Markets Corp.* (2003).

HOLDING:

The California Court of Appeal recently held that an arbitration agreement that was entered into as a contract of adhesion may be upheld. A contract of adhesion is one that is not fully negotiated by the parties. Usually, it is a "take it or leave it" situation, and there is no ability to negotiate the provisions. This particular contract of adhesion involved an arbitration agreement as condition of employment. In most cases, the courts will look at each contract of adhesion to determine whether it is unconscionable, if so, then the contract is thrown out. In this case, the court found the arbitration clause to be the only unconscionable provision. However, the court ruled that this clause was not so unconscionable that it could not be saved. The court further stated that the provision requiring payment of fees can be severed from the balance of the agreement, thus the arbitration provision would be binding. Therefore, McManus would not have to pay unconscionable fees in the arbitration, and the balance of the contract can be upheld.

SUBJECT MATTER: Construction Defect - Statute of Limitations

NAME OF CASE: *Krusi v. S.J. Amoroso Construction Co., Inc.*

HOLDING:

In this case, the Court of Appeal held that the owners of a commercial building, who were in fact the fourth owners during the building's eight-year history, could not bring a negligence action against the building's architects and contractors for construction defects. The reasoning of the Court was rather complex and the Court "harmonized" or discussed conflicting holdings in other cases by other Courts of Appeal. The Court recognized that causes of action for negligence in the design, engineering or construction of the building accrue when the damage or physical injury to the property occurs. In some cases, particularly where the seller and buyer do not know the defect, the new buyer can sue the contractor or design professionals for damages. However, in this case, the prior owners not only knew of the defects, but also sued the architect. The Court recognized that a new cause of action does not arise for the new buyer, otherwise the developers and design professionals could face a virtually endless stream of litigation, without any time limit whatsoever.

SUBJECT MATTER: Construction Defects - Professional Liability of Architect

NAME OF CASE: *Smith v. SHN Consulting Engineers & Geologists, Inc.* (2001)

HOLDING:

The two-year Statute of Limitations, which is the period of time one would need to file a lawsuit for professional negligence, applies to a claim by a general contractor against an architect for economic losses incurred in the course of construction. The Court of Appeal also held that the Statute of Limitations begins to run when the Plaintiff sustains damage and discovers or should have discovered the negligence of the design professional it seeks to sue. In this particular case the contractor had told the engineers that it had been "severely damaged" by a variety of construction delays and errors. The court ruled that was the trigger that started the two-year period to file suit.

SUBJECT MATTER: Construction Defect - Limitation on Claims and Type of Damages

NAME OF CASE: *Aas v. Superior Court (William Lyon Company)* (2000)

HOLDING:

In this very important case from the California Supreme Court, it was held that owners could not recover damages on a negligence claim for the cost to repair, or the diminished value attributable to, construction defects that had not yet caused property damage. This was held true not only as to subcontractors, but also between the owners and the developer where there was an actual contract between them.

In this case, as typical with many construction defect claims, the owners were contending that the contractor had violated provisions of the building code, but conceded that those particular deviations had not yet resulted in actual property damage. As an example, there were allegations that they failed to properly construct shear walls and failed to properly connect shear walls to other building components. It was also alleged that there were failures to properly construct one-hour and two-hour firewalls. There were no allegations that those deviations had caused any "resulting damages" such as cracked walls or foundations, or other damages to the structure.

The owners contended that not only did those items have to be repaired, but the fact that things were not built properly caused there to be "stigma" damages, arguing that the property is worth less than it would have been had it been properly constructed. The court, citing to a number of policy issues, held that home buyers already enjoy protection under contract and warranty law for enforcement of the builders' and seller's obligations, as well as under a number of other areas of the law, but that there is no reason to allow damages to be awarded where the alleged defect has not caused any actual damage to the owners.

SUBJECT MATTER: Statute of Limitations on Latent Defects

NAME OF CASE: *Lantzy et al. v. Centex Homes et al.* (2003)

HOLDING:

The Statute of Limitations is the time period within which a plaintiff may bring a lawsuit. There is a ten-year Statute of Limitations for filing suit on latent defects while repairs are pending. However, this ten-year period is not subject to equitable tolling. Equitable tolling occurs when the defendant partakes in action that prevents the plaintiff from suing on a cause of action. As an example, sometimes attempting to make the necessary repairs will "toll" the statute of limitation. Thus, in order to ensure fundamental practicality and fairness, the court will toll, or delay the Statute of Limitations from running so that the plaintiff's suit is not barred. In effect, equitable tolling causes the limitations period to stop running during the tolling event and begins to run again only when the tolling event has ended. However, for suits on latent defects, where there is a ten-year Statute of Limitations, and where the defendant promises or attempts to remedy the defect, there is no provision for equitable tolling. The court stated that the ten-year period is to protect the contractors from perpetual exposure to liability, and is already a generously long cut-off period for plaintiffs in construction defect suits.

SELECTED CASES COVERING PUBLIC WORKS PREHIRE (PROJECT LABOR) AGREEMENTS

SUBJECT MATTER: Prehire (Project Labor) Agreements

NAME OF CASE: *Associated Builders and Contractors, Inc. (Golden Gate Chapter) v. San Francisco Airport Commission* (1999)

HOLDING:

The California Supreme Court recently held that a "Project Stabilization Agreement" ("PSA"), sometimes called a Project Labor Agreement ("PLA"), was constitutional and enforceable. In the words of California Supreme Court Justice Kathryn Werdegar, San Francisco officials could reasonably conclude that such agreements "offered the most effective way to ensure labor harmony on the project and thereby avoid the undesirable consequences of work disruption."

The use of these agreements on construction projects is growing nationally. The PSAs usually require contractors, whether union or nonunion shops, to follow union grievance procedures and pay union wages and benefits. The particular PSA in question contained clauses prohibiting strikes, requiring the arbitration of jurisdictional disputes among the various crafts, and a promise that the workers continue work despite the expiration of any collective bargaining agreements. In exchange for that PSA, the San Francisco Airport Commission agreed to require all contractors to accept the terms of the PSA, and abide by each craft's procedures for determining discipline or discharge of employees.

The San Francisco PSA also required that any necessary employees above the "core work force" be obtained from the union labor pool. A representative of the builders' association that filed the petition that ultimately made it to the Supreme Court was quoted as stating that the PSA prevents a contractor from hiring a favored employee unless that worker had been part of its ongoing work force in the time immediately proceeding the public project. He was also quoted as stating that such plans do not insure labor peace, noting that a wildcat strike briefly crippled the San Francisco Airport construction in May of this year. Airport personnel countered by stating that the agreement was critical in getting the workers back on the job.

Generally, a PSA is a type of pre-hire agreement designed for large and complex construction projects. It is said to be designed to eliminate potential delays resulting from labor disputes, which should insure a steady supply of skilled labor on projects. The California Supreme Court discussed a recent U.S. Supreme Court case which stated that while the National Labor Relations Act (NLRA) generally prohibits pre-hire agreements, in construction projects PSAs will be allowed to stand.

The argument is that the majority of building projects are relatively short in duration and such agreements are necessary for the employer to know the labor costs before estimating and bidding the project, and also so that the employer can have an available supply of skilled craftsman.

It should be noted that in California the first reason is really a non-issue on publics work projects because of the prevailing wage laws. That is to say, regardless of the existence of a PSA, the employer must pay prevailing wages which are usually the same as or close to the union wages for the territory.

In the present case, the San Francisco Airport Commission was entering into contracts to construct a $2.4 billion dollar expansion of the San Francisco International Airport. On the day that bids were due, the Associated Builders and Contractors Inc., Golden Gate Chapter and the Asian American Contractors Association (referred to jointly as "ABC" herein) appeared together at the San Francisco County Superior Court. They tried to get the court to issue an order stating they would not have to comply with the PSA as required by the bid specifications. Generally non-signatory contractors wanted to land the lucrative contracts without having to comply with all the other requirements. They argued that the PSA was unconstitutional and violated state competitive bidding statutes. The Superior Court denied the petition of those groups and the Court of Appeal upheld that denial.

The Court of Appeal stated that the decision to use a PSA for the Airport Expansion Project was a matter of local concern governed by San Francisco's Administrative Code rather than the California Public Contract Code. However, the Court further stated that regardless of whether state or local law applied, the PSA did not violate the competitive bidding laws and was not unconstitutional.

ABC then appealed to the California Supreme Court. The Supreme Court made a number of rulings in this case, though some of them are not really that important to our discussion.

First, the Supreme Court ruled that it did not matter whether state or local competitive bidding laws applied and it would make no determination on this issue because the answer was not necessary to answer the question before the court of whether or not the PSA was constitutional. All of the parties agreed in this case that the Public Contract Code and the local laws all required the bid to go to the lowest responsible bidder. Therefore, the Court held there was no need for it to determine whether the state or the local competitive bidding laws applied.

The Supreme Court then got to the meat of the case -- whether or not the PSA is consistent with competitive bidding laws. The court stated that the first step was to consider the PSA in light of the purposes of the competitive bidding laws to determine whether it serves those purposes, or instead, has the anti-competitive effect of excluding persons from the project or denying an equal opportunity to any categories of potential bidders. Relying largely on the prevailing wage laws requiring all contractors to pay the "prevailing wage," the Supreme Court ruled that complying with the terms of the PSA did not put the nonunion contractors at a competitive disadvantage to union contractors. The Court also rejected arguments that were made that the PSA deters nonunion contractors from bidding because it requires contractors to sign an agreement with the unions and use only union-supplied labor for any workers needed beyond their "core work force," pay into union benefit funds and adopt union wage rates. Under the California prevailing wage laws, most of the financial results would be the same.

The Supreme Court also cited to the fact that federal law requires unions to refer both union members and nonmembers to available jobs. In this respect, the Supreme Court said that ABC failed to show how the PSA either discriminates or deters non-union contractors from bidding on such projects because of the plan. Accordingly, the Supreme Court of California ruled that such agreements were not unconstitutional.

The Supreme Court also made other rulings that were more legally technical in nature such as whether ABC could represent the rights of individual workers; which party has the burden of proof in writ proceedings; that if union shops are legal, then PSAs must also be legal; and lastly, that because PSAs are legal under federal law, any order denying their use might be illegal as a result of the Federal Supremacy clause of the U.S. Constitution.

In sum, because the PSA did not bar or discriminate against a class of contractors, it did not violate the competitive bidding laws. The agreement was consistent with the competitive bidding laws and a contractor's compliance with the agreement was not an unfair labor practice because it did not interfere with the worker's right to choose their bargaining representation.

A representative of Associated Builders was quoted by the Los Angeles Times as stating the decision would hurt construction firms owned by women and minorities because most are not unionized. The practical reality is that PSAs may cause or prevent any nonunion shop from bidding on large projects where a PSA is in place.

As stated by the Supreme Court, these agreements will be examined on a case-by-case basis. In other words, the issue is not quite dead. For now, until the NLRA may determine otherwise, PSAs will probably continue to be held constitutional.

SUBJECT MATTER: Public Works - Liability To Listed Subcontractors

NAME OF CASE: *R.J. Land And Associates Construction Company v. Kiewit-Shea* (1999)

HOLDING:

In this case, the general contractor bidding on a public works project inadvertently listed two subcontractors for the same work. The general contractor did not realize this error in time to correct its bid pursuant to the Public Contract Code. Thereafter, one of the listed subcontractors for that work sued the general contractor for damages for the contractor's failure to enter into a contract with the subcontractor for the listed work. The general contractor was held to be liable to the subcontractor for its damages (which would be its lost profits) for the general contractor's failure to enter into a contract with the subcontractor, despite the fact that it had listed two contractors for the same work and had already utilized the other contractor to do the work.

SUBJECT MATTER: Public Works Construction Contracts – Liability of Public Entity Based Upon "Abandonment Theory."

NAME OF CASE: *Amelco Electric v. City of Thousand Oaks (2002)*

HOLDING:

A contractor brought suit against the City of Thousand Oaks alleging that it was entitled to additional compensation because there were more than 221 change orders resulting in $1.7 million in additional damages and cost to the contractor. The contractor had argued that because there were so many changes, that "an abandonment of the contract" occurred, which would allow the contractor to be paid on a reasonable value of the work basis. The California Supreme Court ruled that unlike the private works sector, where such an argument may be made, the statutory framework in the Public Contract Code prohibits a claim made under the theory of abandonment of contract.

SUBJECT MATTER: Arbitration – Public's Works Projects

NAME OF CASE: *Brutoco Engineering & Construction, Inc. v. Superior Court* (2003)

HOLDING:

In a public works dispute where a party is a public agency, arbitrations must be conducted by a single arbitrator selected by the parties from a "certified list," to be certified by the Public Works Contract Arbitration Committee. This is governed by the Public Contract Code. Furthermore, while the parties may nominate arbitrators who are not on the certified list to act as their arbitrator, a court cannot select a non-certified person as arbitrator when the parties cannot agree on either a certified or non-certified arbitrator.

SUBJECT MATTER: Charter City Required to Pay Prevailing Wages

NAME OF CASE: *City of Long Beach v. Dpt. of Industrial Rel.* (2003)

HOLDING:

There are laws enacted by the legislature that may not apply to chartered cities. A project by a charter city that is strictly a municipal affair is exempt from state prevailing wage law. The court has determined that the more the effects of the project extend beyond the borders of the municipality, the less the project occupies the realm of "municipal affair." Therefore, a project by a charter city that remains within the borders of the municipality will probably be a municipal affair, and therefore exempt from state prevailing wage law. In this case, the project was going to serve a city function as well as be part of a countywide animal shelter system and was only partly funded with city funds, therefore, the project was subject to the prevailing wage laws.

Review of this case has been granted and therefore this case cannot be cited as authority. However, the logic still applies.

SUBJECT MATTER: Off-Site Work May Be Subject to Prevailing Wage Requirements

NAME OF CASE: *Department of Industrial Relations Decision* (March 4, 2003)

HOLDING:

Prevailing wages must be paid to the employees of contractors and subcontractors engaged in the off-site fabrication or prefabrication of items specially produced for public works projects if the wages are advertised for bid after the date of the determination is posted on the Department of Industrial Relation's website. To determine whether a product is made specially for the public works project or for sale to the general market, the test is if the item was produced in accordance with the plans and specifications of the architects, engineer, and/or shop drawings for the project, so that they are different from generic items. **NOTE:** The Department of Industrial Relations has now issued a Stay Order so that implementation of the above Administrative Decision would be stayed pending administrative appeals. However, the above decision is still note-worthy, as this

Stay Order may be lifted, thus restoring the payment of prevailing wages for off-site fabrication work.

SUBJECT MATTER: Permanent Debarment from Public Work's Projects

NAME OF CASE: *Southern California Underground Contractors, Inc. v. City of San Diego* (2003)

HOLDING:

A public entity can permanently debar a contractor given the proper factual basis. As long as there is ample opportunity for the contractor to present its evidence, cross-examine witnesses, etc., a permanent debarment that is proper should be upheld. However, during the presentation of evidence at the debarment hearing, the public entity is not required to allow the cross-examinations of witnesses to allow for a full and fair hearing, if, as in this case, the contractor had the right to take and submit numerous depositions as well as oral and written argument.

SUBJECT MATTER: Declaration of Non-Responsibility Against Public Works Bidder

NAME OF CASE: *Begl Const. Co. Inc., v. Bd. of Rec. & Parks Comm.* (unpublished 2003) Note: **This is an unpublished case. It cannot be used for authority in another case, but the logic of the decision would likely sway another court in the same manner.**

HOLDING:

Our office recently scored a big victory in the Court of Appeal on behalf of one of our clients. The case concerned an issue regarding contractors performing public works projects. Our client, the contractor, performed work for the City of Los Angeles Department of Recreation and Parks. On the project at issue, the contractor filed a claim with the city, seeking more than $700,000.00 for what the contractor contended were delays and unsigned change orders due entirely to deficient plans and changes sought by the City Department. In response, the City held a hearing to determine whether or not the contractor was a responsible bidder. Pursuant to

City of Los Angeles ordinances, once a bidder is deemed to be non-responsible, he is debarred and may not bid on another city project for five years. He may, however, apply for reinstatement after two years.

At the hearing before the Board of Recreation and Park Commissioners, the City did not give him an opportunity to fully present his case. On top of that, even though the contractor had more than one thousand pages of documents showing how it was not to blame for the problems on the project, and an engineer testified as to the delays, the City Department did not seem to take these documents and testimony into consideration. The City Department summarily declared the contractor to be non-responsible.

We then went to the Superior Court, whose job it is to review the record from the Administrative Hearing. Similarly, the Superior Court upheld the decision of the City Department. Finally, we brought our case to the Court of Appeal. The Court of Appeal took the time to read the documents and testimony our client had brought. Upon reading the evidence, the Court of Appeal declared that our client was denied a fair opportunity to put on evidence of its responsibility and refute the charges against it. The Court of Appeal then ordered the City Department to set aside their determination of non-responsibility.

While all of the above was going on, our client went to trial on its claim against the City of Los Angeles. A 12-0 verdict was obtained in our favor, and the jury award was in excess of $680,000.00.

SELECTED CASES COVERING SURETY LIABILITIES

SUBJECT MATTER: Surety's Liability For Prompt Pay Penalties

NAME OF CASE: *Washington International Insurance Company v. Superior Court* (1998)

HOLDING:

Under the prompt pay laws, a contractor who wrongfully fails to pay progress payments to subcontractors within ten days of receipt from the owner is liable not only for a penalty in the amount of 2% per month, but also is responsible for the attorneys fees incurred to collect the unpaid amount as well. This case holds that the payment bond surety is also liable to the subcontractor for the contractor's failure to pay the amounts due on the subcontract, including the civil penalties (2% per month) and attorneys fees.

SUBJECT MATTER: Stop Notice Release Bonds – Right to attorneys fees and statutory penalties

NAME OF CASE: *National Technical Systems v. Superior Court of Los Angeles County (2002)*

HOLDING:

A subcontractor sought to enforce a stop notice release bond against the surety that issued that bond. The court first ruled that the fact that the subcontractor had already obtained a judgment against the general contractor was not admissible in the suit against the surety. The court stated that it was well established that a judgment against a principal is not binding in a separate action against a surety. However, in what may become a "landmark decision" for contractors, the court held that because a surety's liability is the same as its principal, the surety on the stop notice release bond was liable to the subcontractor for attorneys fees and statutory interest penalties that the contractor was obligated to pay to the supplier.

SUBJECT MATTER: Surety Liabilities - Damages

NAME OF CASE: *Cates Construction, Inc. v. Talbot Partners* (1999)

HOLDING:

In this recent case from the California Supreme Court, the court held that a surety who issued performance bonds on behalf of an owner was liable to the owner for all of the contract damages that the principal (a general contractor) was liable to the owner, including delay damages or damages that result from the delay, such as a loss in the value of the property. In so holding, the court held that a contract which required a performance bond and incorporated the terms of the contract into the performance bond, made the surety liable for all damages caused by the contractor's breach of that contract.

Separately, the Supreme Court was also asked to determine whether or not an owner may collect punitive damages against the surety issuing the bond for their failure to act in good faith in resolving the claims that were made against the bond. The Supreme Court ruled that while the owner of the property was entitled to collect all of its damages stemming from the breach by the contractor or the surety on the bond itself, tort damages which would include emotional distress damages or punitive damages are not available for a breach of a surety bond agreement. The court expressly stated that a surety bond is different than an insurance policy, and as such the type of remedies that are available against insurers for breach of their insurance policies are not available against those persons issuing surety bonds.

SUBJECT MATTER: Surety's Obligation for Attorney's Fees

NAME OF CASE: *Scott Co. of Cal. v. Blount, Inc.* (1999)

HOLDING:

A surety may be held liable to a proper payment bond claimant even though the surety's principal (the contractor) has already resolved its obligations to the claimant. This case adds another wrinkle to the issues concerning surety liability, particularly under public work's payment bonds. This case involved two segments, the first of which ended in a favorable settlement for the subcontractor, Scott. However, Blount, the prime contractor, had made a statutory Offer and Compromise under Code of Civil Procedure section 998, which Scott rejected. A 998 offer is essentially a mechanism that hopes to have the parties reach a settlement before trial. However, if the other party refuses the offer, and the judgment following trial is less favorable than that contained in the offer, then the party rejecting the offer will be required to pay all post-offer costs of the party who made the offer. The result in this first segment of this case was that Scott received a favorable judgment, but subsequently owed Blount $46,000. In the second segment of the case, Scott went against the payment bond sureties, with the argument that the payment bond sureties were liable to it even if the general contractor's liability was resolved. This theory is true – a payment bond surety may be independently liable, and may be liable on certain theories of law even though the general contractor pays any liability it has to the subcontractor. However, the issue was whether the sureties were included in the prior settlement offer by Blount. If they were included in the offer, the liability for fees would not have arisen. The court remanded that portion of the case back for the trial court's factual determination.

APPENDIX F.
SAMPLE CITATIONS

This is the actual citation (Page 1).

Contractors State License Board Citation (Business and Professions Code 7099)

Contractors State License Board
Southern Region
7001 Village Drive, Suite 260
Buena Park, CA 90621-2276   Citation Number: 2982020

To: SAM ABDULAZIZ
6454 Coldwater Canyon Ave.
North Hollywood, CA 91606-1187

License Number: 123456, B

Owner of Project: Chuck Murray
Location of Occurrence: 7001 Village Drive, Suite 260, Buena Park, CA 90621
Approximate Date(s) of Occurrence(s): 01/01/95

An investigation of your contracting activity at the location identified above has been conducted by the Contractors State License Board. This citation is being issued in accordance with the Business and Professions Code Section 7099, for violation(s) which were found during the investigation.

This citation details each violation charged and orders of correction where applicable. **IT IS YOUR RESPONSIBILITY TO READ THIS ENTIRE CITATION.**

Unless contested, this citation shall become a final order of the Registrar on 10/30/98; the corrections are due on or before 11/16/98; and the $3,000.00 civil penalty assessment is due on or before 11/23/98.

Payment of the civil penalty should be made to the REGISTRAR OF CONTRACTORS by cashier's check or money order. Please include the citation number on the payment. Any payment ordered to the project owner should be paid to him/her directly.

You, the licensee, are responsible for notifying the Registrar of Contractors when the correction and/or restitution is made. You are also responsible for providing a release from the project owner, or other proof of correction/restitution.

Proof of correction/restitution must be received at the address on the first page of this document no later than five (5) working days after the correction due date.

Please include citation number on all correspondence.

FAILURE TO RESPOND TO THE CITATION WILL RESULT IN FURTHER DISCIPLINARY ACTION AGAINST YOUR LICENSE AND ANY OTHER LICENSE YOU ARE ASSOCIATED WITH.

COMPLIANCE OF THE ORDER OF CORRECTION DOES NOT WAIVE THE CIVIL PENALTY.

10/08/98
Date

For C Lance Barnett, Ph.D.
Registrar of Contractors
Contractors State License Board

Page 2 of the actual citation

Citation Number: 2982020

VIOLATION SECTION

****ITEM NO: 1

SECTION VIOLATED: 7107

DESCRIPTION OF
VIOLATION: Abandoned the project without legal excuse on 01/01/95 leaving the following work not performed or incomplete:

1) Failed in his stage performance due to bad acting

2) Failed to select an appropriate football team because USC was easier to spell than UCLA.

ORDER OF
CORRECTION: N/A

TIME TO CORRECT: N/A

CIVIL PENALTY: $ 1,000.00 (to his favorite charity)

****ITEM NO: 2

SECTION VIOLATED: 7113

DESCRIPTION OF
VIOLATION: Failed to complete the contracted work for the price states in the contract causing a material injury in the amount of $18,000.00 to the prime contractor Contractors of Southern California who may be compelled to expend funds over the price stated in the contract price in order to have the work completed or corrected by others.

Page 3 of the actual citation

Citation Number: 2982020

ORDER OF
CORRECTION: Pay the amount of $18,000.00 to Ken Grossbart within the lifetime of the date of this order.

TIME TO CORRECT: 20 working days.

****ITEM NO: 3

SECTION VIOLATED: 7110/GOV4216-4216.9

DESCRIPTION
OF VIOLATION: Negligent willful or deliberate disregard and violation of Government Code 4216 through 42163.9 in the following manner:

Absent an emergency, the excavator failed to use hand tools, as prescribed by CC.4216.4, to determine the exact location of the subsurface installation(s) in conflict with the excavation, because a shovel was a foreign object to him and thus needed special instructions.

ORDER OF
CORRECTION: N/A

TIME TO CORRECT: N/A

CIVIL PENALTY: $ 1,000.00 (to his favorite charity)

Page 4 of the citation showing it was mailed by First Class.

DECLARATION OF SERVICE BY FIRST CLASS MAIL

RE: SAM ABDULAZIZ CITATION NO: 2982020

I, Marilou S. Felipe, declare that I am over 18 years of age, and not a party to the within cause; that my business address is 7001 Village Drive, Suite 260, Buena Park, CA 90620; that I served a true copy of the attached **Citation, Notice of Appeal, Statement to a Cited Person, and Government Code Section 11507.5, 11507.6, 11507.7,** by first class mail on each of the following, by placing same in an envelope (or envelopes) addressed (respectively) as follows:

NAME AND ADDRESS

SAM ABDULAZIZ
6454 Coldwater Canyon Ave.
North Hollywood, California 91606-1187

CHARLES W. MURRAY
7001 Village Drive, Suite 260
Buena Park, California 90621

Each said envelope was then, on 10/08/98, sealed and deposited in the United States mail at Orange County, California, the county in which I am employed, as first class mail, with the postage thereon fully prepaid.

Executed on 10/08/98, at Buena Park, Orange County, California.

I declare under penalty of perjury under the laws of the State of California that the foregoing is true and correct.

Marilou Felipe
DECLARANT

Page 5 of the actual citation showing it was mailed certified.

DECLARATION OF SERVICE BY CERTIFIED MAIL

RE: SAM ABDULAZIZ CITATION NO: 2982020

I, Marilou S. Felipe, declare as follows:

I am over 18 years of age, and not a party to the within action; my place of employment and business address is Contractors State License Board, 7001 Village Drive, Suite 260, Buena Park, CA 90620.

On 10/08/98, I served a true copy of the attached Citation, Notice of Appeal, Statement to a Cited Person, and Government Code Section 11507.5, 11507.6, 11507.7, by placing it in an envelope addressed to each of the persons named below at the address set out immediately below each respective name, and by sealing the said envelope, which was then certified with return receipt requested and deposited in the United States Mail at Buena Park, Orange County, California, with certification fees and postage thereon fully prepaid.

NAME AND ADDRESS	CERTIFIED NO:
SAM ABDULAZIZ 6454 Coldwater Canyon Ave. North Hollywood, California 91606-1187	Z 2354877612

I declare under penalty of perjury under the laws of the State of California that the foregoing is true and correct.

Executed on 10/08/98, at Buena Park, Orange County, California.

Marilou Felipe
DECLARANT

This form is used by the contractor to inform the CSLB that the contractor is contesting the citation- There is a time limit to file this. This form is sometimes called *Notice of Defense* instead of *Notice of Appeal.*

Before the Registrar of Contractors of the Contractors State License Board Department of Consumer Affairs, State of California

Notice of Appeal (Contesting Citation)

Region ____________________ Citation No. ______________

In the Matter of the Citation Against: ________________________

(Respondent)

To the Registrar of Contractors:

I hereby acknowledge receipt of the Citation referenced above and notification of my rights to contest the Citation. I do hereby contest the Citation and request a hearing.

I have indicated below which parts of the Citation I am contesting. I am not contesting any parts that I have not checked.

(For each item of the Citation, indicate by marking an X in the corresponding boxes whether you are contesting the violation cited, the order of correction, the time to correct, and/or the civil penalty.)

Item No.	Violation Cited	Order of Correction	Time to Correct	Civil Penalty
	☐	☐	☐	☐
	☐	☐	☐	☐
	☐	☐	☐	☐
	☐	☐	☐	☐
	☐	☐	☐	☐
	☐	☐	☐	☐

Dated: ___________________, 19___

Signed: ________________________

Address: ____

____

Telephone No. ____________________ ____________________

(If there is any change in address of the respondent other than set forth in the Citation, the new address should be indicated on this form so that the address of record can be changed and that the Notice of Hearing can be sent to the corrected address.)

These are instructions to the contractor and relevant code sections.

STATEMENT TO CITED PERSON

Attached is a copy of a Citation issued by the Office of the Registrar of Contractors, which is hereby served upon you.

Unless a written request for a hearing signed by you or on your behalf is delivered or mailed to the Registrar of Contractors within fifteen (15) days after the Citation is personally served on you or mailed you, you will be deemed to have waived your right to hearing and the Citation shall be deemed a final order of the Registrar and not subject to review by any court or agency.

The request for a hearing shall be made by indicating the parts of the Citation to be contested, and signing, and delivering or mailing the enclosed form entitled "Notice of Appeal" to Registrar of Contractors:

CONTRACTORS STATE LICENSE BOARD
7001 Village Drive, Suite 260
Buena Park, CA 90621-2276

The time in which to file a notice of appeal may be extended by the Registrar upon showing of good cause, which determination is within the discretion of the Registrar.

You must comply with the orders in the Citation within the times given unless you appeal.

Copies of Sections 11507.5, 11507.6, and 11507.7 of the Government Code are attached.

If you desire the names and addresses of witnesses or an opportunity to inspect and copy the items mentioned in Section 11507.6 of Government Code in possession, custody, or control of the agency, you may contact the Office of the Registrar at the above address.

You may be, but need not be, represented by a counsel. If you wish to be presented by counsel, you are advised to contact your attorney immediately, so that you may be properly represented in all proceedings.

This is required by law to be sent with the citation.

COPY OF GOVERNMENT CODE SECTIONS 11507.5, 11507.6, and 11507.7 PURSUANT TO GOVERNMENT CODE SECTIONS 11504 and 11505

Discovery In Administrative Proceeding

11507.5. The provisions of Section 11507.6 provide the exclusive right to and method of discovery as to any proceeding governed by this chapter.

11507.6 (Second of two; Operative July 1, 1997) Request for discovery

After initiation of a proceeding in which a respondent or other party is entitled to a hearing on the merits, a party, upon written request made to another party, prior to the hearing and within 30 days after the service by the agency of the initial pleading or within 15 days after the service of an additional pleading, is entitled to (1) obtain the names and addresses of witnesses to the extent known to the other party, including, but not limited to, those intended to be called to testify at the hearing, and (2) inspect and make a copy of any of the following in the possession or custody or under the control of the other party:

(a) A statement of a person, other than the respondent, named in the initial administrative pleading, or in any additional pleading, when it is claimed that the act or omission of the respondent as to this person is the basis for the administrative proceeding;

(b) A statement pertaining to the subject matter of the proceeding made by any party to another party or person;

(c) Statements of witnesses then proposed to be called by the party and of other persons having personal knowledge of the acts, omissions or events which are the basis for the proceeding, not included in (a) or (b) above;

(d) All writings, including, but not limited to, reports of mental, physical and blood examinations and things which the party then proposes to offer in evidence;

(e) Any other writing or thing which is relevant and which would be admissible in evidence;

(f) Investigative reports made by or on behalf of the agency or other party pertaining to the subject matter of the proceeding, to the extent that these reports (1) contain the names and addresses of witnesses or of persons having personal knowledge of the acts, omissions or events which are the basis for the proceeding, or (2) reflect matters perceived by the investigator in the course of his or her investigation, or (3) contain or include by attachment any statement or writing described in (a) to (e), inclusive, or summary thereof.

For the purpose of this section, "statements" include written statements by the person signed or otherwise authenticated by him or her, stenographic, mechanical, electrical, or other recordings, or transcripts thereof, of oral statements by the person, and written reports or summaries of these oral statements.

Nothing in this section shall authorize the inspection or copying of any writing or thing which is privileged from disclosure by law or otherwise made confidential or protected as the attorney's work product.

11507.7 (Second of two; Operative July 1, 1997) Petition to compel discovery; Order

(a) Any party claiming the party's request for discovery pursuant to Section 1507.6 has not been complied with may serve and file with the administrative law judge a motion to compel discovery naming as respondent the party refusing or failing to comply with Section 11507.6. The motion shall state facts showing the respondent party failed or refused to comply with Section 11507.6, a description of the matters sought to be discovered, the reason or reasons why the matter is discoverable under that section, that a reasonable and good faith attempt to contact the respondent for an informal resolution of the issue has been made, and the ground or grounds of respondent's refusal so far known to the moving party.

(b) The motion shall be served upon respondent party and filed within 15 days after the respondent party first evidenced failure or refusal to comply with Section 11507.6 or within 30 days after request was made and the party has failed to reply to the request, or within another time provided by stipulation, whichever period is longer.

(c) The hearing on the motion to compel discovery shall be held within 15 days after the motion is made, or a later time that the administrative law judge may on the judge's own motion for good cause determine. The respondent party shall have the right to serve and file a written answer or other response to the motion before or at the time of the hearing.

(d) Where the matter sought to be discovered is under the custody or control of the respondent party and the respondent party asserts that the matter is not a discoverable matter under the provisions of Section 11507.6, or is privileged against disclosure under those provisions, the administrative law judge may order lodged with it matters provided in subdivision (b) of Section 915 of the Evidence Code and examine the matters in accordance with its provisions.

(e) The administrative law judge shall decide the case on the matters examined in camera, the papers filed by the parties, and such oral argument and additional evidence as the administrative law judge may allow.

(f) Unless otherwise stipulated by the parties, the administrative law judge shall no later than 15 days after the hearing make its order denying or granting the motion. The order shall be in writing setting forth the matters the moving party is entitled to discover under Section 11507.6. A copy of the order shall forthwith be served by mail by the administrative law judge upon the parties. Where the order grants the motion in whole or in part, the order shall not become effective until 10 days after the date the order is served. Where the order denies relief to the moving party, the order shall be effective on the date it is served.

APPENDIX G.
DISCIPLINARY GUIDELINES

RECOMMENDED DISCIPLINARY GUIDELINES

(Rev. 12/11/96)

In assessing a disciplinary penalty against a person who has not had a previous citation, revocation, suspension nor denial of application, as the result of the filing of an accusation or a statement of issues, the Registrar shall give due consideration to the following guidelines. In addition to any penalties imposed, all persons that have had a license disciplined, whether or not the disciplinary action has been stayed, will be required to post a disciplinary bond pursuant to Section 7071.8. Unless otherwise specified, all references are to the Business and Professions Code.

Factors to be Considered

In determining whether revocation, suspension or probation is to be imposed in a given case, factors such as the following should be considered:

1. Nature and severity of the act(s), offenses, or crime(s) under consideration.
2. Actual or potential harm to the public.
3. Performed work that was potentially hazardous to the health, safety, or general welfare of the public.
4. Prior disciplinary record.
5. Number and/or variety of current violations.
6. Mitigation evidence.
7. Rehabilitation evidence.
8. In case of a criminal conviction, compliance with terms of sentence and/or court-ordered probation.

Sections and Recommended Disciplinary Guidelines

125. Conspiracy with an Unlicensed Person

Minimum Penalty: Revocation, stayed, 3 years probation

Maximum Penalty: Revocation

If warranted:

1. Actual suspension of 5 days or more.
2. Standard terms and conditions in cases of probation. (1)
3. Submit copies of construction contracts to the Registrar upon demand during the probation period.
4. If not taken within the past 5 years, take and pass the CSLB law and business examination.
5. Take and pass a course in Contractors License Law or a course related to construction law at an accredited 488community college. All courses must be approved in advance by the Registrar.
6. Community Service time as determined by the Registrar; 5-21 days.
7. Pay CSLB investigation and enforcement costs.

141. Disciplinary Action by Foreign Jurisdiction

Minimum Penalty: Revocation, stayed, 3 years probation

Maximum Penalty: Revocation

If warranted:

1. Actual suspension of 5 days or more.
2. Standard terms and conditions in cases of probation. (1)
3. Pay CSLB investigation and enforcement costs.
4. Community Service as determined by the Registrar; 5-21 days.

490. Conviction of a Crime - Substantial Relationship Required

Minimum Penalty: Revocation, stayed, 3 years probation

Maximum Penalty: Revocation

If warranted:

1. Absent compelling mitigating circumstances, conviction of a crime related to the functions of a contractor is a serious offense that warrants an outright revocation.
2. Actual suspension of at least 30 days.
3. Standard terms and conditions in cases of probation. (1)
4. Make restitution.

5. If not taken within the past 5 years, take and pass the CSLB law and business examination.
6. Prohibit receipt of down payments.
7. Community Service as determined by the Registrar; 5-21 days.
8. Pay CSLB investigation and enforcement costs.

496. Violation of Section 123 - Subversion of Licensee Examinations

Minimum Penalty: Revocation

Maximum Penalty: Revocation

If warranted:

1. Pay CSLB investigation and enforcement costs.

498. Securing a License Through Fraud, Deceit or Knowing Misrepresentation

Minimum Penalty: Revocation

Maximum Penalty: Revocation

If warranted:

1. Pay CSLB investigation and enforcement costs.

499. False Statement in Support of Application

Minimum Penalty: Revocation, stayed, 3 years probation

If warranted:

1. Absent compelling mitigating circumstances, making a false statement in support of an application of another person, is a serious offense that warrants an outright revocation.
2. Actual suspension of at least 30 days.
3. Standard terms and conditions in cases of probation. (1)
4. If not taken within the past 5 years, take and pass the CSLB law and business examination.
5. Take and pass a course in Contractors License Law or a course related to construction law at an accredited community college. All courses must be approved in advance by the Registrar.
6. Community Service as determined by CSLB; 5-21 days.
7. Pay CSLB investigation and enforcement costs.

860. (CCR) Penalty for Failure to Comply with Rules

Minimum Penalty: 5 day suspension, stayed, 1 year probation

Maximum Penalty: Revocation

If warranted:

1. Actual suspension of 5 days or more.
2. Standard terms and conditions in cases of probation. (1)
3. If not taken within the past 5 years, take and pass the CSLB law and business examination.
4. Take and pass a course in Contractors License Law or a course related to construction law at an accredited community college. All courses must be approved in advance by the Registrar.
5. Pay CSLB investigation and enforcement costs.

7018.5. Notice to Owner; Mechanics' Lien Law

Minimum Penalty: 5 day suspension, stayed, 1 year probation

Maximum Penalty: 60 day suspension, 1 year probation

If warranted:

1. Standard terms and conditions in cases of probation. (1)
2. Submit copies of construction contracts to the Registrar upon demand during the probation period.
3. If not taken within the past 5 years, take and pass the CSLB law and business examination.
4. Take and pass a course in Contractors License Law or a course related to construction law at an accredited community college. All courses must be approved in advance by the Registrar.
5. Pay CSLB investigation and enforcement costs.

7027.3. Fraudulent Use of a License Number

Minimum Penalty: Revocation

Maximum Penalty: Revocation

If warranted:

1. Pay CSLB investigation and enforcement costs.

7029.1. Contracting Jointly Without a Joint Venture License

Minimum Penalty: 5 day suspension, stayed, 1 year probation

Maximum Penalty: 60 day suspension, 1 year probation

If warranted:

1. Actual suspension of 5 days or more.
2. Standard terms and conditions in cases of probation.(1)
3. If not taken within the past 5 years, take and pass the CSLB law and business examination.
4. Take and pass a course in Contractors License Law or a course related to construction law at an accredited community college. All courses must be approved in advance by the Registrar.
5. Pay CSLB investigation and enforcement costs.

7029.5. Identification on Vehicle, Plumbing, Electrical Sign, and Well-drilling

Minimum Penalty: 5 day suspension, stayed, 1 year probation

Maximum Penalty: 60 suspension, 1 year probation

If warranted:

1. Standard terms and conditions in cases of probation. (1)
2. Pay CSLB investigation and enforcement costs.

7068.2. Failure to Notify; Disassociation of RMO/RME

Minimum Penalty: 60 day suspension, stayed, 1 year probation

Maximum Penalty: Revocation

If warranted:

1. Standard terms and conditions in cases of probation. (1)
2. If not taken within the past 5 years, take and pass the CSLB law and business examination.
3. Take and pass a course in Contractors License Law or a course related to construction law at an accredited community college. All courses must be approved in advance by the Registrar.
4. Pay CSLB investigation and enforcement costs.

7071.11. Judgment, Admitted Claim or Good Faith Payment on Bond

Minimum Penalty: 60 day suspension, stayed, 1 year probation
Maximum Penalty: Revocation
If warranted:

1. Actual suspension of 5 days or more.
2. Standard terms and conditions in cases of probation.
3. Make restitution.
4. Pay CSLB investigation and enforcement costs.

7071.13. Reference in Advertising; Contractors Bond

Minimum Penalty: 5 day suspension, stayed, 1 year probation
Maximum Penalty: 60 day suspension, 1 year probation
If warranted:

1. Standard terms and conditions in cases of probation. (1)
2. Submit copies of advertisements relating to contracting business to the Registrar prior to their being displayed or published during the probation period.
3. If not taken within the past 5 years, take and pass the CSLB law and business examination.
4. Take and pass a course in Contractors License Law or a course related to construction law at an accredited community college. All courses must be approved in advance by the Registrar.
5. Pay CSLB investigation and enforcement costs.

7071.15. Failure to Maintain a Sufficient Bond

Minimum Penalty: 60 day suspension, stayed, 1 year probation
Maximum Penalty: Revocation
If warranted:

1. Actual suspension of 5 days or more.
2. Standard terms and conditions in cases of probation. (1)
3. If not taken within the past 5 years, take and pass the CSLB law and business examination.

4. Take and pass a course in Contractors License Law or a course related to construction law at an accredited community college. All courses must be approved in advance by the Registrar.
5. Pay CSLB investigation and enforcement costs.

7076. Failure to Notify; Death or Disassociation of Licensee Personnel

Minimum Penalty: 60 day suspension, stayed, 1 year probation

Maximum Penalty: Revocation

If warranted:

1. Standard terms and conditions in cases of probation. (1)
2. If not taken within the past 5 years, take and pass the CSLB law and business examination.
3. Take and pass a course in Contractors License Law or a course related to construction law at an accredited community college. All courses must be approved in advance by the Registrar.
4. Pay CSLB investigation and enforcement costs.

7083. Failure to Notify, Changes of Personnel, Business Name, Address, Bond Exemption, and Multiple License Exemption

Minimum Penalty: 60 day suspension, stayed, 1 year probation

Maximum Penalty: Revocation

If warranted:

1. Standard terms and conditions in cases of probation. (1)
2. If not taken within the past 5 years, take and pass the CSLB law and business examination.
3. Take and pass a course in Contractors License Law or a course related to construction law at an accredited community college. All courses must be approved in advance by the Registrar.
4. Pay CSLB investigation and enforcement costs.

7090. Failure to Obtain Building Permits

Minimum Penalty: 60 day suspension, stayed, 1 year probation

Maximum Penalty: Revocation

If warranted:

1. Actual suspension of 5 days or more.

2. Standard terms and conditions in cases of probation. (1)
3. Make restitution.
4. Submit copies of building permits to the Registrar upon demand for projects undertaken during the probation period.
5. If not taken within the past 5 years, take and pass the CSLB trade examination.
6. Take and pass a course in Contractors License Law or a course related to construction law at an accredited community college. All courses must be approved in advance by the Registrar.
7. Pay CSLB investigation and enforcement costs.

7090.5. Fraud and Repeated Acts, Despite Corrections of Conditions

Minimum Penalty: Revocation, stayed, 3 years probation

Maximum Penalty: revocation

If warranted:

1. Actual suspension of 5 days or more.
2. Standard terms and conditions in cases of probation. (1)
3. Take and pass a course in accounting, bookkeeping and/or business management at an accredited community college. All courses must be approved in advance by the Registrar.
4. Submit copies of building permits to the Registrar upon demand for projects undertaken during the probation period.
5. Submit copies of construction contracts to the Registrar upon demand during the probation period.
6. Prohibit receipt of down payments.
7. Submit to the Registrar a detailed plan setting forth the procedure to be used to provide for direct supervising and control by the qualifying individual.
8. If not taken within the past 5 years, take and pass the CSLB law and business examination.
9. Take and pass a course in Contractors License Law or a course related to business law at an accredited community college. All courses must be approved in advance by the Registrar.
10. If not taken within the past 5 years, take and pass the CSLB trade examination.

11. Take and pass a vocational course(s) related to the trade(s) employed on the project. All courses must be approved in advance by the Registrar.
12. Pay CSLB investigation and enforcement costs.

7099.6. Failure to Comply with a Citation

Minimum Penalty: Revocation, stayed, 1 year probation

Maximum Penalty: Revocation

If warranted:

1. Actual suspension of 5 days or more.
2. Standard terms and conditions in cases of probation. (1)
3. Make restitution.
4. Take and pass a course in Contractors License Law or a course related to construction law at an accredited community college. All courses must be approved in advance by the Registrar.
5. Pay CSLB investigation and enforcement costs.

7103. Disciplinary Action by Another State

Minimum Penalty: Revocation, stayed, 3 years probation.

Maximum Penalty: Revocation

If warranted:

1. Actual suspension of 5 days or more.
2. Standard terms and conditions in cases of probation. (1)
3. Pay CSLB investigation and enforcement costs.

7107. Abandonment

Minimum Penalty: Revocation, stayed, 3 years probation

Maximum Penalty: Revocation

If warranted:

1. Absent compelling mitigating circumstances, abandonment of a project is a serious offense that warrants an actual period of suspension of at least 30 days.
2. Standard terms and conditions in cases of probation. (1)
3. Make restitution.

4. Submit copies of building permits to the Registrar upon demand for projects undertaken during the probation period.
5. Submit copies of construction contracts to the Registrar upon demand during the probation period.
6. Submit to the Registrar a detailed plan setting forth the procedure to be used to provide for direct supervision and control by the qualifying individual.
7. If not taken within the past 5 years, take and pass the CSLB law and business examination.
8. Take and pass a course in Contractors License Law or a course related to construction law at an accredited community college. All courses must be approved in advance by the Registrar.
9. If not taken within the past 5 years, take and pass the CSLB trade examination.
10. Take and pass a vocational course(s) related to the trade(s) employed on the project. All courses must be approved in advance by the Registrar.
11. During the period of probation, provide lien releases to project owners as soon as payment is received.
12. Pay CSLB investigation and enforcement costs.

7108. Misuse of Funds

Minimum Penalty: Revocation, stayed, 3 years probation

Maximum Penalty: Revocation

If warranted:

1. Absent compelling mitigating circumstances, misuse of funds is a serious offense that warrants an actual period of suspension of at least 30 days.
2. If diversion or misuse of funds is for personal use not related to construction work, outright revocation is appropriate.
3. Standard terms and conditions in cases of probation. (1)
4. Make restitution.
5. Take and pass a course in accounting, bookkeeping and/or business management at an accredited community college. All courses must be approved in advance by the Registrar.

6. Submit copies of construction contracts to the Registrar upon demand during the probation period.
7. If not taken within the past 5 years, take and pass the CSLB law and business examination.
8. Take and pass a course in Contractors License Law or course related to construction law at an accredited community college. All courses must be approved in advance by the Registrar.
9. Community Service as determined by CSLB; 5-21 days.
10. Pay CSLB investigation and enforcement costs.

7108.5. Prime Contractors and Subcontractors; Payment Required

Minimum Penalty: 60 day suspension, stayed, 1 year probation

Maximum Penalty: Revocation

If warranted:

1. Actual suspension of 5 days or more.
2. Standard terms and conditions in cases of probation. (1)
3. Make restitution.
4. Take and pass a course in accounting, bookkeeping and/or business management at an accredited community college. All courses must be approved in advance by the Registrar.
5. If not taken within the past 5 years, take and pass the CSLB law and business examination.
6. Take and pass a course in Contractors License Law or a course related to construction law at an accredited community college. All courses must be approved in advance by the Registrar.
7. Pay CSLB investigation and enforcement costs.

7109(a). Departure from Accepted Trade Standards for Workmanship

Minimum Penalty: Revocation, stayed, 2 years probation

Maximum Penalty: Revocation

If warranted:

1. Actual suspension of 5 days or more. If the departure from trade standards is substantial, actual suspension of at least 30 days.
2. Standard terms and conditions in cases of probation. (1)
3. Make restitution.

4. Submit copies of building permits to the Registrar upon demand for projects undertaken during the probationary period.
5. Submit copies of construction contracts to the Registrar upon demand during the probation period.
6. Submit to the Registrar a detailed plan setting forth the procedure to be used to provide for direct supervising and control by the qualifying individual.
7. If not taken within the last 5 years, take and pass the CSLB law and business examination.
8. Take and pass a course in Contractors License Law or a course related to construction law at an accredited community college. All courses must be approved in advance by the Registrar.
9. If not taken within the past 5 years, take and pass the CSLB trade examination.
10. Take and pass a vocational course(s) related to the trade(s) employed on the project. All courses must be approved in advance by the Registrar.
11. Pay CSLB investigation and enforcement costs.

7109(b). Departure from Plans and/or Specifications

Minimum Penalty: Revocation, stayed, 2 years probation

Maximum Penalty: Revocation

If warranted:

1. Actual suspension of 5 days or more. If the departure from plans and/or specifications is substantial, actual suspension of at least 30 days.
2. Standard terms and conditions in cases of probation (1)
3. Make restitution.
4. Submit copies of building permits to the Registrar upon demand for all projects undertaken during the probationary period.
5. Submit copies of construction contracts to the Registrar upon demand during the probation period.
6. Submit to the Registrar a detailed plan setting forth the procedure to be used to provide for direct supervising and control by the qualifying individual.

7. If not taken within the past 5 years, take and pass the CSLB law and business examination.
8. Take and pass a course in Contractors License Law or a course related to construction law at an accredited community college. All courses must be approved in advance by the Registrar.
9. If not taken within the past 5 years, take and pass the CSLB trade examination.
10. Take and pass a vocational course(s) related to the trade(s) employed on the project. All courses must be approved in advance by the Registrar.
11. Pay CSLB investigation and enforcement costs.

7109.5. Violation of Safety Orders

Minimum Penalty: Revocation, stayed, 2 years probation

Maximum Penalty: Revocation

If warranted:

1. Actual suspension of 5 days or more.
2. Standard terms and conditions in cases of probation. (1)
3. If not taken within the past 5 years, take and pass the CSLB law and business examination.
4. Take and pass a course in Contractors License Law or a course related to construction law at an accredited community college. All courses must be approved in advance by the Registrar.
5. Establish a safety program.
6. Pay CSLB investigation and enforcement costs.

7110. Violations of Other Laws; Disciplinary Action

Minimum Penalty: Revocation, stayed, 2 years probation

Maximum Penalty: Revocation

If warranted:

1. Actual suspension of 5 days or more.
2. Standard terms and conditions in cases of probation. (1)
3. Make restitution.
4. Comply with orders or assessments of relevant agency.

5. If not taken within the past 5 years, take and pass the CSLB law and business examination.
6. Take and pass a course in Contractors License Law or a course related to construction law at an accredited community college. All courses must be approved in advance by the Registrar.
7. Submit copies of building permits to the Registrar upon demand for projects undertaken during the probation period.
8. Establish a safety program.
9. Pay CSLB investigation and enforcement costs.

7110.1. Violation of Labor Code Section 206.5; Requiring Release of Claim for Wages

Minimum Penalty: 60 day suspension, stayed, 1 year probation

Maximum Penalty: Revocation

If warranted:

1. Actual suspension of 5 days or more.
2. Standard terms and conditions in cases of probation. (1)
3. If not taken within the past 5 years, take and pass the CSLB law and business examination.
4. Take and pass a course in Contractors License Law or a course related to construction law at an accredited community college. All courses must be approved in advance by the Registrar.
5. Pay CSLB investigation and enforcement costs.

7110.5. Violation Pursuant to Section 98.9 of the Labor Code

Minimum Penalty: 60 day suspension, stayed, 1 year probation

Maximum Penalty: Revocation

If warranted:

1. Actual suspension of 5 days or more.
2. Standard terms and conditions in cases of probation. (1)
3. If not taken within the past 5 years, take and pass the CSLB law and business examination.
4. Take and pass a course in Contractors License Law or a course related to construction law at an accredited community college. All courses must be approved in advance by the Registrar.
5. Pay CSLB investigation and enforcement costs.

7111. Preservation of Records

Minimum Penalty: 60 day suspension, stayed, 1 year probation
Maximum Penalty: Revocation
If warranted:

1. Actual suspension of 5 days or more.
2. Standard terms and conditions in cases of probation. (1)
3. Take and pass a course in accounting, bookkeeping and/or business management at an accredited community college. All courses must be approved in advance by the Registrar.
4. If not taken within the past 5 years, take and pass the CSLB law and business examination.
5. Take and pass a course in Contractors License Law or a course related to construction law at an accredited community college. All courses must be approved in advance by the Registrar.
6. Pay CSLB investigation and enforcement costs.

7111.1. Failure of Licensee to Cooperate in an Investigation of a Complaint

Minimum Penalty: 60 day suspension, stayed, 1 year probation
Maximum Penalty: revocation
If warranted:

1. Actual suspension of 5 days or more.
2. Standard terms and conditions in cases of probation. (1)
3. If not taken within the past 5 years, take and pass CSLB law and business examination.
4. Take and pass a course in Contractors License Law or a course related to construction law at an accredited community college. All courses must be approved in advance by the Registrar.
5. Pay CSLB investigation and enforcement costs.

7112. Misrepresentation on an Application

Minimum Penalty: Revocation, stayed, 3 years probation
Maximum Penalty: Revocation
If warranted:

1. Absent compelling mitigating circumstances, misrepresentation is a serious offense that warrants an outright revocation.

2. Actual suspension of at least 30 days.
3. Standard terms and conditions in cases of probation. (1)
4. Community Service as determined by CSLB; 5-21 days.
5. Pay CSLB investigation and enforcement costs.

7113. Failure to Complete Project for Contract Price

Minimum Penalty: Revocation, stayed, 2 years probation

Maximum Penalty: Revocation

If warranted:

1. Actual suspension of 5 days or more. If injury is substantial, actual suspension of at least 30 days.
2. Standard terms and conditions in cases of probation. (1)
3. Make restitution.
4. Complete an education course in estimating construction costs or a related course in the field of construction science. All courses must be approved in advance by the Registrar.
5. Prohibit receipt of down payments.
6. If not taken within the past 5 years, take and pass the CSLB law and business examination.
7. Take and pass a course in Contractors License Law or a course related to construction law at an accredited community college. All courses must be approved in advance by the Registrar.
8. Pay CSLB investigation and enforcement costs.

7113.5. Settlement of Lawful Obligations

Minimum Penalty: Revocation, stayed, 2 years probation

Maximum Penalty: Revocation

If warranted:

1. Actual suspension of 5 days or more.
2. Standard terms and conditions in cases of probation. (1)
3. Make restitution.
4. Take and pass a course in accounting, bookkeeping and/or business management at an accredited community college. All courses must be approved in advance by the Registrar.

5. Submit a list of all subcontractors used on construction projects to the Registrar upon demand during the probation period.
6. Submit a list of all material suppliers used on construction projects to the Registrar upon demand during the probation period.
7. Pay CSLB investigation and enforcement costs.

7114. Aiding and Abetting an Unlicensed Person

Minimum Penalty: Revocation, stayed, 2 years probation

Maximum Penalty: Revocation

If warranted:

1. Actual suspension of 5 days or more.
2. Standard terms and conditions in cases of probation. (1)
3. If not taken within the past 5 years, take and pass the CSLB law and business examination.
4. Take and pass a course in Contractors License Law or a course related to construction law at an accredited community college. All courses must be approved in advance by the Registrar.
5. Submit a list of all subcontractors used on construction projects to the Registrar upon demand during the probation period.
6. Pay CSLB investigation and enforcement costs.

7114.1. Certifying to False Experience

Minimum Penalty: Revocation, stayed, 3 years probation

Maximum Penalty: Revocation

If warranted:

1. Absent compelling mitigating circumstances, certifying false experience is a serious offense that warrants an outright revocation.
2. Standard terms and conditions in cases of probation. (1)
3. Community Service as determined by CSLB; 5-21 days.
4. Pay CSLB investigation and enforcement costs.

7115. Violation of the Contractors License Law

Minimum Penalty: 5 day suspension, stayed, 1 year probation
Maximum Penalty: Revocation
If warranted:

1. Actual suspension of 5 days or more.
2. Standard terms and conditions in case of probation. (1)
3. Pay CSLB investigation and enforcement costs.

7116. Any Wilful or Fraudulent Act

Minimum Penalty: Revocation, stayed, 3 years probation
Maximum Penalty: revocation
If warranted:

1. Absent compelling circumstances, fraud is a serious offense that warrants an actual suspension of at least 60 days.
2. If the injury is substantial, outright revocation is appropriate.
3. Standard terms and conditions in case of probation. (1)
4. Make restitution.
5. If not taken within the past 5 years, take and pass the CSLB law and business examination.
6. Take and pass a course in Contractors License Law or a course related to construction law at an accredited community college. All courses must be approved in advance by the Registrar.
7. Community Service as determined by CSLB; 5-21 days.
8. Pay CSLB investigation and enforcement costs.

7117. Variance from License as to Name or Personnel

Minimum Penalty: 5 day suspension, stayed, 1 year probation
Maximum Penalty: 364 day suspension, 2 years probation
If warranted:

1. Standard terms and conditions in case of probation. (1)
2. If not taken within the past 5 years, take and pass the CSLB law and business examination.
3. Take and pass a course in Contractors License Law or a course related to construction law at an accredited community college. All courses must be approved in advance by the Registrar.
4. Pay CSLB investigation and enforcement costs.

7117.5. Contracting with an Inactive, Suspended or Expired License

Minimum Penalty: Revocation, stayed, 2 years probation

Maximum Penalty: Revocation

If warranted:

1. Actual suspension of 5 days or more.
2. Standard terms and conditions in case of probation. (1)
3. If not taken within the past 5 years, take and pass the CSLB law and business examination.
4. Take and pass a course in Contractors License Law or a course related to construction law at an accredited community college. All courses must be approved in advance by the Registrar.
5. Pay CSLB investigation and enforcement costs.

7117.6. Contracting Out of Classification

Minimum Penalty: 60 day suspension, stayed, 1 year probation

Maximum Penalty: Revocation

If warranted:

1. Actual suspension of 5 days or more.
2. Standard terms and conditions in case of probation. (1)
3. Submit copies of construction contracts to the Registrar upon demand during the probation period.
4. Submit copies of all advertisements relating to contracting business to the Registrar prior to their being displayed or published during the probation period.
5. Pay CSLB investigation and enforcement costs.

7118. Contracting with an Unlicensed Person

Minimum Penalty: Revocation, stayed, 2 years probation

Maximum Penalty: Revocation

If warranted:

1. Actual suspension of 5 days or more.
2. Standard terms and conditions in cases of probation (1).
3. If not taken within the past 5 years, take and pass the CSLB law and business examination.

4. Take and pass a course in Contractors License Law or a course related to construction law at an accredited community college. All courses must be approved in advance by the Registrar.
5. Submit a list of all subcontractors used on construction projects to the Registrar upon demand during the probation period.
6. Community Service as determined by CSLB; 5-21 days.
7. Pay CSLB investigation and enforcement costs.

7118.4. Asbestos Related Inspection with Knowledge of Report being Required for Loan; Disclosure Required

Minimum Penalty: 60 day suspension, stayed, 1 year probation

Maximum Penalty: Revocation

If warranted:

1. Absent compelling mitigating circumstances, conducting an asbestos related inspection while maintaining a financial relationship with an entity which performs corrective work without disclosing this fact is a serious offense that warrants an actual suspension of 60 days.
2. Standard terms and conditions in cases of probation. (1)
3. If not taken within the past 5 years, take and pass the CSLB law and business examination.
4. Take and pass a course in Contractors License Law or a course related to construction law at an accredited community college. All courses must be approved in advance by the Registrar.
5. Community Service as determined by CSLB; 5-21 days.
6. Pay CSLB investigation and enforcement costs.

7118.5. Asbestos-related Work; Contracting with Uncertified Contractor

Minimum Penalty: 60 day suspension, stayed, 1 year probation

Maximum Penalty: Revocation

If warranted:

1. Absent compelling mitigating circumstances, contracting with an uncertified asbestos contractor to perform asbestos related work is a serious offense that warrants an actual suspension of 60 days.
2. Standard terms and conditions in cases of probation. (1)

3. Submit a list of all subcontractors used on construction projects to the Registrar upon demand during the probation period.
4. Community Service as determined by CSLB; 5-21 days.
5. Pay CSLB investigation and enforcement costs.

7118.6. Asbestos-contracting with an Uncertified Person for Removal or Remedial Action

Minimum Penalty: 60 day suspension, stayed, 1 year probation

Maximum Penalty: Revocation

If warranted:

1. Absent compelling mitigating circumstances, contracting with an uncertified person for removal or remedial asbestos work is a serious offense that warrants an actual suspension of 60 days.
2. Standard terms and conditions in cases of probation. (1)
3. Submit a list of all subcontractors used on construction projects to the Registrar upon demand during the probation period.
4. Community Service as determined by CSLB; 5-21 days.
5. Pay CSLB investigation and enforcement costs.

7119. Lack of Reasonable Diligence

Minimum Penalty: 60 day suspension, stayed, 1 year probation

Maximum Penalty: Revocation

If warranted:

1. Actual suspension of 5 days or more.
2. Standard terms and conditions in cases of probation. (1)
3. Make restitution.
4. Prohibit receipt of down payments.
5. Pay CSLB investigation and enforcement costs.

7120. Failure to Pay Money

Minimum Penalty: 60 day suspension, stayed, 1 year probation

Maximum Penalty: Revocation

If warranted:

1. Actual suspension of 5 days or more.
2. Standard terms and conditions in cases of probation. (1)

3. Take and pass a course in accounting, bookkeeping and/or business management at an accredited community college. All courses must be approved in advance by the Registrar.
4. If not taken within the past 5 years, take and pass the CSLB law and business examination.
5. Take and pass a course in Contractors License Law or a course related to construction law at an accredited community college. All courses must be approved in advance by the Registrar.
6. Submit a list of all subcontractors used on construction projects to the Registrar upon demand during the probation period.
7. Submit a list of all material suppliers used on construction projects to the Registrar upon demand during the probation period.
8. Prohibit the receipt of down payments.
9. Provide lien releases to project owners on all future construction projects upon receipt of payments.
10. Pay CSLB investigation and enforcement costs.

7121. Prohibition against Association

Minimum Penalty: Revocation, stayed, 2 years probation

Maximum Penalty: Revocation

If warranted:

1. Actual suspension of 5 days or more.
2. Standard terms and conditions in cases of probation. (1)
3. Make restitution.
4. If not taken within the past 5 years, take and pass the CSLB law and business examination.
5. Take and pass a course in Contractors License Law or a course related to construction law at an accredited community college. All courses must be approved in advance by the Registrar.
6. Pay CSLB investigation and enforcement costs.

7123. Conviction of a Crime

Minimum Penalty: Revocation, stayed, 3 years probation

Maximum Penalty; Revocation

If warranted:

1. Absent compelling mitigating circumstances, conviction of a crime related to the functions of a contractor is a serious offense and warrants an outright revocation.
2. Actual suspension of at least 30 days.
3. Standard terms and conditions in cases of probation. (1)
4. Make restitution.
5. If not taken within the past 5 years, take and pass the CSLB law and business examination.
6. Take and pass a course in Contractors License Law or a course related to construction law at an accredited community college. All courses must be approved in advance by the Registrar.
7. Prohibit the receipt of down payments.
8. Community Service as determined by CSLB; 5-21 days.
9. Pay CSLB investigation and enforcement costs.

7123.5. Violation of Prohibition Against Overpricing Following an Emergency or Disaster (Penal Code Section 396)

Minimum Penalty: 6 month suspension, 3 years probation

Maximum Penalty: Revocation

If warranted:

1. Absent compelling mitigating circumstances, overpricing following an emergency or disaster is a serious offense and warrants an outright revocation.
2. Actual suspension of 6 months.
3. Standard terms and conditions in cases of probation. (1)
4. Make restitution.
5. If not taken within the past 5 years, take and pass the CSLB law and business examination.
6. Take and pass a course in Contractors License Law or a course related to construction law at an accredited community college. All courses must be approved in advance by the Registrar.
7. Prohibit the receipt of down payments.
8. Community Service as determined by CSLB; 5-21 days.
9. Pay CSLB investigation and enforcement costs.

7125(b). Filing False Workers' Compensation Exemption Reports

Minimum Penalty: Revocation, stayed, 2 years probation

Maximum Penalty: Revocation

If warranted:

1. Actual suspension of 5 days or more.
2. Standard terms and conditions in cases of probation. (1)
3. If not taken within the past 5 years, take and pass the CSLB law and business examination.
4. Take and pass a course in Contractors License Law or a course related to construction law at an accredited community college. All courses must be approved in advance by the Registrar.
5. Submit a list of persons employed on construction related projects to the Registrar upon demand during the probation period.
6. Make restitution.
7. Pay CSLB investigation and enforcement costs.

7154. Employment of a Nonregistered Home Improvement Salesperson

Minimum Penalty: 60 day suspension, stayed, 1 year probation

Maximum Penalty: Revocation

If warranted:

1. Actual suspension of 5 days or more.
2. Standard terms and conditions in cases of probation. (1)
3. If not taken within the past 5 years, take and pass the CSLB law and business examination.
4. Take and pass a course in Contractors License Law or a course related to construction law at an accredited community college. All courses must be approved in advance by the Registrar.
5. Pay CSLB investigation and enforcement costs.

7155. Violation of Contractors License Law by Home Improvement Salesperson

Minimum Penalty: 60 day suspension, stayed, 1 year probation

Maximum Penalty: Revocation

If warranted:

1. Actual suspension of 5 days or more.
2. Standard terms and conditions in cases of probation. (1)
3. Submit copies of construction contracts to the Registrar upon demand during the probation period.
4. If not taken within the past 5 years, take and pass the CSLB law and business examination.
5. Take and pass a course in Contractors License Law or a course related to construction law at an accredited community college. All courses must be approved in advance by the Registrar.
6. Pay CSLB investigation and enforcement costs.

7155.5. Liability of a Contractor for a Home Improvement Salesperson

Minimum Penalty: Suspension, stayed, 1 year probation

Maximum Penalty: Revocation

If warranted:

1. Actual suspension of 5 days or more.
2. Standard terms and conditions in cases of probation. (1)
3. If not taken within the past 5 years, take and pass the CSLB law and business examination.
4. Take and pass a course in Contractors License Law or a course related to construction law at an accredited community college. All courses must be approved in advance by the Registrar.
5. Submit copies of construction contracts to the Registrar upon demand during the probation period.
6. Prohibit the receipt of down payments.
7. Pay CSLB investigation and enforcement costs.

7156. Registered Salespersons Violations

Minimum Penalty: 60 day suspension, stayed, 1 year probation

Maximum Penalty: Revocation

If warranted:

1. Actual suspension of 5 days or more.
2. Standard terms and conditions in cases of probation. (1)
3. Submit copies of construction contracts to the Registrar upon demand during the probation period.

4. Pay CSLB investigation and enforcement costs.

7157. Home Improvement Inducements

Minimum Penalty: 60 day suspension, stayed, 1 year probation

Maximum Penalty: Revocation

If warranted:

1. Actual suspension of at least 5 days.
2. Standard terms and conditions in cases of probation. (1)
3. If not taken within the past 5 years, take and pass the CSLB law and business examination.
4. Take and pass a course in Contractors License Law or a course related to construction law at an accredited community college. All courses must be approved in advance by the Registrar.
5. Submit copies of advertisements relating to contracting business to the Registrar prior to their being displayed or published during the probation period.
6. Prohibit the receipt of down payments.
7. Pay CSLB investigation and enforcement costs.

7158. False Completion Certificate

Minimum Penalty: Revocation, stayed, 3 years probation

Maximum Penalty: Revocation

If warranted:

1. Absent compelling circumstances, knowingly using a false certificate is a serious offense that warrants an actual suspension of at least 30 days.
2. Standard terms and conditions in cases of probation. (1)
3. If not taken within the past 5 years, take and pass the CSLB law and business examination.
4. Take and pass a course in Contractors License Law or a course related to construction law at an accredited community college. All courses must be approved in advance by the Registrar.
5. Make restitution.
6. Submit copies of construction contracts to the Registrar upon demand during the probation period.
7. Prohibit receipt of down payments.

8. Community Service as determined by CSLB; 5-21 days.
9. Pay CSLB investigation and enforcement costs.

7159. Home Improvement Contract Requirements

Minimum Penalty: 60 day suspension, stayed, 1 year probation
Maximum Penalty: Revocation
If warranted:

1. If any injuries are involved, actual suspension of at least 30 days.
2. Standard terms and conditions in cases of probation. (1)
3. If not taken within the past 5 years, take and pass the CSLB law and business examination.
4. Take and pass a course in Contractors License Law or a course related to construction law at an accredited community college. All courses must be approved in advance by the Registrar.
5. Submit copies of construction contracts to the Registrar upon demand during the probation period.
6. Prohibit receipt of down payments.
7. Community Service as determined by CSLB; 5-21 days.
8. Pay CSLB investigation and enforcement costs.

7161. Misrepresentation; False Advertisement

Minimum Penalty: Revocation, stayed, 3 years probation
Maximum Penalty: Revocation
If warranted:

1. Absent compelling mitigating circumstances, misrepresentation and false or deceptive advertising are serious offenses that warrant an actual period of suspension of at least 30 days.
2. If injury is substantial, outright revocation is appropriate.
3. Standard terms and conditions in cases of probation. (1)
4. If not taken within the past 5 years, take and pass the CSLB law and business examination.
5. Take and pass a course in Contractors License Law or a course related to construction law at an accredited community college. All courses must be approved in advance by the Registrar.

6. Submit copies of construction contracts to the Registrar upon demand during the probation period.
7. Submit copies of advertisements relating to contracting business to the Registrar prior to their being displayed or published during the probation period.
8. Prohibit the receipt of down payments.
9. Community Service as determined by CSLB; 5-21 days.
10. Pay CSLB investigation and enforcement costs.

7162. Representation with Respect to Trademark or Brand Name; Quantity or Size

Minimum Penalty: Revocation, stayed, 2 years probation

Maximum Penalty: Revocation

If warranted:

1. Actual suspension of 5 days or more.
2. Standard terms and conditions in cases of probation. (1)
3. If not taken within the past 5 years, take and pass the CSLB law and business examination.
4. Take and pass a course in Contractors License Law or a course related to construction law at an accredited community college. All courses must be approved in advance by the Registrar.
5. Make restitution.
6. Submit copies of construction contracts to the Registrar upon demand during the probation period.
7. Submit copies of advertisements relating to contracting business to the Registrar prior to their being displayed or published during the probation period.
8. Prohibit the receipt of down payments.
9. Pay CSLB investigation and enforcement costs.

7164. Contract Form for Single Family Dwelling

Minimum Penalty: 60 day suspension, stayed, 1 year probation

Maximum Penalty: Revocation

If warranted:

1. Actual suspension of 5 days or more.
2. Standard terms and conditions in cases of probation. (1)

3. If not taken within the past 5 years, take and pass the CSLB law and business examination.
4. Take and pass a course in Contractors License Law or a course related to construction law at an accredited community college. All courses must be approved in advance by the Registrar.
5. Submit copies of construction contracts to the Registrar upon demand during the probation period.
6. Pay CSLB investigation and enforcement costs.

7165. Swimming Pool Construction Contract

Minimum Penalty: 60 day suspension, stayed, 1 year probation

Maximum Penalty: Revocation

If warranted:

1. Actual suspension of 5 days or more.
2. Standard terms and conditions in cases of probation. (1)
3. If not taken within the past 5 years, take and pass the CSLB law and business examination.
4. Take and pass a course in Contractors License Law or a course related to construction law at an accredited community college. All courses must be approved in advance by the Registrar.
5. Submit copies of construction contracts to the Registrar upon demand during the probation period.
6. Pay CSLB investigation and enforcement costs.

7183.5. Asbestos; Certification Obtained under False Pretenses

Minimum Penalty: Revocation, stayed, 3 years probation

Maximum Penalty: Revocation

If warranted:

1. Absent compelling mitigating circumstances, obtaining an asbestos certification under false pretenses is a serious offense and warrants an outright revocation.
2. Actual suspension of at least 30 days.
3. Standard terms and conditions in cases of probation. (1)
4. Community Service as determined by CSLB; 5-21 days.
5. Pay CSLB investigation and enforcement costs.

7189. Asbestos Certification; Conflicts of Interest

Minimum Penalty: 60 day suspension, stayed, 1 year probation

Maximum Penalty: Revocation

If warranted:

1. Absent compelling circumstances, a person defined as an "asbestos consultant" or a "site surveillance technician", having financial or proprietary interest in an asbestos contractor's company is a serious offense that warrants an actual suspension period of at least 30 days.
2. Standard terms and conditions in cases of probation. (1)
3. Submit copies of construction contracts to the Registrar upon demand during the probation period.
4. Prohibit the receipt of down payments.
5. Community Service as determined by CSLB; 5-21 days.
6. Pay CSLB investigation and enforcement costs.

All Other Violations

Minimum Penalty: 5 day suspension, stayed, 1 year probation

Maximum Penalty: Revocation

If warranted:

1. Actual suspension of 5 days or more.
2. Standard terms and conditions in cases of probation. (1)
3. If not taken within the past 5 years, take and pass the CSLB law and business examination.
4. Take and pass a course in Contractors License Law or a course related to construction law at an accredited community college. All courses must be approved in advance by the Registrar.
5. If not taken within the past 5 years, take and pass the CSLB trade examination.
6. Take and pass a vocational course(s) related to the trade(s) employed on the project. All courses must be approved in advance by the Registrar.
7. Submit copies of construction contracts to the Registrar upon demand during the probation period.
8. Make restitution
9. Pay CSLB investigation and enforcement costs.

(1) *Standard Terms and Conditions to be Included in all Cases of Probation*

1. Obey All Laws: Respondent shall comply with all federal, state and local laws governing the activities of a licensed contractor in California.
2. Interviews With Regional Deputy: Respondent and any of respondent's personnel of record shall appear in person for interviews with the Regional Deputy or designee upon request and reasonable notice.
3. Completion Of Probation: Upon successful completion of probation, the contractor's license will be fully restored.
4. Violation Of Probation: If respondent violates probation in any respect, the Registrar, after giving notice and opportunity to be heard, may revoke probation and impose the disciplinary order that was stayed. If the decision contains an order to make restitution, the Registrar may impose the disciplinary order without giving the respondent an opportunity to be heard should the respondent fail to comply with the restitution order.
5. Respondent shall submit copies of documents directly related to the person's construction operations to the Registrar upon demand during the probation period.

Article 8. Citation

880. Order of Correction -- Practical Feasibility.

Before including an order of correction in a citation, due consideration shall be given to the practical feasibility of correction in accordance with, but not limited to, the following criteria:

(a) An order of correction is appropriate where it would not result in excessive destruction of or substantial waste of existing acceptable construction.

(b) An order of correction is appropriate where the owner of the construction project is willing to allow the cited licensee to correct.

(c) An order of correction is appropriate where it appears to the Registrar that the cited licensee has competence or ability to correct.

(Authority cited: Sections 7008 and 7099.1, Business and Professions Code. Reference: Sections 7099 and 7099.1, Business and Professions Code.)

881. Order of Correction -- Alternative Compliance.

A cited licensee may comply with an order of correction by having and paying for another licensee to do the corrective work. The cited licensee remains responsible, however, for any failure to fully comply with the order of correction.

An order of correction may, but need not, contain the alternative that the cited person may pay a specified sum to the owner of the construction project in lieu of correcting.

(Authority cited: Sections 7008 and 7099.1, Business and Professions Code. Reference: Sections 7099 and 7099.1, Business and Professions Code.)

882. Order of Correction -- Time Required to Correct.

Where an order of correction is included in a citation, due consideration shall be given to the time required to correct in accordance with, but not limited to, the following criteria:

(a) Accepted industry practice in that area relating to performance of such work under certain climate or weather conditions.

(b) A reasonable time in which to obtain necessary materials.

(c) The number of working days the construction project will be made accessible by the owner for corrections.

(Authority cited: Sections 7008 and 7099.1, Business and Professions Code. Reference: Sections 7099 and 7099.1, Business and Professions Code.)

883. Order of Correction -- Extension of Time to Correct.

If the cited person, after exercising substantial efforts and reasonable diligence, is unable to complete the correction within the time allowed because of conditions beyond his control, he may request an extension of time in which to correct. Such request must be made in writing, and must be made prior to the expiration of the time allowed in the order of correction. An extension may be granted upon showing of good cause which determination is within the discretion of the Registrar. If a request for extension of time is not made prior to the expiration of time allowed in the order of correction, failure to correct within the time allowed shall constitute a violation of the order of correction whether or not good cause for an extension of time existed.

(Authority cited: Sections 7008 and 7099.1, Business and Professions Code. Reference: Sections 7099 and 7099.1, Business and Professions Code.)

884. Recommended Assessments of Civil Penalties.

In assessing a civil penalty against a person who has not previously been cited for violation of the same or similar section of the Contractors License Law, the Registrar shall give due consideration to the following guidelines:

Section Violated	*Recommended Minimum Civil Penalty*	*Recommended Maximum Civil Penalty*
7030	$50.00	$100.00
7030.5	50	100
7071.13	50	100
7075	50	100
7083	50	100
7083.1	50	100
7018.5	50	150
7027.1	50	150
7029.5	50	150
7034	50	150
7068.2	50	150
7110.1	50	150
7117	50	150
7125	50	150
7028.5	50	500
7071.11	50	500
7111	50	500
7113.5	50	500
7154	50	500
7157	50	500
7110	50	1000
7068.1	50	1000
7076	50	1000
7099.10	50	1000
7099.11	50	1000
7111.1	50	1000
7114.1	50	1000

Section Violated	*Recommended Minimum Civil Penalty*	*Recommended Maximum Civil Penalty*
7118.4	50	1000
7118.5	50	1000
7159	50	1000
7162	50	1000
7164	50	1000
7107	100	1000
7108	100	1000
7108.5	100	1000
7108.6	100	1000
7119	100	1000
7120	100	1000
7109	50	1500
7109.5	50	1500
7113	50	1500
7116	50	1500
7158	50	1500
7161	50	1500
7123	500	1500
7125.1	500	1500
7028	200	2000
7029.1	200	2000
7117.5	200	2000
7117.6	200	2000
7114	200	15000
7118	200	15000

(a) The minimum and maximum civil penalties as set forth above are advisory only. Where there is more than one violation, where, in the judgment of the Registrar, a person has exhibited bad faith or where, in the judgment of the Registrar, the violation is grave, the maximum recommended civil penalty shall be $2,000.00.

(b) Where a cited person has a history of violations of the same or similar sections of the Contractors License Law, the maximum recommended civil penalty shall be $2,000.00.

As discussed elsewhere in this book, the Legislature changed the maximum civil penalty to be assessed from $2,000 to $5,000. However, the penalty for aiding and abetting an unlicensed contractor remains at a maximum of $15,000.

Above is the regulation that deals with this issue. Note that the regulation only allows for a maximum civil penalty of $2,000. Whether a civil penalty can be assessed in the amount of $5,000 without a new regulation is questionable.

Where a citation lists more than one violation the amount of assessed civil penalty shall be stated separately for each section violated.

(c) Where a citation lists more than one violation and each of the violations relates to the same construction project, the total penalty assessment in each citation shall not exceed $2,000.00.

(d) Notwithstanding subsections (a), (b) or (c) a civil penalty of $15,000 may be assessed for a violation of Section 7114 or 7118 if the cited person has a history of violations of the same or similar sections of the Contractors License Law or in the judgment of the Registrar the cited person has exhibited bad faith or the violation is grave.

(Authority cited: Sections 7008 and 7099.2, Business and Professions Code. Reference: Sections 7099 and 7099.1, Business and Professions Code.)

A

Accusation....258
Active Conduct....185
Advertising. 59, 64, 70, 83, 262, 270, 279
After Suspension Bonds....69
AIA....159, 169
Aiding Unlicensed Persons....74
Appeal....280
Appendix....281
Applicable Contract Provisions....179
Arbitration....71, 166, 220
  Clauses....83
  of Disputes....83
Arrangement....74
Asbestos....60, 75, 83, 263

B

Bid Bond....193
  Chiseling....161
  Peddling....161
  Shopping....161, 162
Bidding....61
Bond Notice Contents....197
  Premium....198
  Rights....245
Bonding Obligations....199
Bonds....195, 226, 247
Breach of Contract....74
Business & Professions
  Code....200, 201
  Section....261, 264
Business Continuation....71

C

CAL OSHA....89
California
  20-Day Preliminary Notice....320
  Constitution....89, 236
  Government....89
  Mechanics' Lien Law....128, 173
  State University....254
California Supreme Court....4, 91, 160, 162, 167
Cancellation Notice Exception....133
Certification....107
CGL Insurance Policy....202
  Policy....202, 205, 206
Citation....61, 259, 262
Claim Against Bond....69
  Made Policies....209
Classifications of Licensing....104
Compensatory Damages....163
Composition....74
Concept of Indemnification 183, 187, 203
Conduit Clauses....167
Construction Bonding....193
  Contracts....147, 156
Contract Items....166
  Requirements....119, 165
Contracting.... 60, 62, 75, 261, 263, 264
  Without License....60
Contractor Defined....58
  Identification....62
  Judgment Bonds....201
  Regulations....97
Contractor's Bond....69
  License Law....57, 298
Conviction as Cause....76
Corporation business....71
Corporations....330
County Recorder....284
Coverage....205
Criminal....257, 263

D

Damages....163, 167
Declaration of a Disaster....131, 176
Definition of Contractor....87
Denial of License....103
Denied application....69
Department of Consumer
  Affairs....86, 92, 93
Disassociation of Partners....76
Disciplinary Bonds....201
  Proceedings....72
Discipline....69
Discipline and Disciplinary Statutes.257
  in Another State....72
  in California....72

Disclosure 63
Dispute Evasion 217
Disputes 84, 217
Disregard of Plans 73
Drennan v. Star Paving 160
Duty to Defend 213

E

Emergency Act Violation 76
  Repair Exception 133, 178
Emotional Distress Damages 332
Employment Penalty 78
Enforcement 109
Enforcing Stop Notice 244
Examination 69, 102
Exemption 303
  Certificate 275
Experience 102
Express Conditions 162
  Indemnity 162, 183, 184
Extension of Credit 235, 285

F

Failure to Cooperate 74
False Advertising 82
  Completion Certificate 79
  Representation 82
Falsified Experience 74
Federal Public Works 198, 246
Filing False Claim 58
  Suit 248, 251
Fire Protection Installation 59
Fraud 75
Fraudulent Use 60

G

General Building Contractor 66, 86, 104
General Engineering Contractor 104

H

Home Depot 66, 87
Home Improvement.... 107, 116, 170, 179, 263
  Act 143, 144, 145
  Commercial General Liability Insurance form 122, 136
  Contract ... 77- 79, 130, 134, 176, 316
  Contract Form 79
  Defined 119
  Regulations 119
  Salesperson 77
Home Solicitation Act 144, 145, 180, 318

I

Illegal Indemnity Provisions 191
Implied Conditions 162
  Indemnity 183
Inactive License Contracting 75
Indemnification 168, 182, 203
  Agreement 184, 187, 188, 201
Independent Contractor 99
Individual License 61
Injunction 61
Insurance 202
  Certificates 215
  Policy Contents 203
Investigative Reports 58

J

Joint Venture License 61
Judgment 70
  Bond 70

K

Kickbacks 78, 142

L

Landscape Contractor 60
License Bond 200
  Cancellation 71
License Qualification 101
  Renewal 103
  Required for Permits 64
Licenses 66
Licensing and Regulation of Contractors 86
  Requirement 98
Licensure Exemption 65, 98

Lien Foreclosure....... 285, 286, 287, 288
  Rights.............................. 64, 236, 237
  Rights Release.............................. 239
Limitation of Liability 199
Liquidated Damages.......................... 164
Litigation.. 220
Local Business Taxes 58

M

Mechanics' Lien 222, 223, 230
  Contents.. 234
  Release Bond 200, 243
Minor Work 99
  Exception............................... 65, 179
  Exemption . 65, 66, 180, 257, 303, 305
Miscellaneous Exemptions 100
Misuse of Funds.................................. 72
Modified Occurrence Policies .. 211, 212
  Risk policy.................................... 212

N

Non-transferable license...................... 70
Not Requiring a License 100
Notice of Cancellation...... 130-134, 144, 175, 176, 177, 179, 180
  Cessation of Labor. 232, 233, 285, 287
  Completion .. 197, 228, 232, 233, 244, 249, 251, 284-289
Notice Requirements................. 134, 195
Notice to Owner. 58, 81, 128, 171, 173, 224, 264, 280

O

Out of Classification Contracting........ 75
Owner's Own Work............................. 99

P

Participation in Violation 78
Passive Conduct................................ 185
Pay if Paid................................ 159, 167
Pay when Paid.................................. 167
Payment and Performance Bond....... 120, 128, 171, 174, 277
Payment Bond........... 195, 245, 250, 251
Payment of Dump Truck Carriers....... 72
  of Subcontractor 72
  schedule 80, 120, 171, 277
Penalty 59, 60, 82
Performance and Payment Bond 80, 102, 103, 120, 171, 195, 224, 277, 280
Performance Bond............................. 195
Personnel Variance.............................. 75
Policies.. 208
Portions of the Law............................ 118
Preliminary Notice............ 128, 173, 226
Pre-printed Forms 133, 179
Probationary License 107
Procedural Requirements.................... 98
Progress Payments 252-254, 255
Prohibited Clauses 64
Prompt Payment Laws 252
Proper License 88
Public Work Defined......................... 247
  Procedure...................................... 246
Punitive Damages 164

Q

Qualification 67, 101
Qualifying responsibility...................... 67

R

Reasonable Diligence.......................... 76
Recommended Civil Penalties 264
Record preservation............................ 74
Reference to Bond 70
Referrals.. 142
Registrar of Contractors 64, 92, 94, 96, 267, 275
Regulations.. 97
  in General 89
Release Bond 200, 245
Reporting Changes to Board 71
Required Contract Statements 62
  License Number.............................. 64
Reservation of Rights 213
Resolve Liabilities 77
Responsible Managing Employee 101
  Officer... 101
Retention Payments.......... 253, 254, 255
RME........................... 68, 101, 102, 262
RMO.................. 68, 101, 102, 261, 262

S

Salesman Penalty 78
Salesperson Registration 78
Small Claims 220, 221, 222
Specialty Contractor59, 67, 88, 105, 106, 224
  Classified 105
Specific Requirements........................ 169
Stale Liens 242
State License Board ...87, 89, 92-96, 104, 118, 134, 146, 169, 180, 201, 257-259, 261, 265
  Public Works 248
Statutes.. 97
Statutory Lien Releases 129, 175
Stop Notice............................... 222, 244
Subcontractor 255, 283
Substantial Compliance...................... 308
Substitution of Examinee..................... 68
Suspensions.. 114
Swimming Pool Contract....83, 106, 170, 263
  Contracting..................................... 116
  Work Regulations.......................... 119

T

Termination 157, 168, 169
Transferability of License..................... 71
Trigger of Coverage............................ 207
Types of Indemnity............................. 186
  of Insurance Policies 207

U

Under Contract Performance............. 162
Underground Storage Tanks................ 60
Uniform Commercial Code 156
Unlicensed Contractors......... 61, 64, 179

V

Violation 262
  of Labor Code 73
  of Laws 73
Violations of Safety Orders.................. 73

W

Waiver and Release .. 129, 130, 175, 240, 241
Waiver of Lien Rights 64, 237
Warning letter..................................... 280
Withholding Money 76
Worker's Compensation........ 76, 77, 263
  Certificate 77